Gary M. Lepper

A
BIBLIOGRAPHICAL
INTRODUCTION
TO SEVENTY-FIVE
MODERN AMERICAN
AUTHORS

Serendipity Books
Berkeley 1976

Designed by the Poltroon Press. Composition by Alastair Johnston
and paste-up by Dave Bullen at the West Coast Print Center.
Printed in the U.S.A. by Braun-Brumfield.

Serendipity Books
1790 Shattuck Avenue
Berkeley, California 94709

To Mrs. Louis Henry Cohn.

ACKNOWLEDGMENTS

During the past six years, I have had to ask questions of many people. Some have kindly answered individual inquiries; some authors have graciously reviewed their own checklists. I am grateful to them all. However, there are those whom I have asked repeated or lengthy questions and I offer them my special appreciation:

Leslie S. Clarke (University of California, Berkeley), Mrs. Louis Henry Cohn (House of Books, Ltd., New York), Seamus Cooney (Kalamazoo, Michigan), Allan Covici (The Invisible Bookman, Berkeley), Norman H. Davis (Santa Cruz, California), Elsa Glines (California State College, Hayward), Robert Hawley (Oyez, Berkeley), I. T. Holtzman (Birmingham, Michigan), William Heyen (Brockport, New York), Marvin Malone (Stockton, California), John Martin (Black Sparrow Press, Santa Barbara, California), Thomas Nicely (Leaves of Grass, Ann Arbor, Michigan), John Nomland (Los Angeles), Stathis Orphanos (R. Sylvester & S. Orphanos Books, Los Angeles), William Pieper (William Pieper Books, Los Nietos, California), D. A. Sachs (Oakland, California), Jack Shoemaker (Sand Dollar Books, Berkeley), Ralph Bruno Sipper (Joseph the Provider Books, Santa Barbara, California), David Streeter (Pomona, California), Beverly Ruth Vander Kooy (State University of New York, Buffalo) and Henry W. Wenning (Byram, Connecticut).

I am particularly grateful to Peter Howard (Berkeley) and George Bixby (Ampersand Books, New York), who tirelessly shared their remarkable knowledge with me through dozens of hours of consultation, criticism and advice.

GML

Table of Contents

Introduction

This book is a compendium of checklists of the writings of seventy-five American poets and novelists who have achieved literary prominence since 1945.

Criteria for Inclusion

Each checklist includes primary work (books, playscripts, etc.), fugitive matter (broadsides, postcards, other ephemerae) and translations, if any, by a particular author. Sheet music, phonograph and tape recordings and edited books are omitted.

The checklists describe the first printings of first editions, whether American (the usual case) or foreign (e.g. the British publication of WHO LOST AN AMERICAN? by Nelson Algren). Reprints and reissues are acknowledged only if (1) the author revised or expanded the original text or (2) the author signed a specific portion of the new printing; such cases are mentioned under the heading "ALSO". All entries have been examined personally except those followed by an asterisk. Although items marked by asterisks are potential "ghosts", they are included because of the reliability of my sources for information.

Review copies and uncorrected proofs in specially printed wrappers enjoy much collector and some bibliographical interest. They are mentioned in the "NOTES". Galley and page proofs presumably exist for most books but are rarely bound for circulation; they are excluded. The occasional unique copy of a book gift bound by the publisher for the author is also excluded. Acting editions of plays are included only if they are known to precede all other editions. A problem arises with respect to unpublished playscripts and screenplays, which are normally reproduced only for private purposes. Such scripts are noted only if the existence of multiple copies (reproduced by whatever means) has been confirmed. Academic theses (e.g. THE OLD MEN by John Gardner) are treated identically.

Terms of Description

The authors are arranged alphabetically; each checklist of primary works is arranged chronologically through 1975, followed by the translations, also listed chronologically.

Title: The "title" of an entry is that which is found on the title page of a book or at the head of a broadside, postcard, script, etc. If there is no title page, the cover title is cited. A title has been supplied in a very few instances (for POEMS by Donald Hall; for the unseen PATERSON SOCIETY broadsides). Untitled broadsides are entered by the title of the first poem (if there are several titled poems) or by the opening words of the first or only poem. Subtitles are included only when particularly illuminative.

Publisher, Place of Publication, Date: If the publisher, city or date of publication appears on the face of the same sheet as the title, each is shown without parentheses; if not, it is shown within parentheses, regardless of the source of the parenthetical information. Often the state as well as the city appears in these facts of publication, but major cities (including Berkeley) are consistently entered without state.

Binding or Format: "Hardcover" refers to all hardcover issues: cloth, half-cloth, boards, leather, etc. A dustwrapper is specified when known to exist and is a paper dustwrapper unless otherwise described. "Broadside" is a single sheet designed to display text appearing on one side only. A broadside is listed separately even if it bears the same title as a related book printed earlier or later than the broadside. I abandon the term "broadside" if another description is required for clarity (e.g. "postcard", "bookmark", "bumpersticker"). I have tried to be precise in describing works manufactured by quick service reproduction. Dittoed, mimeographed, hectographed and photocopied sheets circulate commonly, susceptible to further reproduction by xerographic process. When unable to identify an exact method of reproduction, I have resorted to the phrase "mechanically reproduced sheets." "Wrappers" is a term used variously to describe entries which are neither "hardcover" nor "broadside" nor "photocopied or mechanically reproduced sheets". For example, "wrappers" may describe a single folded sheet not designed to be displayed as a broadside. "Offprint" refers to a section of a larger publication which has been printed separately from either the same type setting or the same plates as the original.

Priority of Issue: The chronological priority (if any) of multiple "issues" is always signaled by the phrase "priority as listed" or "no priority". The usual joint issues are "hardcover" and "wrappers". The size of an edition and points of issue are described when known.

Identification of First Edition: Whenever applicable, the statement on the copyright page is transcribed ("first edition", "First Printing", etc.). I use the phrase "No statement of first edition" if a major publisher or university press does not identify the first edition on the copyright page. I do not usually provide an explicit identification of the first edition status of a small press publication, because it normally has only one printing. If necessary, however, further information (e.g. "$1.25" on cover; "sky-crappers" on page 105) is supplied to identify the first edition.

Illustration: An illustrator is named only if the work includes either his signature or an original illustration, or both.

Series Title: A series or group title of which an entry is a part is always given (e.g. "Maya Quarto Five", "Unicorn Folio: Series One, Number Four").

This is not a definitive work. I look forward to corrections and improvements and welcome correspondence to those ends.

Gary M. Lepper
Concord, California
March, 1976

Nelson Algren

SOMEBODY IN BOOTS. New York: Vanguard Press (1935).
    Hardcover, dustwrapper.
    No statement of first edition.
    ALSO: New York: Avon Publications (ca. 1957).
        Wrappers.
        No statement of first edition.
        NOTE: 1). Retitled *The Jungle*.
              2). Abridged edition.
    ALSO: (NewYork): Berkley Publishing Co. (1965).
        Wrappers.
        "BERKLEY MEDALLION EDITION, AUGUST, 1965"
        NOTE: New preface by the author.

NEVER COME MORNING. New York: Harper & Bros. (1942).
    Hardcover, dustwrapper.
    "FIRST EDITION"
    ALSO: New York: Avon Publications #185 (1948).*
        Wrappers.
        No statement of first edition.
        NOTE: Revised edition.
    ALSO: New York: Harper & Row (1963).
        Wrappers.
        "First HARPER COLOPHON Edition..."
        NOTE: New preface by the author.

THE NEON WILDERNESS. Garden City, N.Y.: Doubleday, 1947.
    Hardcover, dustwrapper; priority as listed:
        1). Advertisements for other books on back cover of dustwrapper.
        2). Critical excerpt on back cover of dustwrapper.
   "first edition"

THE MAN WITH THE GOLDEN ARM. Garden City, N.Y. : Doubleday, 1949.
   Hardcover, dustwrapper; no priority:
      1). Trade edition.
      2). Unknown number of copies, signed by the author on a tipped-in sheet.
   "FIRST EDITION"

CHICAGO. Garden City, N.Y. : Doubleday, 1951.
   Hardcover, dustwrapper.
   "First Edition"
   NOTE: Uncorrrected proofs in printed wrappers preceded publication.
   ALSO: Sausalito, Calif. : Contact Editions, 1961.
      Wrappers.
      NOTE: New introduction by the author.
   ALSO: Oakland: Angel Island Publications (1961).
      Wrappers, priority as listed:
         1). Epilogue entitled *Ode To Kissassville.*
         2). Epilogue entitled *Ode To Lower Finksville.*
      "Third Edition"
      NOTE: New epilogue by the author.

A WALK ON THE WILD SIDE.   New York: Farrar, Straus & Cudahy (1956).
   Hardcover, dustwrapper.
   "First printing, 1956"
   ALSO: Greenwich, Conn. : Fawcett (1963).*
      Wrappers.
      NOTE: Revised edition.

WHO LOST AN AMERICAN? (London): Andre Deutsch (1963).
   Hardcover, dustwrapper.
   No statement of first edition.

CONVERSATIONS WITH NELSON ALGREN. New York: Hill and Wang (1964).
   Hardcover, dustwrapper.
   "First edition October 1964"
   NOTE: 1). Only H. E. F. Donahue is noted as the author.
      2). The words of Algren comprise most of the text.
      3). A brochure, with excerpts from the book, preceded publication.

NOTES FROM A SEA DIARY. New York: Putnam (1965).
   Hardcover, dustwrapper.
   No statement of first edition.

THE LAST CAROUSEL. New York: Putnam (1973).
   Hardcover, dustwrapper.
   No statement of first edition.
   NOTE: Uncorrected proofs in printed wrappers preceded publication.

John Ashbery

TURANDOT. New York: Tibor de Nagy Gallery, 1953.
>Wrappers.
>300 copies.
>NOTE: There were an unknown number of unnumbered copies.

SOME TREES. New Haven, Conn.: Yale University Press, 1956.
>Hardcover, dustwrapper.
>No statement of first edition.
>Yale Series of Younger Poets Volume 52.

THE POEMS. New York: Tiber Press (1960).
>Hardcover, acetate dustwrapper; no priority:
>>1). 200 copies, numbered in Arabic, signed by the author and illustrator.
>>2). 25 copies, numbered in Roman, signed by the author and illustrator.
>Illustrated by Joan Mitchell.
>NOTE: Issued in box with *Permanently* by Kenneth Koch, *Odes* by Frank O'Hara and
>>*Salute* by James Schuyler.

ARTISTS' THEATRE: FOUR PLAYS. New York/London: Grove Press/Evergreen Books
>(1960).
>Wrappers.
>"First Evergreen Edition 1960"
>NOTE: Plays by four authors; Ashbery contributed *The Heroes*.

THE TENNIS COURT OATH. Middletown, Conn.: Wesleyan University Press (1962).
>Two issues, no priority:
>>1). Hardcover, dustwrapper.
>>2). Wrappers.
>"FIRST EDITION"

THE TICKET. (Rome: Angelo Savelli, 1963).*
>Broadside.
>110 copies.

THE FUCK YOU QUOTE OF THE WEEK #2. New York: Fuck You Press, 1964.
Broadside.

A CONVERSATION. Tucson: Interview Press (ca. 1965).
Wrappers.
NOTE: With Kenneth Koch.

BALANCE OF PAYMENTS. Spoleto, Italy: Spoleto Festival, 1965.*
Mimeographed sheets.
NOTE: The Italian text was published simultaneously.

JOE BRAINARD. (New York): Alan Gallery (1965).
Wrappers.

RIVERS AND MOUNTAINS. New York: Holt, Rinehart & Winston (1966).
Two issues, no priority:
1). Hardcover, dustwrapper.
2). Wrappers.
"First Edition"

SELECTED POEMS. London: Jonathan Cape (1967).
Hardcover, dustwrapper; priority as listed:
1). Lines 7-8 of the copyright statement read "c 1957, 1959, 1960, 1961, 1962
by John Ashbery"
2). Errata slip pasted in so that lines 7-8 read: "Now reprinted by permission of
Wesleyan University Press c 1959, 1962, 1957, and 1960 (respectively) by…"
3). Correction integral.
No statement of first edition.
NOTE: Uncorrected proofs in printed wrappers preceded publication.

THREE MADRIGALS. (New York: Poets Press, 1968).
Wrappers, no priority:
1). 150 copies, numbered, signed by the author.
2). 12 copies, for the use of the author.
NOTE: There were an unknown number of copies (1) unnumbered and unsigned and
(2) asterisked and signed.

SUNRISE IN SUBURBIA. New York: Phoenix Book Shop, 1968.
Wrappers, wove paper, no priority:
1). 100 copies, numbered, signed by the author.
2). 26 copies, lettered, signed by the author.
NOTE: 1). 6 copies of uncorrected proofs on laid paper, stapled, preceded publication.
2). There were an unknown number of "out of series" copies, unnumbered and
unsigned.

A NEST OF NINNIES. New York: Dutton, 1969.
    Hardcover, dustwrapper.
    "First Edition"
    NOTE: With James Schuyler.

A WHITE PAPER. (New York: Museum of Modern Art, 1969).
    Plastic sheet with raised letters.

FRAGMENT. Los Angeles: Black Sparrow Press, 1969.
    Two issues, no priority:
        1). Hardcover, acetate dustwrapper; no priority:
            a). 250 copies, numbered, signed by the author and illustrator.
            b). 20 copies, lettered, signed by the author, with an original drawing by
                the illustrator, boxed.
            c). 5 special copies, for the publisher, author, illustrator, printer & binder.
        2). Wrappers.
            750 copies.
    Illustrated by Alex Katz.

EVENING IN THE COUNTRY. San Francisco: Spanish Main Press (1970).
    Broadside.

THE DOUBLE DREAM OF SPRING. New York: Dutton, 1970.
    Two issues, priority as listed:
        1). Hardcover, dustwrapper; priority as listed:
            a). Cover measures 8 5/16" x 6 1/8"; round spine.
            b). Cover measures 8 1/8" x 6"; flat spine.
        2). Wrappers.
    "First Edition"
    NOTE: Uncorrected proofs in ring-bound wrappers preceded publication.

THE NEW SPIRIT. New York: Adventures In Poetry (1970).
    Wrappers, no priority:
        1). 100 copies.
        2). 65 copies, numbered, signed by the author.

PINK PURPLE AND BLUE. (New York: Privately published, 1971).*
    Broadside.
    12 copies (approximately).

EUROPA. New York: EENU (1971).
    Sheets in acetate in clip folder.
    NOTE: The text is entirely in Spanish.

I OPEN MY EYES. (Kent, Ohio: Kent State University Libraries, 1971).
>   Broadside, no priority:
>   >   1). 450 copies.
>   >   2). 50 copies, signed by the author.
>   NOTE: Laid in portfolio entitled *Six Poems/Seven Prints*, which is itself *Occasional Papers #6*.

THREE POEMS. New York: Viking Press (1972).
>   Two issues, no priority:
>   >   1). Hardcover, dustwrapper.
>   >   2). Wrappers.
>   No statement of first edition.
>   NOTE: Uncorrected proofs in printed wrappers preceded publication.

FROM THE NEW SPIRIT. (Brockport, N.Y.: Department of English, State University College, 1972).
>   Wrappers.
>   NOTE: Cover title is *Writer's Forum*.

THE SERIOUS DOLL. (Syracuse, N.Y.: Kermani Press, 1975).
>   Wrappers.
>   50 copies, numbered, signed by the author.

THE VERMONT NOTEBOOK. Los Angeles: Black Sparrow Press, 1975.
>   Two issues, no priority:
>   >   1). Hardcover, acetate dustwrapper; no priority:
>   >   >   a). 250 copies, numbered, signed by the author and illustrator.
>   >   >   b). 26 copies, lettered, signed by the author and illustrator, with an original drawing by the illustrator.
>   >   >   c). 6 special copies, for the publisher, author, illustrator, printer, binder and publisher's file.
>   >   2). Wrappers.
>   >   2190 copies.
>   Illustrated by Joe Brainard.

SELF-PORTRAIT IN A CONVEX MIRROR. New York: Viking Press (1975).
>   Hardcover, dustwrapper.
>   No statement of first edition.

*COMPILER'S NOTE: Only one artist's exhibition catalogue is listed above, although Ashbery contributed to many. I did not examine most of those and, therefore, do not know which would meet my criteria for inclusion here.The reader should consult the "E" section of David K. Kermani's fine bibliography of Ashbery (New York: Garland Publishing, 1976) for additional information.

Translations.

Jean-Jacques Mayoux.
MELVILLE. New York : Grove Press (1960).
    Wrappers.
    No statement of first edition.
    Evergreen Profile Book 9.

Noel Vexin.
MURDER IN MONTMARTRE. (New York) : Dell (1960).*
    Wrappers.
    "First Dell printing — November, 1960"
    NOTE : 1). Translated as "Jonas Berry."
        2). Translated with Lawrence G. Blochman.

Genevieve Manceron.
THE DEADLIER SIN. (New York) : Dell (1961).*
    Wrappers.
    "First Dell printing — April, 1961"
    NOTE : 1). Translated as "Jonas Berry."
        2). Translated with Lawrence G. Blochman.

Louis Auchinloss

THE INDIFFERENT CHILDREN. New York: Prentice-Hall (1947).
    Hardcover, dustwrapper.
    No statement of first edition.
    NOTE: Written as "Andrew Lee."

THE INJUSTICE COLLECTORS. Boston:Houghton Mifflin, 1950.
    Hardcover, dustwrapper.
    Date on title page.

SYBIL. Boston: Houghton Mifflin, 1952.
    Hardcover, dustwrapper.
    Date on title page.

A LAW FOR THE LION. Boston: Houghton Mifflin, 1953.
    Hardcover, dustwrapper.
    Date on title page.

THE ROMANTIC EGOISTS. Boston: Houghton Mifflin, 1954.
    Hardcover, dustwrapper.
    Date on title page.

THE GREAT WORLD AND TIMOTHY COLT. Boston: Houghton Mifflin, 1956.
    Hardcover, dustwrapper.
    "FIRST PRINTING: OCTOBER 1956"

VENUS IN SPARTA. Boston: Houghton Mifflin, 1958.
    Hardcover, dustwrapper.
    "FIRST PRINTING"

PURSUIT OF THE PRODIGAL. Boston: Houghton Mifflin, 1959.
    Hardcover, dustwrapper.
    "FIRST PRINTING"
    NOTE: Review copies in printed wrappers preceded publication.

THE HOUSE OF FIVE TALENTS. Boston: Houghton Mifflin, 1960.
    Hardcover, dustwrapper.
    "First Printing"

REFLECTIONS OF A JACOBITE. Boston: Houghton Mifflin (1961).
    Hardcover, dustwrapper.
    "FIRST PRINTING"

EDITH WHARTON. Minneapolis: University of Minnesota Press (1961).
    Wrappers.
    No statement of first edition.
    University of Minnesota Pamphlets on American Writers #12.

PORTRAIT IN BROWNSTONE. Boston: Houghton Mifflin, 1962.
    Hardcover, dustwrapper.
    "First Printing"

POWERS OF ATTORNEY. Boston: Houghton Mifflin, 1963.
    Hardcover, dustwrapper.
    "First printing"

THE RECTOR OF JUSTIN. Boston: Houghton Mifflin, 1964.
    Hardcover, dustwrapper.
    "First Printing"

ELLEN GLASGOW. Minneapolis: University of Minnesota Press (1964).
    Wrappers.
    No statement of first edition.
    University of Minnesota Pamphlets on American Writers Number 33.

PIONEERS & CARETAKERS. Minneapolis: University of Minnesota Press (1965).
    Hardcover, dustwrapper.
    No statement of first edition.

THE EMBEZZLER. Boston: Houghton Mifflin, 1966.
    Hardcover, dustwrapper.
    "First Printing"

TALES OF MANHATTAN. Boston: Houghton Mifflin, 1967.
    Hardcover, dustwrapper.
    "First Printing"

EDITH WHARTON AND HER LETTERS. (New York: Hofstra Review, 1967).*
    Wrappers.
    NOTE: Offprint from *Hofstra Review*, Winter 1967.

ON SISTER CARRIE. (New York): Charles E. Merrill, 1968.
    Wrappers.
    "First Printing" on verso of cover.
    500 copies.

A WORLD OF PROFIT. Boston: Houghton Mifflin, 1968.
    Hardcover, dustwrapper; no known priority:
        1). Dustwrapper with drawing of birds.
        2). Dustwrapper with drawing of urban skyline.
    "First Printing"

MOTIVELESS MALIGNITY. Boston: Houghton Mifflin, 1969.
    Hardcover, dustwrapper.
    "First Printing"

SECOND CHANCE. Boston: Houghton Mifflin, 1970.
    Hardcover, dustwrapper.
    "First Printing"

EDITH WHARTON. New York: Viking Press (1971).
    Hardcover, dustwrapper.
    No statement of first edition.

HENRY ADAMS. Minneapolis: University of Minnesota Press (1971).
    Wrappers.
    No statement of first edition.
    University of Minnesota Pamphlets on American Writers Number 93.

I COME AS A THIEF. Boston: Houghton Mifflin, 1972.
    Hardcover, dustwrapper.
    "First Printing"
    NOTE: Uncorrected proofs in printed wrappers preceded publication.

RICHELIEU. New York: Viking Press (1972).
    Hardcover, dustwrapper.
    No statement of first edition.

THE PARTNERS. Boston: Houghton Mifflin, 1974.
    Hardcover, dustwrappers.
    "First Printing"
    NOTE: Uncorrected proofs in printed wrappers preceded publication.

A WRITER'S CAPITAL. Minneapolis: University of Minnesota Press (1974).
    Hardcover, dustwrapper.
    No statement of first edition.

READING HENRY JAMES. Minneapolis: University of Minnesota Press (1975).
    Hardcover, dustwrapper.
    No statement of first edition.

James Baldwin

GO TELL IT ON THE MOUNTAIN. New York: Knopf, 1953.
    Hardcover, dustwrapper; no known priority:
        1). Tan binding.
        2). Green binding.*
    "FIRST EDITION"
    NOTE: 500 review copies in printed wrappers preceded publication.

NOTES OF A NATIVE SON. Boston: Beacon Press (1955).
    Hardcover, dustwrapper; priority as listed:
        1). Dustwrapper with no review quotations on back panel.
        2). Dustwrapper with review quotations on back panel.
    No statement of first edition.

GIOVANNI'S ROOM. New York: Dial Press, 1956.
    Hardcover, dustwrapper.
    No statement of first edition.

NOBODY KNOWS MY NAME. New York: Dial Press, 1961.
    Hardcover, dustwrapper.
    No statement of first edition.
    NOTE: Uncorrected proofs in printed wrappers preceded publication.

THIS MORNING, THIS EVENING, SO SOON. Frankfurt am Main: Verlag Moritz
    Diesterweg (1962).*
    Wrappers.

ANOTHER COUNTRY. New York: Dial Press, 1962.
    Hardcover, dustwrapper.
    No statement of first edition.

THE FIRE NEXT TIME. New York: Dial Press, 1963.
    Hardcover, dustwrapper.
    No statement of first edition.
    NOTE: Review copies in printed wrappers preceded publication.

BLUES FOR MISTER CHARLIE. New York: Dial Press, 1964.
  Hardcover, dustwrapper.
  No statement of first edition.

NOTHING PERSONAL. (New York: Atheneum, 1964).
  Hardcover, boxed.
  No statement of first edition.

GOING TO MEET THE MAN. London: Michael Joseph (1965).
  Hardcover, dustwrapper.
  No statement of first edition.

THE AMEN CORNER. New York: Dial Press, 1968.
  Hardcover, dustwrapper.
  "First Printing, 1968"
  NOTE: Reportedly, there was a mimeographed script for the 1955 production in
    Washington, D.C.

TELL ME HOW LONG THE TRAIN'S BEEN GONE. New York: Dial Press, 1968.
  Hardcover, dustwrapper.
  "First Printing, 1968"
  NOTE: Uncorrected proofs in printed wrappers preceded publication.

AN OPEN LETTER TO MY SISTER, MISS ANGELA DAVIS.   (New York): New York
    Committee to Free Angela Davis (ca. 1970).
  Broadside.
  NOTE: An offprint from *The New York Review of Books*.

A RAP ON RACE. Philadelphia: Lippincott (1971).
  Hardcover, dustwrapper.
  "First edition"
  NOTE: With Margaret Mead.

NO NAME IN THE STREET. London: Michael Joseph (1972).
  Hardcover, dustwrapper.
  No statement of first edition.

ONE DAY, WHEN I WAS LOST. London: Michael Joseph (1972).
  Hardcover, dustwrapper.
  No statement of first edition.

A DIALOGUE. Philadelphia: Lippincott (1973).
  Two issues, no priority:
        1). Hardcover, dustwrapper.
        2). Wrappers.
    "First edition"
  NOTE: With Nikki Giovanni.

IF BEALE STREET COULD TALK. New York: Dial Press, 1974.
  Hardcover, no priority:
    1). Trade edition, dustwrapper.
    2). 250 copies, numbered, signed by the author, boxed.
  "First Printing"
  NOTE: 1). Uncorrected proofs in printed wrappers preceded publication.
    2). An unknown number of copies bear a proof dustwrapper, which is blank
        except for a pictorial likeness of the author.
    3). A Formosan piracy of the first edition, in reduced format, has been examined.

John Barth

THE FLOATING OPERA. New York: Appleton-Century-Crofts (1956).
   Hardcover, dustwrapper.
   "(1)" following text on page 280.
   ALSO: Garden City, N.Y.: Doubleday, 1967.
      Hardcover, dustwrapper.
      "This Doubleday edition has been revised by the author."

THE END OF THE ROAD. Garden City, N.Y.: Doubleday, 1958.
   Hardcover, dustwrapper.
   "First Edition"
   ALSO: Garden City, N.Y.: Doubleday, 1967.
      Hardcover, dustwrapper.
      "Revised Edition"

THE SOT-WEED FACTOR. Garden City, N.Y.: Doubleday, 1960.
   Hardcover, dustwrapper.
   "First Edition"
   ALSO: Garden City, N.Y.: Doubleday, 1967.
      Hardcover, dustwrapper.
      "REVISED EDITION"

GILES GOAT-BOY. Garden City, N.Y.: Doubleday, 1966.
   Hardcover, no priority:
      1). Trade Edition, dustwrapper; priority unknown:
         a). $6.95 in upper right corner of front flap of dustwrapper.
         b). $6.95 in lower right corner of front flap of dustwrapper.
      2). 250 copies, numbered, signed by the author, boxed.
   "H18" in bottom right corner of page 710.
   NOTE: Uncorrected proofs in printed wrappers preceded publication.

LOST IN THE FUNHOUSE. Garden City, N.Y.: Doubleday, 1968.
   Hardcover, no priority:
      1). Trade edition, dustwrapper.
      2). 250 copies, numbered, signed by the author, boxed.
   "First Edition"
   NOTE: Uncorrected proofs in printed wrappers preceded publication.

CHIMERA. New York: Random House (1972).
      Hardcover, no priority:
          1). Trade edition, dustwrapper.
          2). 300 copies, numbered, signed by the author, boxed.
     "First Edition"
     NOTE: Uncorrected proofs in printed wrappers preceded publication.

A CONVERSATION WITH JOHN BARTH. (Schenectady: Union College, 1972).
     Wrappers.
     NOTE: A special issue of *The Idol*.

NATIONAL BOOK AWARD ACCEPTANCE REMARKS. (New York: Privately published)
     1973.
     Photocopied sheet.

Donald Barthelme

COME BACK, DR. CALIGARI. Boston: Little, Brown (1964).
    Hardcover, dustwrapper.
    "FIRST EDITION"
    NOTE: Review copies preceded publication; no known priority:
           1). Two stories on unbound sheets, laid in box labeled "An Advance
              Preview."
           2). Uncorrected proofs, tied in printed wrappers.

SNOW WHITE. New York: Atheneum, 1967.
    Hardcover, dustwrapper.
    "First Edition"

UNSPEAKABLE PRACTICES, UNNATURAL ACTS. New York: Farrar, Straus & Giroux
    (1968).
    Hardcover, dustwrapper.
    "First printing, 1968"

CITY LIFE. New York: Farrar, Straus & Giroux (1970).
    Hardcover, dustwrapper; priority as listed:
           1). No black dot on rear cover.
           2). Black dot on rear cover.
    "First Printing, 1970"

THE SLIGHTLY IRREGULAR FIRE ENGINE. New York: Farrar, Straus & Giroux (1971).
    Hardcover, dustwrapper.
    "First edition, 1971"
    NOTE: A National Book Award sticker was later placed on the front of the
        dustwrapper.

SADNESS. New York: Farrar, Straus & Giroux (1972).
    Hardcover, dustwrapper.
    "First printing, 1972"
    NOTE: Uncorrected proofs in printed wrappers preceded publication; text differs from
        the trade edition.

GUILTY PLEASURES. New York: Farrar, Straus & Giroux (1974).
    Hardcover, dustwrapper.
    "First printing, 1974"
    NOTE: Uncorrected proofs in printed wrappers preceded publication.

THE DEAD FATHER. New York: Farrar, Straus & Giroux (1975).
    Hardcover, dustwrapper.
    "First printing, 1975"
    NOTE: The *Manual For Sons* section was photocopied in galley form and sent, with a
        letter from the author and publisher, to salesmen.

Saul Bellow

DANGLING MAN. New York: Vanguard Press (1944).
    Hardcover, dustwrapper.
    No statement of first edition.

THE VICTIM. New York: Vanguard Press (1947).
    Hardcover, dustwrapper.
    No statement of first edition.

THE ADVENTURES OF AUGIE MARCH. New York: Viking Press, 1953.
    Hardcover, priority as listed:
        1). Orange topstain; copyright page notes Vail-Ballou as printer.
        2). No topstain; copyright page notes Wolff as printer.
    Dustwrapper, priority as listed:
        1). No excerpts from reviews.
        2). Several excerpts from reviews.
    No statement of first edition.

SEIZE THE DAY. New York: Viking Press, 1956.
    Hardcover, dustwrapper.
    No statement of first edition.

HENDERSON THE RAIN KING. New York: Viking Press, 1959.
    Hardcover, dustwrapper; priority as listed:
        1). Yellow topstain.
        2). No topstain.
    No statement of first edition.

DESSINS. Paris: Editions Cahiers d'Art (1960).
    Hardcover, dustwrapper.
    No statement of first edition.
    NOTE: This is often listed as a "translation" by Bellow; it is not. It is a book of reproductions of the art of Jesse Reichek. The only text consists of two pages (in French) by Christian Zervos and one page (in English) by Bellow.

RECENT AMERICAN FICTION. Washington, D. C. : Library of Congress, 1963.
Wrappers.

HERZOG. New York : Viking Press (1964).
 Hardcover, dustwrapper; priority as listed:
  1). Printing of text generally light throughout.
  2). Printing of text generally darker throughout.
 No statement of first edition.
 NOTE : 1). The issue point is legitimate, but uncertainly identified. The first printing
  was received as described, found unsatisfactory and another printing was
  ordered. The subsequent printing arrived, but, because of the volume of
  orders, both sets of sheets were bound as the first edition. Confusion results
  from the fact that the inking of the second printing is not very superior to that of
  the first.
  2). Uncorrected proofs in ringbound printed wrappers, with the publication
  price noted as $5.00, preceded publication. At least one copy has revised
  sheets pasted over the printed sheets underneath.
  3). Sewn signatures, laid in the finished dustwrapper, with a slip announcing
  the date of publication and a change in price from $5.00 to $5.95, preceded
  publication.

FROM A STATEMENT BY SAUL BELLOW ABOUT HERZOG. New York : Viking Press
 (ca. 1964).
 Mechanically reproduced sheet.

ACCEPTANCE SPEECH, NATIONAL BOOK AWARD. New York : Privately published,
 1965.*
 Mechanically reproduced sheet.

THE LAST ANALYSIS. New York : Viking Press (1965).
 Hardcover, dustwrapper.
 No statement of first edition.
 NOTE : Reportedly, this play appeared earlier, entitled *Bummidge,* in an edition of
  mimeographed sheets for the use of the New York cast.

KEYNOTE ADDRESS. New York : P. E. N., 1966.
 Mimeographed sheets.

MOSBY'S MEMOIRS. New York : Viking Press (1968).
 Hardcover, dustwrapper.
 No statement of first edition.
 NOTE : Uncorrected proofs in printed wrappers, ringbound, preceded publication.

MR. SAMMLER'S PLANET. New York : Viking Press (1970).
 Hardcover, dustwrapper.
 No statement of first edition.
 NOTE : Uncorrected proofs in printed wrappers preceded publication.

ACCEPTANCE SPEECH, NATIONAL BOOK AWARD. New York: (Privately published), 1971.*

Mechanically reproduced sheets.

THE PORTABLE SAUL BELLOW. New York: Viking Press, 1974.

  Two issues, no priority:

  1). Hardcover, no priority:

  a). Trade edition, dustwrapper.

  b). Library edition, with special binding.

  2). Wrappers.

No statement of first edition.

HUMBOLDT'S GIFT. New York: Viking Press (1975).

  Hardcover, dustwrapper; no priority:

  1). Trade edition.

  2). Unknown number of copies, signed by the author on a tipped-in sheet.

No statement of first edition.

NOTE: Uncorrected proofs in printed wrappers preceded publication.

TRANSLATION.

I. B. Singer.
GIMPEL THE FOOL. New York: Farrar, Straus & Giroux, 1967.*
    Hardcover, dustwrapper.
    NOTE : It is the practice of this publisher to indicate first printing.

Thomas Berger

CRAZY IN BERLIN. New York: Scribner's (1958).
    Hardcover, dustwrapper; priority as listed:
        1). No rear flyleaf.
        2). Rear flyleaf added.
    "A" on copyright page.

REINHART IN LOVE. New York: Scribner's (1962).
    Hardcover, dustwrapper.
    "A" on copyright page.
    ALSO: London:Eyre & Spottiswoode (1963).
    Hardcover, dustwrapper.
    No statement of first edition.
    NOTE: Includes a sentence omitted from the first American edition.

LITTLE BIG MAN. New York: Dial Press, 1964.
    Hardcover, dustwrapper.
    No statement of first edition.

KILLING TIME. New York: Dial Press, 1967.
    Hardcover, dustwrapper.
    "First Printing 1967"
    NOTE: Uncorrected proofs in printed wrappers preceded publication.

VITAL PARTS. New York: Baron, 1970.
    Hardcover, dustwrapper.
    No statement of first edition.
    NOTE: Uncorrected proofs in printed wrappers preceded publication, priority as listed:
        1). Grey wrappers.
        2). Narrow yellow wrappers.

REGIMENT OF WOMEN. New York: Simon & Schuster (1973).
    Hardcover, dustwrapper.
    "FIRST PRINTING"
    NOTE: Uncorrected proofs in printed wrappers preceded publication.

SNEAKY PEOPLE. New York: Simon & Schuster (1975).
    Hardcover, dustwrapper.
    "1 2 3 4 5 6 7 8 9 10" on copyright page.
    NOTE: Uncorrected proofs in printed wrappers preceded publication.

Daniel Berrigan

TIME WITHOUT NUMBER. New York: Macmillan, 1957.
    Hardcover, dustwrapper.
    "First Printing"

THE BRIDE. New York: Macmillan, 1959.
    Hardcover, dustwrapper.
    "First Printing"

ENCOUNTERS. Cleveland: World (1960).
    Hardcover, dustwrapper.
    "FIRST EDITION"
    ALSO: New York: Associated Artists, 1965.
        Wrappers, no priority:
            1). 60 copies, numbered in Arabic, signed by the illustrator.
            2). 10 copies, lettered, signed by the illustrator.
            3). 5 copies, numbered in Roman, signed by the illustrator.
        Illustrated by Robert E. Marx.

THE BOW IN THE CLOUDS. New York: Coward-McCann (1961).*
    Hardcover, dustwrapper.

THE WORLD FOR WEDDING RING. New York: Macmillan (1962).
    Hardcover, dustwrapper.
    "First Printing"

NO ONE WALKS WATERS. New York: Macmillan (1966).
    Hardcover, dustwrapper.
    "First Printing"

THEY CALL US DEAD MEN. New York: Macmillan (1966).
    Hardcover, dustwrapper.
    "First Printing"

THE WORLD SHOWED ME ITS HEART. (St. Louis: National Sodality Service Center, 1966).
    Wrappers.

CONSEQUENCES. New York: Macmillan (1967).
    Hardcover, dustwrapper.
    "FIRST PRINTING"

TEN COMMANDMENTS FOR THE PEACEABLE. (Ithaca: Cornell United Religious Work, 1967).
    Mechanically reproduced sheet.
    NOTE: Anonymous.

THE FREE AND LASTING UNIVERSITY. (Ithaca: Cornell United Religious Work, 1967).
    Mechanically reproduced sheet.

GO FROM HERE. San Francisco: Open Space, 1968.
    Wrappers.
    NOTE: Suppressed before publication and never sewn into covers.

GOD. (Santa Barbara, Calif.: Unicorn Press, 1968).
    Broadside.

CRIME POEMS / TRIAL POEMS. (Ithaca: Glad Day Press, 1968).
    Folded sheets.
    NOTE: Laid loosely in *The First Issue, #9*.

LOVE, LOVE AT THE END. New York: Macmillan (1968).
    Hardcover, dustwrapper.
    "FIRST PRINTING"

NIGHT FLIGHT TO HANOI. New York: Macmillan (1968).
    Hardcover, dustwrapper.
    "FIRST PRINTING"

HANOI POEMS. (Ithaca: Cornell United Religious Work, 1968).
    Mechanically reproduced sheets.

LAUREL. (Ithaca: Cornell United Religious Work, 1968).
    Mechanically reproduced sheets.
    NOTE: 1). An untitled collection of poems, the first of which is *Laurel*.
        2). Anonymous.

IN BALTIMORE. (Ithaca: Cornell United Religious Work, 1968).
    Mechanically reproduced sheets.
    NOTE: 1). Anonymous.
        2). An untitled collection of poems, the first of which is *In Baltimore*.

I HAD A SENSE. (Ithaca:Cornell United Religious Work, 1968).
  Mechanically reproduced sheets.
  NOTE: 1). Anonymous.
      2). An untitled collection of poems, the first of which is *I Had a Sense.*

NOTES OF A FUGITIVE. N.p., (ca. 1968).
  Mechanically reproduced sheets.
  NOTE: *Letter #1* from Berrigan; *Letter #2* from Allen Ginsberg.

FALSE GODS, REAL MEN. (New York): Macmillan (1969).
  Hardcover, dustwrapper.
  "First Printing"

THE TRIAL OF THE CATONSVILLE NINE. Boston: Beacon Press (1970).
  Two issues, no priority:
      1). Hardcover, dustwrapper.
      2). Wrappers.
  No statement of first edition.

TRIAL POEMS. Boston: Beacon Press (1970).
  Hardcover, dustwrapper.
  No statement of first edition.
  NOTE: With Thomas Lewis.

CRIME TRIAL. Boston: Impressions Workshop (1970).
  Sheets in portfolio, boxed; no priority:
      1). 75 copies, portfolio signed by the author and illustrator; each etching signed
         by the illustrator, numbered.
      2). 15 copies of each etching in black and white, signed by the illustrator; there
         is no text.
  Illustrated by Robert E. Marx.

NO BARS TO MANHOOD. Garden City, N.Y.: Doubleday, 1970.
  Hardcover, dustwrapper.
  "FIRST EDITION"

FATHER BERRIGAN'S LETTER TO THE WEATHERMEN. (Nyack, N.Y.: Fellowship
  Publications, ca. 1971).
  Sheet photocopied on both sides.
  NOTE: From *The Village Voice,* January 21, 1971.

THE GEOGRAPHY OF FAITH. Boston: Beacon Press (1971).
  Hardcover, dustwrapper.
  No statement of first edition.

THE DARK NIGHT OF RESISTANCE. Garden City, N.Y.: Doubleday, 1971.
  Hardcover, dustwrapper.
  "First Edition"

AMERICA IS HARD TO FIND. Garden City, N.Y.: Doubleday, 1972.
    Hardcover, dustwrapper.
    "First Edition"

ABSURD CONVICTIONS, MODEST HOPES. New York: Random House (1972).
    Hardcover, dustwrapper.
    "First Edition"
    NOTE: With Les Lockwood.

PRISON POEMS. (Greensboro, N.C.): Unicorn Press, 1973.
    Hardcover, dustwrapper.
    No statement of first edition.
    NOTE: Review copies in printed wrappers preceded publication.

SELECTED AND NEW POEMS. Garden City, N.Y.: Doubleday, 1973.
    Hardcover, dustwrapper.
    "FIRST EDITION"

JESUS CHRIST. Garden City, N.Y.: Doubleday, 1973.
    Hardcover, dustwrapper.
    "First Edition"

VIETNAMESE LETTER. (Nyack, N.Y.): Hoa Binh Press (1974).
    Wrappers.
    250 copies, numbered, signed by the author and illustrator; Berrigan's signature is
    only "Daniel."
    Illustrated by Thomas Lewis.
    NOTE: There were an unknown number of copies, unnumbered, with the author's
        facsimile signature printed in full.

CONTEMPLATION AND RESISTANCE. (Nyack, N.Y.: Fellowship of Reconciliation,
    ca. 1974).
    Wrappers.
    NOTE: With Nhat Hanh.

LIGHTS ON IN THE HOUSE OF THE DEAD. Garden City, N.Y.: Doubleday, 1974.
    Hardcover, dustwrapper.
    "First Edition"

Ted Berrigan

THE SONNETS. (New York): Lorenz and Ellen Gude, 1964.
    Wrappers.
    300 copies, numbered.
    NOTE: There were an unknown number of unnumbered copies.

A NEW BABY WAS BORN. (N. p.: Privately published, 1965).
    Broadside.
    NOTE: Birth announcement collage.

LIVING WITH CHRIS. (New York): Boke Press (ca. 1965).
    Wrappers.

SOME THINGS. N.p., (ca. 1966).
    Mimeographed sheet in folder.
    NOTE: With Ron Padgett.

BEAN SPASMS. (New York: Kulchur Press, 1967).
    Two issues, no priority:
        1). Hardcover, acetate dustwrapper.
        2). Wrappers.
    NOTE: With Ron Padgett.

MANY HAPPY RETURNS TO DICK GALLUP. (New York: Angel Hair, 1967).
    Wrappers, no priority:
        1). 200 copies.
        2). 4 copies, lettered, signed by the author.
    ALSO: New York: Corinth Books, 1969.
        Wrappers, no priority:
            1). 1450 copies.
            2). 50 copies, numbered, signed by the author and illustrator.
        Illustrated by Joe Brainard.
    NOTE: Retitled *Many Happy Returns*.

DOUBLETALK. (Iowa City: Privately published, 1969).
    Wrappers.
    240 copies, signed by the authors.
    NOTE: With Anselm Hollo.

PEACE. Detroit: Alternative Press (1969).
    Broadside.

NOH. (N. p.: Lines Press, 1969).
    Broadside.
    50 copies, numbered, signed by the authors.
    Linesheet 1.
    NOTE: With Ron Padgett.

A FRAGMENT. (London: Cape Goliard Press, 1969).
    Broadside in folder, no priority:
        1). 267 copies, numbered.
        2). 60 copies, numbered, signed by the author and illustrator.
    Illustrated by Jim Dine.

GUILLAUME APOLLINAIRE IST TOT. (Frankfurt, Germany): Marz Verlag (1970).
    Wrappers, dustwrapper.
    NOTE: Bilingual edition containing material yet to appear in the United States.

SCORPION, EAGLE & DOVE. (N. p.: Privately published) 1970.
    Broadside, no priority:
        1). Trade edition.
        2). 50 copies, numbered, signed by the author.

IN THE EARLY MORNING RAIN. London: Cape Goliard Press, 1970.
    Hardcover, no priority:
        1). Trade edition.
        2). 100 copies, numbered, signed by the author.
    "This first edition..."

POEMS, IN BRIEF. Bolinas, Calif.: (Privately published) 1971.
    Wrappers, manila folder.
    12 copies, numbered, signed by the author.
    NOTE: Comprises the only issue of *The Synthetic Magazine.*

MEMORIAL DAY. (New York: Poetry Project, St. Mark's Church In-the-Bowery, 1971).
    Wrappers.
    NOTE: With Anne Waldman.

AN INTERVIEW WITH TED BERRIGAN. London, 1971.*
    Wrappers.

BACK IN BOSTON AGAIN. (New York): Telegraph Books (1972).
    Wrappers, no priority:
        1). Trade edition.
        2). 50 copies, numbered, signed by the authors.
    "FIRST EDITION"
    NOTE: With Tom Clark and Ron Padgett.

THE DRUNKEN BOAT. (New York): Adventures In Poetry (1974).
    Wrappers.

A FEELING FOR LEAVING. (New York): Frontward Books (1975).
    Wrappers, no priority:
        1). 375 copies.
        2). 25 copies, numbered, signed by the author.
        3). 3 copies, hors commerce.

Wendell Berry

NATHAN COULTER. Boston: Houghton Mifflin, 1960.
    Hardcover, dustwrapper.
    "First printing"

THE BROKEN GROUND. New York: Harcourt, Brace & World (1964).
    Hardcover, dustwrapper.
    "first edition"

NOVEMBER TWENTY SIX NINETEEN HUNDRED SIXTY THREE. New York: George
    Braziller (1964).
    Hardcover, boxed; no priority:
        1). Trade edition.
        2). Limited edition, signed by the author and illustrator, with an original
        illustration by the illustrator.
    "FIRST EDITION"
    Illustrated by Ben Shahn.

A PLACE ON EARTH. New York: Harcourt, Brace & World (1967).
    Hardcover, dustwrapper.
    "F IRST EDITION"

OPENINGS. New York: Harcourt, Brace & World (1968).
    Hardcover, dustwrapper.
    "First edition"

THE RISE. (Lexington, Ky.: University of Kentucky Library Press, 1968).
    Hardcover.
    100 copies, numbered, signed by the author.

A SECULAR PILGRIMAGE. (N. p.: Privately published) 1968.
    Mechanically reproduced sheets.

FINDINGS. (Iowa City, Iowa): Prairie Press, 1969.
    Hardcover, dustwrapper.

AWAKE AT NIGHT; THE WAR; THREE HAIKU. (Palo Alto, Calif.:Privately published, 1969).
   Mimeographed sheet.

PRAYER AND SAYINGS OF THE MAD FARMER; THE GRANDMOTHER. (Palo Alto, Calif.: Privately published, 1969).
   Mimeographed sheets.

THE BIRTH (NEAR PORT WILLIAM). (Palo Alto, Calif.: Privately published, 1969).
   Mimeographed sheets, no known priority:
      1). 3 unnumbered pages.
      2). 5 numbered pages.

THE LONG-LEGGED HOUSE. New York: Harcourt, Brace & World (1969).
      Two issues, no priority:
         1). Hardcover, dustwrapper.
         2). Wrappers.
      "First edition"

FARMING. New York: Harcourt, Brace Jovanovich (1970).
      Two issues, no priority:
         1). Hardcover, dustwrapper.
         2). Wrappers.
      No statement of first edition.
      NOTE: The second printing bears the letters "BCDEFG" on the copyright page; none of the copies examined had the letter "A", either alone or in sequence.

RALPH EUGENE MEATYARD. (Lexington, Ky.): Gnomon Press (1970).
      Wrappers.
      NOTE: With Arnold Gassan.

THE HIDDEN WOUND. Boston: Houghton Mifflin, 1970.
      Hardcover, dustwrapper.
      "FIRST PRINTING"

THE UNFORESEEN WILDERNESS. Lexington, Ky.: University Press of Kentucky, 1971.
      Hardcover, dustwrapper.
      No statement of first edition.

CIVILIZING THE CUMBERLANDS. (Lexington, Ky.: King Library Press, University of Kentucky, 1972).
      Hardcover.
      100 copies, numbered.
      NOTE: With *Mountain Passes of the Cumberland* by James Lane Allen.

A CONTINUOUS HARMONY. New York: Harcourt, Brace Jovanovich (1972).
      Hardcover, dustwrapper.
      "First edition"

THE COUNTRY OF MARRIAGE. New York: Harcourt, Brace Jovanovich (1973).
    Hardcover, dustwrapper.
    "First edition"

THE MEMORY OF OLD JACK. New York: Harcourt, Brace Jovanovich (1974).
    Hardcover, dustwrapper.
    "First edition"

AN EASTWARD LOOK. Berkeley: Sand Dollar, 1974.
    Wrappers, no priority:
        1). 350 copies.
        2). 26 copies, numbered, signed by the author.
    Sand Dollar 11.

FALLING ASLEEP. (Austin: Cold Mountain Press, 1974).
    Postcard.
    Cold Mountain Press Poetry Post Card Series II, Number 8.

HORSES. (Monterey, Ky.: Larkspur Press, 1975).
    Wrappers.
    949 copies.

SAYINGS & DOINGS. (Lexington, Ky.): Gnomon (1975).
    Two issues, no priority:
        1). Hardcover, dustwrapper.
        2). Wrappers.

TO WHAT LISTENS. (Crete, Neb.: Best Cellar Press, 1975).
    Wrappers.

John Berryman

FIVE YOUNG AMERICAN POETS. Norfolk, Conn.: New Directions (1940).
  Hardcover, dustwrapper.
  No statement of first edition.
  NOTE: Mary Barnard, Randall Jarrell, W.R.Moses, and George Marion O'Donnell
    also contributed.

POEMS. Norfolk, Conn.: New Directions (1942).
  Two issues, no priority:
    1). Hardcover, dustwrapper.
    2). Wrappers.
  No statement of first edition.
  NOTE: Review copies in printed wrappers, preceding publication, have been reported.

TWO POEMS. (N.p.: Privately published) 1942.
  Wrappers.
  60 copies.

THE DISPOSSESSED. New York: William Sloane Associates (1948).
  Hardcover, dustwrapper.
  "First printing"

A CRITICAL SUPPLEMENT TO POETRY. (Chicago: Modern Poetry Association) 1949.
  Wrappers.

STEPHEN CRANE. (New York): William Sloane (1950).
  Hardcover, dustwrapper.
  "First Printing"
  ALSO: Cleveland: World (1962).
    Wrappers.
    "First Meridian printing February 1962"
    NOTE: New preface by the author.

HOMAGE TO MISTRESS BRADSTREET. New York: Farrar, Straus & Cudahy (1956).
Hardcover, dustwrapper.
"First printing, 1956"
ALSO: New York: Noonday Press (1968).
Wrappers.
"First printing, 1968"
NOTE: 1). Retitled *Homage to Mistress Bradstreet and Other Poems.*
2). New introduction by the author.

HIS THOUGHT MADE POCKETS & THE PLANE BUCKT. Pawlet, Vt.: Claude
Fredericks, 1958.
Two issues, no priority:
1). Hardcover.
26 copies, lettered, signed by the author.
2). Wrappers.
500 copies, numbered.

THE ARTS OF READING. New York: Thomas Y. Crowell (1960).
Hardcover, dustwrapper.
No statement of first edition.
NOTE: With Ralph Ross and Allen Tate.

77 DREAM SONGS. New York: Farrar, Straus & Co. (1964).
Hardcover, dustwrapper.
"First printing, 1964"

TWO DREAM SONGS. (Minneapolis: Privately published) 1965.
Wrappers.
150 copies.

BERRYMAN'S SONNETS. New York: Farrar, Straus & Giroux (1967).
Hardcover, dustwrapper.
"First printing, 1967"

JOHN BERRYMAN. Dublin: Graduates Club (1967).
Wrappers.

SHORT POEMS. New York: Farrar, Straus & Giroux (1967).
Hardcover, dustwrapper.
"First printing, 1967"

HIS TOY, HIS DREAM, HIS REST. New York: Farrar, Straus & Giroux (1968).
Hardcover, dustwrapper.
"First printing, 1968"
NOTE: Uncorrected proofs in printed wrappers preceded publication.

NATIONAL BOOK AWARD IN POETRY 1969 ACCEPTANCE SPEECH 3/12/69.
New York: (National Book Committee) 1969.
Mimeographed sheet.

THE DREAM SONGS. New York: Farrar, Straus & Giroux (1969).
Hardcover, dustwrapper.
"First printing, 1969"

TWO DREAM SONGS. (Minneapolis: Privately published) 1969.
Wrappers, printed.

TWO DREAM SONGS. (Minneapolis: Privately published) 1969.
Wrappers, photocopied.
NOTE: Entirely different text from the preceding entry.

LOVE & FAME. New York: Farrar, Straus & Giroux, 1970.
Hardcover, no priority:
1). Trade edition, dustwrapper.
2). 250 copies, indiscriminately numbered in Arabic or Roman, or lettered in
Roman or Greek, signed by the author.
"FIRST EDITION, 1970"
NOTE: 1). Photocopies of the typescript and a letter from the author to "a dozen of my
friends," soliciting criticism, were circulated by the publisher; in consequence
Berryman revised some poems before publication.
2). Uncorrected proofs in printed wrappers preceded publication and include
poems not in the published edition.
ALSO: London: Faber & Faber (1971).
Hardcover, dustwrapper.
No statement of first edition.
NOTE: New *Afterword* by the author.
ALSO: New York: Farrar, Straus & Giroux (1972).
Wrappers.
"SECOND EDITION, 1972"
NOTE: Revised edition, with a new introduction by the author.

DREAM SONG 14. (Brockport, N.Y.: Department of English, State University College,
1970).
Wrappers.
NOTE: Cover title is *Department of English State University College Brockport.*

TWO POEMS. (New York: Privately published) 1970.
Wrappers.

DELUSIONS, ETC. New York: Farrar, Straus & Giroux (1972).
Hardcover, dustwrapper.
"FIRST EDITION, 1972"

SELECTED POEMS 1938-1968. London: Faber & Faber (1972).
   Wrappers.
   No statement of first edition.

RECOVERY. New York: Farrar, Straus & Giroux (1973).
   Hardcover, dustwrapper.
   "FIRST EDITION, 1973"
   NOTE: Uncorrected proofs in printed wrappers preceded publication.

Paul Blackburn

THE DISSOLVING FABRIC. (Palma de Mallorca): Divers Press, 1955.
    Wrappers.

BROOKLYN-MANHATTAN TRANSIT. New York: Totem Press (1960).
    Wrappers.
    Totem Blueplate #3.

PATERSON SOCIETY. Cambridge, Mass.: Paterson Society, ca. 1960.*
    Broadside.

THE NETS. New York: Trobar (1961).
    Wrappers.

SING-SONG. (New York): Caterpillar (1966).
    Brown wrappers.
    Colphon must state only: "100 copies were mimeographed in New York City
        December 1966."
    Caterpillar IV.

16 SLOPPY HAIKU & A LYRIC FOR ROBERT REARDON. Cleveland: 400 Rabbit Press,
    1966.
    Wrappers.
    45 copies.

THE CITIES. New York: Grove Press (1967).
    Wrappers.
    "First Printing"

IT MIGHT AS WELL BE SPRING. (Madison, Wisc.): Perishable Press, 1967.
    Broadside.
    100 copies.

THE REARDON POEMS. Madison, Wisc.: Perishable Press, 1967.
    Two issues, no priority:
        1). Hardcover, no priority:
            a). Gathered in three signatures.
                40 copies.
            b). Gathered in twelve signatures.
                3 copies.
        2). Wrappers.
            100 copies.

BRYANT PARK. (London: Cape Goliard Press, 1968).
    Broadside.

IN. ON. OR ABOUT THE PREMISES. London: Cape Goliard Press, 1968.
    Two issues, no priority:
        1). Hardcover, no priority:
            a). Acetate dustwrapper.
                1300 copies.
            b). Tissue dustwrapper.
                100 copies, numbered, signed by the author.
        2). Wrappers.
            3500 copies.
    NOTE: 2000 copies in wrappers and 750 hardcover copies were distributed in the United
    States by Grossman; "Grossman" was added to the title page of these copies.

A McCLURE POEM. San Francisco: (Privately published) 1969.
    Broadside.
    20 copies, numbered, signed by the author.

TWO NEW POEMS. (Madison, Wisc.): Perishable Press (1969).
    Wrappers.
    10 copies.

THE ASSASSINATION OF PRESIDENT McKINLEY. Mt. Horeb, Wisc.: Perishable Press,
    1970.
    Wrappers.
    "125 copies or less," according to the colophon.

THREE DREAMS AND AN OLD POEM. (Buffalo: Intrepid Press, 1970).
    Wrappers, no priority:
        1). 900 copies.
        2). 100 copies, numbered, signed by the author.
    Beau Fleuve Series Number One.

GIN. Mt. Horeb, Wisc.: Perishable Press (1970).
    Hardcover.
    136 copies.

THE JOURNALS. Mt. Horeb, Wisc.: Perishable Press, 1971.
    Hardcover.
    125 copies, numbered.
    ALSO: Los Angeles: Black Sparrow Press, 1975.
        Two issues, no priority:
            1). Hardcover, acetate dustwrapper; no priority:
                a). 500 copies.
                b). 50 copies, numbered, signed by the editor (Robert Kelly).
            2). Wrappers.
        NOTE: Expanded edition.

BAGGS. New York: Doctor Generosity Press (ca. 1971).
    Broadside.

EARLY SELECTED Y MAS. Los Angeles: Black Sparrow Press, 1972.
    Two issues, no priority:
        1). Hardcover, acetate dustwrapper; no priority:
            a). 200 copies, numbered, signed by the author.
            b). 26 copies, lettered, signed by the author.
        2). Wrappers.
            1500 copies.
    NOTE: A flyer (*Broadside/Flyer #4*), printing a poem from the book, preceded
    publication.

HALFWAY DOWN THE COAST. (Northampton, Mass.): Mulch Press (1975).
    Two issues, priority as listed:
        1). Wrappers.
        2). Hardcover.*

Translations.

PROENSA. (Palma de Mallorca): Divers Press, 1953.
    Wrappers.

POEM OF THE CID. New York: American R.D.M.Corporation (1966).
    Wrappers.

Julio Cortazar.
END OF THE GAME. New York: Pantheon (1967).
    Hardcover, dustwrapper.
    "First Printing"
    NOTE: Later issued by Collier Books as *Blow-Up and Other Stories.*

Pablo Picasso.
HUNK OF SKIN. (San Francisco): City Lights Books (1968).
    Wrappers.
    "First American Edition"

Julio Cortazar.
CRONOPIOS AND FAMAS. New York: Pantheon (1969).
    Hardcover, dustwrapper.
    "FIRST AMERICAN EDITION"

TWO CHINESE POEMS. New York: Doctor Generosity Press (ca. 1970).
    Broadside, no known priority:
        1). "A Doctor Generosity Broadside" in bold-faced lettering at the head of the
            broadside.
        2). Only the title at the head of the broadside.
    NOTE: Translated with Elma Seto.

PEIRE VIDAL. New York/Amherst: Mulch Press, 1972.
    Two issues, no priority:
        1). Hardcover, dustwrapper.
        2). Wrappers.
    "1st Printing"
    NOTE: Uncorrected proofs in printed wrappers preceded publication.

Robert Bly

A BROADSHEET AGAINST THE NEW YORK TIMES BOOK REVIEW. (Madison, Minn.) :
    Sixties Press, 1961.
    Wrappers.

THE LION'S TAIL AND EYES. (Madison, Minn.) : Sixties Press, 1962.
    Two issues, no priority :
        1). Hardcover, dustwrapper.
        2). Wrappers.
    NOTE : James Wright and William Duffy also contributed.

SILENCE IN THE SNOWY FIELDS. Middletown, Conn. : Wesleyan University Press (1962).
    Two issues, no priority :
        1). Hardcover, dustwrapper.
        2). Wrappers.
    "First Edition"
    ALSO : London : Jonathan Cape (1967).
        Hardcover, dustwrapper.
        No statement of first edition.
    NOTE : Enlarged edition.

DUCKS. (Menomonie, Wisc. : Ox Head Press, 1966).
    Wrappers.
    50 copies (approximately).

CHRYSANTHEMUMS. (Menomonie, Wisc.) : Ox Head Press, 1967.
    Wrappers.
    350 copies, numbered.

THE LIGHT AROUND THE BODY. New York: Harper & Row (1967).
Two issues, no priority:
    1). Hardcover, dustwrapper.
    2). Wrappers.
"FIRST EDITION"
ALSO: London: Rapp & Whiting (1968).
Hardcover, dustwrapper; no priority:
    1). Trade edition.
    2). 50 copies, numbered, signed by the author.
No statement of first edition.

OPENING AN OYSTER. (Santa Barbara, Calif.): Unicorn Press, 1967.
Broadside, no priority:
    1). 200 copies.
    2). 26 copies, lettered, signed by the author.

DEAR MR. STEVENS. (Santa Barbara, Calif.: Unicorn Press) 1968.
Broadside.
325 copies.
NOTE: Laid in portfolio entitled *Unicorn Folio: Series One, Number Four*, numbered.

IN A BOAT ON BIG STONE LAKE. (Santa Barbara, Calif.: Unicorn Press) 1968.
Broadside.
Unicorn Broadsheet Two.
NOTE: There were an unknown number of copies signed by the author.
    2). A postcard printing of this poem was later produced, with an unknown
    number of copies signed by the author.

ACCEPTANCE SPEECH BY ROBERT BLY ON WINNING THE NATIONAL BOOK
AWARD FOR POETRY. (New York: Privately published, 1968).
Mechanically reproduced sheets.

THREE SHORT POEMS. (N.p.: Privately published, ca. 1968).
Broadside.

THE MORNING GLORY. (Santa Cruz, Calif.: Kayak Press, 1969).
Wrappers.
800 copies.
ALSO: (Santa Cruz, Calif.: Kayak Press, 1970).
Wrappers.
1500 copies.
NOTE: Expanded edition.
ALSO: New York: Harper & Row (1975).
Two issues, no priority:
    1). Hardcover, dustwrapper.
    2). Wrappers.
"FIRST EDITION" and "75 76 77 78 79 10 9 8 7 6 5 4 3 2 1"
NOTE: Further expanded edition.

TWO POEMS. (Amherst, Mass.: Massachusetts Review, 1969).
Wrappers.

THE TEETH-MOTHER NAKED AT LAST. (Madison, Minn.: American Writers Against
the Vietnam War, 1970).
Wrappers.
ALSO: (San Francisco): City Lights Books (1970).
Wrappers.
No statement of first edition.
Pocket Poets Series Number Twenty-six.
NOTE: Revised edition.

COUNTING SMALL-BONED BODIES. Palo Alto, Calif.: Free Poetry Institute For the
Study of Non-Violence (1970).
Broadside, priority as listed:
1). Yellow stock.
2). Blue stock, without publisher's name and location on face.

LOOKING INTO A FACE. (Brockport, N.Y.: Department of English, State University
College, 1970).
Wrappers.
NOTE: Cover title is *Department of English, State University College, Brockport.*

OUTHOUSE POEM. Santa Barbara, Calif.: Unicorn Press (1971).
Postcard, no priority:
1). Trade edition.
2). 50 copies, signed by the author.

HEARING GARY SNYDER READ. (Santa Barbara, Calif.: Unicorn Press, 1971).
Broadside.
Unicorn Broadsheet Series Two Number Three.

POEMS FOR TENNESSEE. Martin, Tenn.: Tennessee Poetry Press, 1971.
Wrappers.
NOTE: William Stafford and William Matthews also contributed.

SNOWFALL IN THE AFTERNOON. (Brockport, N.Y.: Department of English, State
University College, 1971).
Wrappers.
NOTE: Cover title is *Department of English, State University College, Brockport.*

RACHEL REBEKAH BLY. (N.p.: Privately published) 1971.
Broadside.

WILD HAY. (Amherst, Mass.: Wang Hui-Ming) 1971.
Broadside.

FOUR IMAGES FOR DEATH. (Amherst, Mass.: Slow Loris Press, 1971).
  Broadside, no priority:
       1). 175 copies.
       2). 25 copies, numbered, signed by the author.

A CRICKET IN THE WAINSCOTING. Detroit: Alternative Press (ca. 1972).
  Broadside.

STRIPS OF AUGUST SUN COME IN THROUGH SHUTTERS. (Detroit: Alternative
  Press, ca. 1972).
  Postcard.

SLEEPERS JOINING HANDS. New York: Harper & Row (1972).
  Two issues, no priority:
       1). Hardcover, dustwrapper.
       2). Wrappers.
  "FIRST EDITION"
  NOTE: Reportedly, there are two states of the first edition dustwrapper, the first of
    which is orange, mauve and grey on white stock.

SIX WINTER PRIVACY POEMS. Cambridge, Mass.: Pomegranate Press, 1972.
  Broadside, no priority:
       1). 100 copies.
       2). 150 copies, numbered, signed by the author and illustrator.
  Illustrated by Karyl Klopp.

WATER UNDER THE EARTH. Rushden, Northamptonshire, England: Sceptre Press
  (1972).
  Wrappers, no priority:
       1). 100 copies, numbered.
       2). 50 copies, numbered, signed by the author.

CHRISTMAS EVE SERVICE AT MIDNIGHT AT ST. MICHAEL'S. (Rushden, Northamptonshire, England, 1972).
  Wrappers, no priority:
       1). 70 copies, numbered.
       2). 30 copies, numbered, signed by the author.

ANOTHER DOING NOTHING POEM and JUMPING OUT OF BED and NOVEMBER
  DAY AT McCLURE's. (San Francisco: Panjandrum Press, 1972).
  Broadside.
  NOTE: Laid in portfolio, which is laid in a box, both of which are entitled *Panjandrum
    Number One.*

SUNDAY MORNING IN TOMALES BAY. (San Francisco: Panjandrum Press, 1972).
    Broadside.
    NOTE: Laid in portfolio, which is laid in a box, both of which are entitled *Panjandrum
        Number One.*

JUMPING OUT OF BED. Barre, Mass.: Barre Publishers, 1973.
    Wrappers.

THE DEAD SEAL NEAR McCLURE'S BEACH. Rushden, Northamptonshire, England:
    Sceptre Press (1973).
    Wrappers, no priority.
        1). 100 copies, numbered.
        2). 50 copies, numbered, signed by the author.

POINT REYES POEMS. Half Moon Bay, Calif.: Mudra, 1974.
    Sewn in wrappers, no priority:
        1). 250 copies.
        2). 50 copies, numbered, signed by the author.
    NOTE: There is a subsequent printing, stapled in wrappers.

BUFFALO. (St. Paul, Minn.: Smith Park Poetry Series, 1974).*
    Broadside.

THE HOCKEY POEM. (Duluth, Minn.): Knife River Press, 1974.
    Wrappers.
    500 copies.

A MAN WRITES TO A PART OF HIMSELF. (New York): Y(WCA) Poetry Center (1974).
    Broadside.

OLD MAN RUBBING HIS EYES. Greensboro, N.C.: Unicorn Press, 1975.
    Two issues, no priority:
        1). Hardcover, no priority:
            a). 200 copies, numbered.
            b). 35 copies, numbered, signed by the author and illustrator.
        2). Wrappers.
    Illustrated by Franz Albert Richter.

THE FIR. Morris, Minn.: Prairie Gate Press (1975).
    Wrappers.
    200 copies.

GRASS FROM TWO YEARS and LET'S LEAVE. (Denver: Ally Press, 1975).
> Two issues, no priority:
>> 1). Hardcover.
>>> 50 copies, numbered, signed by the author.
>> 2). Wrappers.
>>> 150 copies, numbered, signed by the author.
> NOTE: *Let's Leave* is Bly's translation of work by Kabir.

LEAPING POETRY. Boston: Beacon Press (1975).
> Two issues, no priority:
>> 1). Hardcover, dustwrapper.
>> 2). Wrappers.
> "9 8 7 6 5 4 3 2 1" on copyright page.

THE ILLUSTRATED BOOK ABOUT REPTILES AND AMPHIBIANS OF THE WORLD.
New York: Grosset & Dunlap (1960).*
Hardcover, dustwrapper.

George Trakl.
TWENTY POEMS. (Madison, Minn.): Sixties Press, 1961.
    Two issues, no priority:
        1). Hardcover, dustwrapper.
        2). Wrappers.
    note: Translated with James Wright.

Cesar Vallejo.
TWENTY POEMS. (Madison, Minn.): Sixties Press, 1962.
    Two issues, no priority:
        1). Hardcover, dustwrapper.
        2). Wrappers.
    note: Translated with James Wright and John Knoepfle.

Selma Lagerlof.
THE STORY OF GOSTA BERLING. (New York): New American Library (1962).
    Wrappers.
    "first printing, may 1962"

Tomas Transtromer.
THREE POEMS. (Lawrence, Kan.: Terence Williams, 1966).
    Wrappers.
    Formula Series #3.
    note: Translated with Eric Sellin and Thomas R. Buckman.

Pablo Neruda.
TWENTY POEMS. (Madison, Minn.): Sixties Press, 1967.
    Two issues, no priority:
        1). Hardcover, dustwrapper.
        2). Wrappers.
    note: Translated with James Wright.

Juan Ramon Jimenez.
FORTY POEMS. (Madison, Minn.): Sixties Press, 1967.
    Two issues, no priority:
        1). Hardcover, dustwrapper.
        2). Wrappers.

Knut Hamsun.
HUNGER. New York: Noonday (1967).
    Hardcover, dustwrapper.
    "First Noonday Press printing, 1967"

Gunnar Ekelof.
LATE ARRIVAL ON EARTH. London: Rapp & Carroll (1967).
    Hardcover, dustwrapper.
    No statement of first edition.
    NOTE: Translated with Christina Paulston.

Gunnar Ekelof.
I DO BEST ALONE AT NIGHT. Washington: Charioteer Press, 1968.
    Hardcover, dustwrapper.
    300 copies.
    NOTE: Translated with Christina Paulston.

Yvan Goll.
SELECTED POEMS. (San Francisco: Kayak Press, 1968).
    Wrappers.
    1200 copies.
    Illustrated by Jean Verda.
    NOTE: Translated with George Hitchcock, Galway Kinnell and Paul Zweig.

Issa.
TEN POEMS. N.p. (1969).
    Wrappers.

Pablo Neruda.
LETTER TO MIGUEL OTERO SILVA, IN CARACAS (1948). (San Francisco: Cranium
    Press, ca. 1970).
    Wrappers.

Tomas Transtromer.
TWENTY POEMS. (Madison, Minn.): Seventies Press, 1970.
    Two issues, no priority:
        1). Hardcover, dustwrapper.
        2). Wrappers.

Tomas Transtromer.
NIGHT VISION. (Northwood Narrows, N.H.: Lillabulero Press, 1971).
    Wrappers.
    ALSO: (London): London Magazine Editions, 1972.
        Hardcover, dustwrapper.
        NOTE: Revised edition.

Kabir.
THE FISH IN THE SEA IS NOT THIRSTY. (Northwood Narrows, N.H.: Lillabulero Press,
    1971).
    Wrappers.

Pablo Neruda and Cesar Vallejo.
SELECTED POEMS. Boston: Beacon Press (1971).
    Two issues, no priority:
        1). Hardcover, dustwrapper.
        2). Wrappers.
    No statement of first edition.
    NOTE: Translated with James Wright and John Knoepfle.

BASHO. San Francisco: Mudra, 1972.
    Wrappers.

Miguel Hernandez and Blas de Otero.
SELECTED POEMS. Boston: Beacon Press (1972).
    Two issues, no priority:
        1). Hardcover, dustwrapper.
        2). Wrappers.
    No statement of first edition.
    NOTE: Translated with Timothy Balanz, Hardie St. Martin and James Wright.

Andrei Voznesensky.
DOGALYPSE. (San Francisco): City Lights Books (1972).
    Wrappers.
    No statement of first edition.
    Pocket Poets Series Number 29.
    NOTE: Translated with Maureen Sager, Catherine Leech, Vera Reck, Vera Dunham
        and Lawrence Ferlinghetti.

Rainer Maria Rilke.
TEN SONNETS TO ORPHEUS. (San Francisco): Zephyrus Image (1972).
    Wrappers, no known priority:
        1). A few copies had rose on front cover in red and green.
        2). Most copies had rose on front cover in black.
    Zephyrus Image Magazine Number One

Kabir.
THE MUSK INSIDE THE DEER. (N.p.: ca. 1972).
    Broadside.

Tomas Transtromer.
ELEGY and SOME OCTOBER NOTES. Rushden, Northamptonshire, England: Sceptre
    Press (1973).
    Wrappers, no priority:
        1). 100 copies, numbered.
        2). 50 copies, numbered, signed by the translator.

Garcia Lorca and Juan Ramon Jimenez.
SELECTED POEMS. Boston: Beacon Press (1973).
    Two issues, no priority:
        1). Hardcover, dustwrapper.
        2). Wrappers.
    "9 8 7 6 5 4 3 2 1" on copyright page.

Pablo Neruda.
ODE TO SOME YELLOW FLOWERS. Austin: Cold Mountain Press, 1973.
    Broadside.
    1000 copies.

Pablo Neruda.
THE DICTATORS. (Buffalo: Slow Loris Press, 1973).
    Broadside, no priority:
        1). 175 copies.
        2). 25 copies, numbered, signed by the translator.

Kabir.
THE FLUTE. (Austin: Cold Mountain Press, 1974).
    Postcard.
    Cold Mountain Press Poetry Post Card Series II, Number 5.

Kabir.
THE RADIANCE. (East Lansing, Mich.: Old Marble Press, 1974).
    Wrappers.
    300 copies.

Harry Martinson, Gunnar Ekelof and Tomas Transtromer.
FRIENDS, YOU DRANK SOME DARKNESS. Boston: Beacon Press (1975).
    Two issues, no priority:
        1). Hardcover, dustwrapper.
        2). Wrappers.
    "9 8 7 6 5 4 3 2 1" on copyright page.

Paul Bowles

TWO POEMS. (New York: Modern Editions Press, ca. 1934).
    Wrappers.
    The Poetry Series: Pamphlet 5.

THE SHELTERING SKY. London: John Lehmann (1949).
    Hardcover, dustwrapper.
    No statement of first edition.

A LITTLE STONE. London: John Lehmann (1950).
    Hardcover, dustwrapper; priority as listed:
        1). Light green binding.
        2). Dark green binding.
    No statement of first edition.

THE DELICATE PREY. (New York): Random House (1950).
    Hardcover, dustwrapper.
    "first printing"

LET IT COME DOWN. New York: Random House (1952).
    Hardcover, dustwrapper.
    "FIRST PRINTING"

THE SPIDER'S HOUSE. New York: Random House (1955).
    Hardcover, dustwrapper.
    "FIRST PRINTING"

YALLAH. Zurich: Manesse, 1956.*
    Hardcover, dustwrapper.
    ALSO: New York: McDowell, Obolensky (1957).
        Hardcover, dustwrapper.
        No statement of first edition.

THE HOURS AFTER NOON. London: Heinemann (1959).
    Hardcover, dustwrapper.
    No statement of first edition.

A HUNDRED CAMELS IN THE COURTYARD. (San Francisco): City Lights Books (1962).
Wrappers.
Thirty-three other books advertised on inside rear cover.

THEIR HEADS ARE GREEN AND THEIR HANDS ARE BLUE. New York: Random House
(1963).
Hardcover, dustwrapper.
"FIRST PRINTING"

UP ABOVE THE WORLD. New York: Simon & Schuster (1966).
Hardcover, dustwrapper.
"First printing"

THE TIME OF FRIENDSHIP. New York: Holt, Rinehart & Winston (1967).
Hardcover, dustwrapper.
"First Edition"

PAGES FROM COLD POINT. London: Peter Owen (1968).
Hardcover, dustwrapper.
"First British Commonwealth edition 1968"

SCENES. Los Angeles: Black Sparrow Press, 1968.
        Two issues, no priority:
                1). Hardcover, no priority:
                        a). 50 copies, numbered, signed by the author.
                        b). 4 special copies, for the publisher, author, printer and binder.
                2). Wrappers.
                250 copies, numbered, signed by the author.

THE THICKET OF SPRING. Los Angeles: Black Sparrow Press, 1972.
        Two issues, no priority:
                1). Hardcover, acetate dustwrapper; no priority:
                        a). 200 copies, numbered, signed by the author.
                        b). 26 copies, lettered, signed by the author.
                        c). 4 special copies, for the publisher, author, printer and binder.
                2). Wrappers
                1000 copies.

WITHOUT STOPPING. New York: Putnam (1972).
Hardcover, dustwrapper.
No statement of first edition.
NOTE: Uncorrected proofs with text different from the trade edition, in printed
        wrappers, preceded publication.

THREE TALES. (New York): Frank Hallman, 1975.
    Two issues, no priority:
        1). Hardcover.
           100 copies, numbered, signed by the author.
        2). Wrappers.
           1000 copies.

TRANSLATIONS.

Roger Frison-Roche.
THE LOST TRAIL OF THE SAHARA. New York: Prentice-Hall (1952).
    Hardcover, dustwrapper.
    "FIRST AMERICAN EDITION"

Jean-Paul Sartre.
NO EXIT. New York: Samuel French (1958).
    Wrappers.
    NOTE: This is an "acting edition," "adapted" by Bowles.

Driss ben Hamed Charhadi.
A LIFE FULL OF HOLES. New York: Grove Press (1964).
    Hardcover, dustwrapper.
    "First Printing"

Mohammed Mrabet.
LOVE WITH A FEW HAIRS. London: Peter Owen (1967).
    Hardcover, dustwrapper.
    No statement of first edition.

Mohammed Mrabet.
THE LEMON. London: Peter Owen (1969).
    Hardcover, dustwrapper.
    No statement of first edition.

Mohammed Mrabet.
M'HASHISH. (San Francisco): City Lights Books (1969).
    Wrappers.
    No statement of first edition.

Mohammed Mrabet.
THE BOY WHO SET THE FIRE. Los Angeles: Black Sparrow Press, 1974.
    Two issues, no priority:
        1). Hardcover, acetate dustwrapper; no priority:
            a). 250 copies, numbered, signed by the author and translator.
            b). 26 copies, lettered, signed by the author and translator.
        2). Wrappers.
           1777 copies.

Mohamed Choukri.
JEAN GENET IN TANGIER. New York: Ecco Press (1974).
    Hardcover, dustwrapper.
    No statement of first edition.

Isabelle Eberhardt.
THE OBLIVION SEEKERS. (San Francisco): City Lights (1975).
    Wrappers.
    No statement of first edition.

Mohammed Mrabet.
HADIDAN AHARAM. (Los Angeles): Black Sparrow Press, 1975.
    Wrappers.
    Sparrow 37.

Richard Brautigan

FOUR NEW POETS. (San Francisco): Inferno Press (1957).
  Wrappers.
  NOTE: Martin Hoberman, Carl Larsen and James M. Singer also contributed.

THE RETURN OF THE RIVERS. (San Francisco): Inferno Press (1958).
  Wrappers.

THE GALILEE HITCH-HIKER. (San Francisco: White Rabbit Press, 1958).
  Wrappers.
  200 copies.
  ALSO: (San Francisco: David Sandberg, 1966).
      Wrappers, no priority:
        1). 700 copies.
        2). 16 copies, numbered, signed by the author.

LAY THE MARBLE TEA. San Francisco: Carp Press, 1959.
  Wrappers.

THE OCTOPUS FRONTIER. San Francisco: Carp Press, 1960.
  Wrappers.

A CONFEDERATE GENERAL FROM BIG SUR. New York: Grove Press (1964).
  Hardcover, dustwrapper.
  No statement of first edition.

SEPTEMBER CALIFORNIA. (San Francisco: San Francisco Arts Festival Commission, 1964).
  Broadside.
  300 copies, most of which were signed by the author and illustrator.
  Illustrated by Richard Correll.
  NOTE: Laid in portfolio entitled *San Francisco Arts Festival: A Poetry Folio: 1964*.

KARMA REPAIR KIT. (San Francisco): Communication Company (1967).
    Broadside.

ALL WATCHED OVER BY MACHINES OF LOVING GRACE. (San Francisco):
    Communication Company (1967).
    Broadside, priority as listed:
        1). Faint illustration, the most prominent portion of which is the phrase
          Loudspeaker Current.
        2). Bold illustration, consisting of hand-drawn small animals and a photo-
          graph of a computer bank.

ALL WATCHED OVER BY MACHINES OF LOVING GRACE. (San Francisco):
    Communication Company (1967).
    Wrappers.
    1500 copies.

THE BEAUTIFUL POEM. (San Francisco): Communication Company (ca. 1967).
    Broadside.

LOVE POEM. (San Francisco): Communication Company (ca. 1967).
    Broadside.

FLOWERS FOR THOSE YOU LOVE. (San Francisco): Communication Company
    (ca. 1967).
    Broadside.

TROUT FISHING IN AMERICA. San Francisco: Four Seasons Foundation, 1967.
    Wrappers.
    Writing 14.

PLEASE PLANT THIS BOOK. (San Francisco: Graham Mackintosh, 1968).
    Folder with eight seed packets; poem on each packet.

THE PILL VERSUS THE SPRINGHILL MINE DISASTER. San Francisco: Four Seasons
    Foundation (1968).
    Two issues, no priority:
        1). Hardcover.
          50 copies, numbered, signed by the author.
        2). Wrappers.
    Writing 20.

IN WATERMELON SUGAR. San Francisco: Four Seasons Foundation (1968).
    Two issues, no priority:
        1). Hardcover.
          50 copies, numbered, signed by the author.
        2). Wrappers.
    Writing 21.

THE SAN FRANCISCO WEATHER REPORT. (San Francisco): Graham Mackintosh
(1968).
Broadside.

SPINNING LIKE A GHOST ON THE BOTTOM OF A TOP, I'M HAUNTED BY ALL
THE SPACE THAT I WILL LIVE WITHOUT YOU. (San Francisco, ca. 1969).
Broadside.
NOTE: 1). Anonymous.
2). One leaf of an unbound anthology in wrappers entitled *Free City*; it also
circulated separately.

YOU'VE GOT. (Berkeley: Privately published, ca. 1970).
Broadside.

ROMMEL DRIVES DEEP INTO EGYPT. New York: Delacorte Press (1970).
Two issues, no priority:
1). Hardcover, dustwrapper.
"First Printing"
2). Wrappers.
"First Delta Printing — April 1970"

FIVE POEMS. (Berkeley): Serendipity Books, 1971.
Broadside.

THE ABORTION. New York: Simon & Schuster (1971).
Two issues, no priority:
1). Hardcover, dustwrapper.
2). Wrappers.
"First printing"
NOTE: Uncorrected proofs in printed wrappers preceded publication.

REVENGE OF THE LAWN. New York: Simon & Schuster (1971).
Two issues, no priority:
1). Hardcover, dustwrapper; presumed priority:
a). Green topstain.
b). No topstain.
2). Wrappers.
"First printing"

THE HAWKLINE MONSTER. New York: Simon & Schuster (1974).
Two issues, priority as listed:
1). Hardcover, dustwrapper.
2). Wrappers.
"1 2 3 4 5 6 7 8 9 10" on copyright page.
NOTE: Uncorrected proofs in printed wrappers preceded publication.

WILLARD AND HIS BOWLING TROPHIES. New York: Simon & Schuster (1975).
   Hardcover, dustwrapper.
      "1 2 3 4 5 6 7 8 9 10" on copyright page.

Charles Bukowski

20 TANKS FROM KASSELDOWN. (Washington, D. C.: Black Sun Press, 1946).
Broadside.
Portfolio III Leaf Eight.
NOTE: Laid in portfolio entitled *Portfolio III.*

HIS WIFE, THE PAINTER. (Eureka, Calif.: Hearse Press) 1960.
Broadside.
Hearse Broadside #1.
NOTE: Laid in portfolio entitled *Coffin 1.*

THE PAPER ON THE FLOOR. (Eureka, Calif.: Hearse Press, 1960).
Wrappers.
150 copies.
NOTE: Laid in portfolio entitled *Coffin 1.*

THE OLD MAN ON THE CORNER. (Eureka, Calif.: Hearse Press, 1960).
Broadside.
150 copies.
NOTE: Laid in portfolio entitled *Coffin 1.*

WASTE BASKET. (Eureka, Calif.: Hearse Press, 1960).
Broadside.
150 copies.
NOTE: Laid in portfolio entitled *Coffin 1.*

FLOWER, FIST AND BESTIAL WAIL. (Eureka, Calif.): Hearse Press (1960).
Wrappers.
200 copies.
Hearse Chapbooks #5.

A SIGNATURE OF CHARLES BUKOWSKI. (Albuquerque: Targets Magazine, 1960).
Wrappers.
NOTE: An offprint from the magazine *Targets 4.*

SIGNATURE 2. (Albuquerque: Targets Magazine, 1961).
    Folded sheet.
    NOTE: A few copies were made up from the magazine *Targets 7* for the use of the
    author.

POEMS AND DRAWINGS. (Crescent City, Fla.: Epos) 1962.
    Wrappers.
    NOTE: An *Epos Extra Issue* of *Epos: A Quarterly of Poetry*.

LONGSHOT POEMS FOR BROKE PLAYERS. New York: 7 Poets Press (1962).
    Wrappers.

RUN WITH THE HUNTED. Chicago: Midwest Poetry Chapbooks (1962).
    Wrappers.
    Midwest Poetry Chapbooks, 1.

THE PRIEST AND THE MATADOR. N.p.: Penny Poetry (ca. 1962).
    Broadside.

IT CATCHES MY HEART IN ITS HANDS. (New Orleans): Loujon Press (1963).
    Wrappers, no priority:
        1). Trade edition.
        2). An unknown number of copies (reported to be approximately 20) were
           signed by the author.
    777 copies.
    "First printing, October 1963"
    Gypsy Lou Series No. 1.

GRIP THE WALLS. (Storrs, Conn.: Wormwood Review Press, 1964).
    Wrappers, no priority:
        1). 600 copies.
        2). 24 copies, signed, dated, with original drawings by the author.
    NOTE: Issued as an insert in the magazine *The Wormwood Review*, Vol 4, No. 4.

CRUCIFIX IN A DEATH-HAND. New York: Loujon Press/Lyle Stuart (1965).
    Wrappers, no priority:
        1). 3100 copies (approximately).
        2). 26 copies, lettered, with drawings and letter signed by the author laid in.
        3). 12 copies, numbered, with letter by the author tipped in, dustwrapper.
        4). 12 copies, unnumbered, with letter by the author tipped in, dustwrapper.
        5). 12 copies, inscribed by the author, dustwrapper.
        6). 10 copies, numbered, with drawing(s) or statement signed by the author
           tipped in, dustwrapper.
        7). 5 copies, numbered, with self-portrait tipped in, dustwrapper.
    Gypsy Lou Series, #2.

COLD DOGS IN THE COURTYARD. (Chicago: Literary Times — Cyfoeth
    Publications, 1965).
    Wrappers.
    500 copies.

CONFESSIONS OF A MAN INSANE ENOUGH TO LIVE WITH BEASTS.
    Bensenville, Ill.: Mimeo Press, 1965.
    Wrappers, no priority:
        1). Trade edition.
            500 copies.
        2). 25 copies (approximately) with original drawing signed by the author.
    "First printing: 1965"

THE GENIUS OF THE CROWD. (Cleveland: 7 Flowers Press, 1966).
    Wrappers.
    103 copies.

ALL THE ASSHOLES IN THE WORLD AND MINE. (Bensenville, Ill.: Open Skull
    Press, 1966).
    Wrappers.
    400 copies.
    "first printing: 1966"

THE EARTH ROSE. Santa Monica, Calif.: (Privately published, ca. 1966).*
    Broadside.

TRUE STORY. Los Angeles: Black Sparrow Press, 1966.
    Broadside, no priority:
        1). 27 copies, numbered, signed by the author.
        2). 3 copies, lettered, signed by the author.

ON GOING OUT TO GET THE MAIL. Los Angeles: Black Sparrow Press, 1966.
    Broadside, no priority:
        1). 27 copies, numbered, signed by the author.
        2). 3 copies, lettered, signed by the author.

TO KISS THE WORMS GOODNIGHT. Los Angeles: Black Sparrow Press, 1966.
    Broadside, no priority:
        1). 27 copies, numbered, signed by the author.
        2). 3 copies, lettered, signed by the author.

THE GIRLS and FOR THE MERCY-MONGERS. Los Angeles: Black Sparrow Press,
    1966.
    Broadside, no priority:
        1). 27 copies, numbered, signed by the author.
        2). 3 copies, lettered, signed by the author.

THE FLOWER LOVER and I MET A GENIUS. Los Angeles: Black Sparrow Press, 1966.
  Broadside, no priority:
      1). 27 copies, numbered, signed by the author.
      2). 3 copies, lettered, signed by the author.

NIGHT'S WORK. (Storrs, Conn.: Wormwood Review Press, 1966).
  Wrappers, no priority:
      1). 600 copies.
      2). 24 copies, numbered, signed by the author.
  NOTE: Issued as an insert in *The Wormwood Review*, Vol. 6, No. 4.

2 POEMS. (Los Angeles: Black Sparrow Press, 1967).
  Wrappers, no priority:
      1). 96 copies, numbered, signed by the author.
      2). 3 copies, lettered, signed by the author.
  NOTE: 12 review copies, unnumbered and unlettered, preceded publication.

THE CURTAINS ARE WAVING AND PEOPLE WALK THROUGH THE AFTERNOON HERE AND IN BERLIN AND IN NEW YORK CITY AND IN MEXICO. (Los Angeles: Black Sparrow Press, 1967).
  Wrappers, no priority:
      1). 107 copies (approximately), numbered, signed by the author.
      2). 15 copies (approximately), numbered, signed, with a drawing by the author laid in.
      3). 3 copies, lettered, signed by the author.

POEMS WRITTEN BEFORE JUMPING OUT OF AN 8 STORY WINDOW. (Glendale, Calif.: Poetry X/Change, 1968).
  Wrappers, no priority:
      1). Trade edition.
      2). 25 copies, with original drawings by the author in the center of the book, replacing *Cows in Art Class*.
  "A Litmus first edition"
  ALSO: (Gersthofen, Germany): Maro Verlag (1974).
      Wrappers.
      "Erstausgabe/First Printing April 1974"
      NOTE: 1). Titled *Gedichte Die Einer Schrieb Bevor Er Im 8. Stockwer Aus Dem Fenster Sprank*.
               2). Expanded edition, which prints two letters and three new poems in English as well as German.
  ALSO: (Salt Lake City: Litmus, 1975).
      Wrappers.
      "first edition with correspondence" and "second edition"
      NOTE: Five letters by the author appear as an addendum.

AT TERROR STREET AND AGONY WAY. Los Angeles: Black Sparrow Press, 1968.
  Two issues, priority as listed:
      1). Hardcover, no priority:
          a). 75 copies, numbered, signed with a drawing by the author tipped
          in.
          b). 4 special copies, for the publisher, author, printer and binder.
      2). Wrappers, priority as listed:
          a). 18 copies with "Sreet" on front cover.
          b). 747 copies with title corrected by glued-on label.

A BUKOWSKI SAMPLER. Madison, Wisc.: Quixote Press (1969).
  Wrappers.
  ALSO: Madison, Wisc.: Druid Books (1971).
    Wrappers.
    NOTE: Expanded edition.

NOTES OF A DIRTY OLD MAN. North Hollywood, Calif.: Essex House (1969).
  Wrappers.

IF WE TAKE. (Los Angeles: Black Sparrow Press, 1969).
  Wrappers, no priority:
      1). 300 copies.
      2). 100 copies, numbered, signed by the author.
      3). 4 special copies, for the publisher, author, printer and binder.

THE DAYS RUN AWAY LIKE WILD HORSES OVER THE HILLS. Los Angeles:
  Black Sparrow Press, 1969.
  Two issues, priority as listed:
      1). Wrappers, priority as listed:
          a). "1943" on page 19, line 15.
          b). Correction slip, changing "1943" to "1843", laid in.
          1250 copies (according to the publisher, only 1243 were actually
          published, of which only "a few" contained the correction slip).
      2). Hardcover, acetate dustwrapper; no priority:
          a). 250 copies, numbered, signed by the author.
          b). 50 copies, numbered, signed, with an original drawing by the
          author tipped in.
          c). 5 copies, for presentation.

FIRE STATION. Santa Barbara, Calif.: Capricorn Press, 1970.
  Two issues, no priority:
      1). Hardcover, tissue dustwrapper.
          100 copies.
      2). Wrappers.

CHILLED GREEN. (Detroit): Alternative Press (1970).
    Postcard.

ANOTHER ACADEMY. (Los Angeles: Black Sparrow Press, 1970).
    Wrappers, no priority:
        1). 250 copies, numbered, signed by the author.
        2). 26 copies, lettered, signed, with an original drawing by the author.

POST OFFICE. Los Angeles: Black Sparrow Press, 1971.
    Two issues, no priority:
        1). Hardcover, acetate dustwrapper; no priority:
            a). 250 copies, numbered, signed by the author.
            b). 50 copies, numbered, signed, with an original drawing by the author.
            c). 4 special copies, for the publisher, author, printer and binder.
        2). Wrappers.
        2000 copies.

MOCKINGBIRD WISH ME LUCK. Los Angeles: Black Sparrow Press, 1972.
    Two issues, no priority:
        1). Hardcover, acetate dustwrapper; no priority:
            a). 250 copies, numbered, signed by the author.
            b). 50 copies, signed, with an original drawing by the author.
            c). 4 special copies, for the publisher, author, printer and binder.
        2). Wrappers.
        2500 copies.
    NOTE: A flyer ("Broadside/Flyer No. 2"), printing an excerpt from the book, preceded publication.

ERECTIONS, EJACULATIONS, EXHIBITIONS AND GENERAL TALES OF ORDINARY MADNESS. (San Francisco): City Lights Books (1972).
    Wrappers.
    No statement of first edition.
    NOTE: Selections from this book were published as *Life and Death In the Charity Ward* by London Magazine Press in 1974.

ME AND YOUR SOMETIMES LOVE POEMS. (Los Angeles: Kisskill Press, 1971).
    Wrappers.
    100 copies.
    NOTE: With Linda King.

WHILE THE MUSIC PLAYED. (Los Angeles): Black Sparrow Press, 1973.
    Wrappers.
    Sparrow 5.

LOVE POEM TO MARINA. (Los Angeles): Black Sparrow Press, 1973.
    Broadside, no priority:
        1). Trade edition.
        2). 100 copies, numbered, signed by the author.

SOUTH OF NO NORTH. Los Angeles: Black Sparrow Press, 1973.
    Two issues, no priority:
        1). Hardcover, acetate dustwrapper; no priority:
           a). 300 copies, numbered, signed by the author.
           b). 50 copies, numbered, with an original drawing by the author.
        2). Wrappers.
           4100 copies.

BURNING IN WATER, DROWNING IN FLAME. Los Angeles: Black Sparrow Press, 1974.
    Two issues, no priority:
        1). Hardcover, acetate dustwrapper; no priority:
           a). 300 copies, numbered, signed by the author.
           b). 50 copies, numbered, with an original drawing by the author.
           c). Library edition.
                221 copies.
        2). Wrappers.
           3873 copies.

AFRICA, PARIS, GREECE. (Los Angeles): Black Sparrow Press, 1974.
    Wrappers.
    Sparrow 30.
    NOTE: 20 copies were "published" by the author in hardcover, acetate dustwrapper, with an original numbered drawing.

FACE OF A POLITICAL CANDIDATE ON A STREET BILLBOARD. (East Lansing, Mich.): Old Marble Press, 1975.
    Broadside, no priority:
        1). 550 copies.
        2). 50 copies, numbered, signed by the author.

FACTOTUM. Los Angeles: Black Sparrow Press, 1975.
    Two issues, no priority:
        1). Hardcover, acetate dustwrapper; no priority:
           a). 750 copies.
           b). 250 copies, numbered, signed by the author.
           c). 75 copies, numbered, with an original drawing by the author.
        2). Wrappers.

WINTER. (Evanston, Ill.): No Mountains Poetry Project, 1975.
    Broadside.
    199 copies, numbered and signed by the author.

William S. Burroughs

JUNKIE. New York: Ace Books (1953).
> Wrappers.
> No statement of first edition.
> NOTE: 1). Written as "William Lee."
>> 2). An Ace Doublebook, with *Narcotic Agent* by Maurice Helbrand.
> ALSO: Milan, 1962.*
>> Hardcover.
>> NOTE: 1). Entitled *La Scimmia Sulla Schiena.*
>>> 2). Contains the first appearance of *Opium Jones* as an appendix.

LETTER FROM A MASTER ADDICT TO DANGEROUS DRUGS. (Privately published, ca. 1957).*
> Stapled sheets.
> NOTE: Offprint from *The British Journal of Addiction*, vol. 53, no. 2, January 1957.

THE NAKED LUNCH. Paris: Olympia Press (1959).
> Wrappers, dustwrapper.
> Title page has a green border; price on rear wrapper is "Francs: 1,500" (later converted to New Francs by rubber stamp).
> NOTE: Reported, but unexamined, is a special edition, boxed.
> ALSO: New York: Grove Press (1962).
>> Hardcover, dustwrapper.
>> No statement of first edition.
>> NOTE: 1). Revised edition.
>>> 2). An advertising brochure, containing an excerpt from the book and critical comments, preceded publication.

EXCERPT FROM PANTAPON ROSE. (San Francisco: Wallace Berman, 1959).
> Broadside.
> NOTE: Laid in portfolio entitled *Semina 4.*

MINUTES TO GO. (Paris): Two Cities Editions (1960).
    Wrappers, no priority:
        1). Trade edition.
        2). 5 copies, numbered, signed by Burroughs & Gysin: the *Edition Originale.*
    NOTE: With Brion Gysin, Gregory Corso and Sinclair Beiles.

THE EXTERMINATOR. (San Francisco): Auerhahn Press, 1960.
    Wrappers.
    NOTE: With Brion Gysin.

THE SOFT MACHINE. Paris: Olympia Press (1961).
    Wrappers, dustwrapper.
    Price on rear wrapper is "15 N.F."
    ALSO: Paris: Olympia Press (1963).*
        Wrappers, dustwrapper.
        NOTE: "New revised and augmented edition: February, 1963."
    ALSO: New York: Grove Press (1966).
        Hardcover, dustwrapper.
        "First Printing"
        NOTE: Further revised and expanded edition.
    ALSO: London: Calder & Boyars, 1968.
        Wrappers.
        No statement of first edition.
        NOTE: Further revised and expanded edition.

THE TICKET THAT EXPLODED. Paris: Olympia Press (1962).
    Wrappers, dustwrapper.
    Price on rear wrapper is "18 N.F."
    ALSO: New York: Grove Press (1967).
        Hardcover, dustwrapper.
        "First Printing"
        NOTE: Revised edition.
    ALSO: London: Calder & Boyars, 1968.
        Wrappers.
        No statement of first edition.
        NOTE: Further revised edition.

THE YAGE LETTERS. (San Francisco): City Lights Press (1963).
    Wrappers.
    NOTE: With Allen Ginsberg.

DEAD FINGERS TALK. London: John Calder (1963).
    Hardcover, dustwrapper.
    No statement of first edition.
    NOTE: Uncorrected proofs in wrappers, with the final dustwrapper, preceded
        publication.

TAKIS. (New York: Iolas Gallery, 1963).*
    Wrappers.

DAVID B. EXHIBITION. (Paris: Privately published) 1964.
    Mechanically reproduced sheet.
    NOTE: Translated into French by Michael Thudotte.

ROOSEVELT AFTER INAUGURATION BY "WILLIE LEE" ALIAS WILLIAM S.
    BURROUGHS. (New York: Fuck You Press, 1964).
    Wrappers.

THE COLDSPRING NEWS. Flint, Mich.: Spero, 1964.*
    Broadside, priority as listed:
        1). Copyright notice at bottom.
        2). No copyright notice at bottom.
    NOTE: Issued separately or bound into *Spero*, vol. 1, no. 1.

NOVA EXPRESS. New York: Grove Press (1964).
    Hardcover, dustwrapper.
    "First Printing"

TIME. New York: "C" Press, 1965.
    Two issues, no priority:
        1). Hardcover, no priority:
            a). 10 copies, lettered, with a page of manuscript and an original draw-
                ing by the illustrator.
            b). 4 copies, hors commerce, with a page of manuscript and an original
                drawing by the illustrator.
        2). Wrappers, no priority:
            a). 886 copies.
            b). 100 copies, numbered, signed by the author and illustrator.
    Illustrated by Brion Gysin.

VALENTINE'S DAY READING. New York: East End Theatre, 1965.
    Wrappers.

WILT CAUGHT IN TIME. (New Orleans: Loujon Press, ca. 1965).
    Broadside.

APO-33 BULLETIN, A METABOLIC REGULATOR. (San Francisco: Mary Beach, 1967).
    Wrappers.
    Beach Books No. 1.

SO WHO OWNS DEATH TV? (San Francisco): Beach Books (1967).
  Wrappers, no known priority:
      1). Black wrappers, printed in silver.
      2). White wrappers, printed in red and black.
  NOTE: With Claude Pelieu and Carl Weissner.
  ALSO: Frankfurt am Main, Germany: Nova Press, 1969.*
      Wrappers.
      NOTE: 1). A facsimile letter added.
          2). Entitled *Fernseh-Tuberkulose.*

THE DEAD STAR. San Francisco: Nova Broadcast Press, 1969.
  Wrappers.
  NOVA Broadcast 5.

THE JOB. Paris: Pierre Belfond, 1969.*
  Wrappers.
  ALSO: London: Jonathan Cape (1969).
      Hardcover, dustwrapper.
      No statement of first edition.
      NOTE: 1). Revised edition.
          2). Uncorrected proofs in printed wrappers preceded publication.
  ALSO: New York: Grove Press (1970).*
      Hardcover, dustwrapper.
      NOTE: Further revised edition.
  ALSO: New York: Grove Press (1974).*
      Hardcover, dustwrapper.
      NOTE: Further revised edition.

ACADEMY SERIES. Brighton, England: Urgency Press Rip Off (ca. 1969).
  Wrappers.
  650 copies.

SCIENTOLOGY REVISITED. N.p. (ca. 1969).*
  Stapled sheets.

THE LAST WORDS OF DUTCH SCHULTZ. London: Cape Goliard Press, 1970.
  Hardcover, no priority:
      1). Trade edition, dustwrapper.
      2). 100 copies, numbered, signed by the author; tissue dustwrapper.
  "This first edition..." opposite title page.

THE WILD BOYS. New York: Grove Press (1971).
  Hardcover, dustwrapper.
  "First Printing"

ELECTRONIC REVOLUTION 1970-71. (London: Henri Chopin, 1971).
    Wrappers, no priority:
        1). 450 copies, numbered.
        2). 50 copies, numbered,signed by the author, with two silkscreened illus-
            trations signed by the illustrator; boxed.
    Illustrated by Brion Gysin.
    NOTE: Gottingen, Germany: 1972.*
        Wrappers, no priority:
            1). Trade edition.
            2). 100 copies, numbered, signed by the author.
        NOTE: Entitled *Die Elektronische Revolution.*

ALI'S SMILE. (Brighton, England): Unicorn Books, 1971.
    Hardcover.
    NOTE: The exact number of copies is difficult to determine because of the ambiguity
        of the colophon: "This first publication in any form of *Ali's Smile* issued in
        an edition of 99 numbered and signed copies of which numbers 1 to 90 are for
        sale and numbers 1 to 99 are hors commerce."

EXTERMINATOR! New York: Viking Press (1973).
    Hardcover, dustwrapper.
    "First Printing"
    NOTE: Uncorrected proofs in printed wrappers, numbered, preceded publication.

WHITE SUBWAY. London: Aloes (1974).
    Wrappers, no priority:
        1). 975 copies.
        2). 25 copies, perfect-bound, numbered, signed by the author.
    NOTE: There was a prepublication edition which was saddlestitched in wrappers.

THE BOOK OF BREETHING. Ingatestone, Essex, England: Henri Chopin (1974).
    Two issues, no priority:
        1). Hardcover.
            50 copies, numbered in Roman, signed by the author.
        2). Wrappers.
            350 copies, numbered in Arabic.
    NOTE: There were an unknown number of copies in wrappers, unnumbered.

PORTFOLIO 1. London: Ruby Editions, 1974.*
    Sheets in portfolio.
    100 copies, signed by the artists.
    NOTE: Silkscreened illustrations by Burroughs, Cozette de Charmoy and Henri
        Chopin.

PORT OF SAINTS. London/Ollon, Switzerland: Covent Garden Press/Am Here Books
      (1975).
      Hardcover, dustwrapper; no priority:
            1). 100 copies.
            2). 100 copies, numbered, signed by the author, boxed.
      NOTE: Although the title page states "1973," this was not published until 1975.

SNACK... (London): Aloes Books (1975)
      Wrappers.
      NOTE: Two tape transcripts: a radio broadcast by Eric Mottram and a meeting
      between Mottram and Burroughs.

Hortense Calisher

IN THE ABSENCE OF ANGELS. Boston: Little, Brown, 1951.
   Hardcover, dustwrapper.
   "FIRST EDITION"

FALSE ENTRY. Boston: Little, Brown (1961).
   Hardcover, dustwrapper.
   "FIRST EDITION"

TALE FOR THE MIRROR. Boston: Little, Brown (1962).
   Hardcover, dustwrapper.
   "FIRST EDITION"

TEXTURES OF LIFE. Boston: Little, Brown (1963).
   Hardcover, dustwrapper.
   "FIRST EDITION"

EXTREME MAGIC. Boston: Little, Brown (1964).
   Hardcover, dustwrapper.
   "FIRST EDITION"

JOURNAL FROM ELLIPSIA. Boston: Little, Brown (1965).
   Hardcover, dustwrapper.
   "FIRST EDITION"

THE RAILWAY POLICE and THE LAST TROLLEY RIDE. Boston: Little, Brown (1966).
   Hardcover, dustwrapper.
   "FIRST EDITION"

WHAT NOVELS ARE. Claremont, Calif.: Scripps College, 1969.
   Wrappers.

THE NEW YORKERS. Boston: Little, Brown (1969).
  Hardcover, dustwrapper.
  "FIRST EDITION"
  NOTE: Uncorrected proofs in printed wrappers preceded publication.

QUEENIE. New York: Arbor House (1970).
  Hardcover, dustwrapper.
  "FIRST EDITION"

STANDARD DREAMING. New York: Arbor House (1972).
  Hardcover, dustwrapper.
  No statement of first edition.

HERSELF. New York: Arbor House (1972).
  Hardcover, dustwrapper, priority as listed:
    1). First line of text on rear panel of dustwrapper reads "On Women...".
    2). First line of text on rear panel of dustwrapper reads "Men on women...".
  No statement of first edition.
  NOTE: An advertising brochure containing an excerpt from the book preceded
    publication.

EAGLE EYE. New York: Arbor House (1973).
  Hardcover, dustwrapper.
  No statement of first edition.
  NOTE: Uncorrected proofs in printed wrappers preceded publication.

SECRET LIFE IN THE UNITED STATES. New York: Arbor House (1975).*
  Hardcover, dustwrapper.

THE COLLECTED STORIES. New York: Arbor House (1975).*
  Hardcover, dustwrapper.

Truman Capote

OTHER VOICES, OTHER ROOMS. New York: Random House (1948).
    Hardcover, dustwrapper.
    "FIRST PRINTING"
    ALSO: New York: Random House (1968).*
        Hardcover, dustwrapper.
        NOTE: New introduction by the author.

A TREE OF NIGHT. New York: Random House (1949).
    Hardcover, dustwrapper.
    "FIRST PRINTING"

LOCAL COLOR. New York: Random House (1950).
    Hardcover, dustwrapper.
    "First Printing"

THE GRASS HARP. (New York): Random House (1951).
    Hardcover, dustwrapper; priority as listed:
        1). Rough linen cloth binding.
        2). Smooth linen cloth binding.
    "First Printing"

THE GRASS HARP: A PLAY. New York: Random House (1952).
    Hardcover, dustwrapper.
    "FIRST PRINTING"

BEAT THE DEVIL. London: Romulus-Santana Productions (ca. 1953).
    Wrappers.
    NOTE: A screenplay; the copy examined was designated a "post-production script."

THE MUSES ARE HEARD. New York: Random House (1956).
    Hardcover, dustwrapper.
    "First Printing"

BREAKFAST AT TIFFANY'S. New York: Random House (1958).
    Hardcover, dustwrapper.
    "First Printing"

OBSERVATIONS. (New York: Simon & Schuster, 1959).
    Hardcover, acetate dustwrapper, boxed.
    No statement of first edition.

THE INNOCENTS. London: Achilles Film Productions, 1961.
    Wrappers.
    NOTE: A screenplay.

SELECTED WRITINGS. New York: Random House (1963).
    Hardcover, dustwrapper.
    "FIRST PRINTING"

IN COLD BLOOD. New York: Random House (1965).
    Hardcover, no priority:
        1). Trade edition, dustwrapper; no known priority:
            a). "1/66" in lower right corner of front flap of dustwrapper.
            b). No marking in lower right corner.
        2). 500 copies, numbered, signed by the author, acetate dustwrapper, boxed.
    "FIRST PRINTING"
    NOTE: 1). 500 review copies in printed wrappers preceded publication.
        2). A Formosan piracy of the first edition, in reduced format, has been examined.

A CHRISTMAS MEMORY. New York: Random House (1966).
    Hardcover, boxed; no priority:
        1). Trade edition.
        2). 600 copies, numbered, signed by the author.
    No statement of first edition.

THE THANKSGIVING VISITOR. New York: Random House (1967).
    Hardcover, boxed; no priority:
        1). Trade edition.
        2). 300 copies, numbered, signed by the author.
    "First Printing"

HOUSE OF FLOWERS. New York: Random House (1968).
    Hardcover, dustwrapper.
    "First Printing"
    NOTE: With Harold Arlen.

TRILOGY. (New York): Macmillan (1969).
    Hardcover, dustwrapper.
    "First Printing"

THE DOGS BARK. New York: Random House (1973).
    Hardcover, dustwrapper.
    "First Edition"
    NOTE: Uncorrected proofs in printed wrappers preceded publication.

John Cheever

THE WAY SOME PEOPLE LIVE. New York: Random House (1943).
Hardcover, dustwrapper.
"FIRST PRINTING"

THE ENORMOUS RADIO. New York: Funk & Wagnalls, 1953.
Hardcover, dustwrapper.
"1" on copyright page.

STORIES. New York: Farrar, Straus & Cudahy (1956).
Hardcover, dustwrapper.
"First Printing, 1956"
NOTE: Jean Stafford, Daniel Fuchs and William Maxwell also contributed.

THE WAPSHOT CHRONICLE. New York: Harper & Bros. (1957).
Hardcover, dustwrapper.
"FIRST EDITION"
ALSO: New York: Time-Life (1956).*
Wrappers.
NOTE: New introduction by the author.

THE HOUSEBREAKER OF SHADY HILL. New York: Harper & Bros. (1958).
Hardcover, dustwrapper.
"FIRST EDITION"

SOME PEOPLE, PLACES & THINGS THAT WILL NOT APPEAR IN MY NEXT NOVEL.
New York: Harper & Bros. (1961).
Hardcover, dustwrapper.
"FIRST EDITION"

THE WAPSHOT SCANDAL. New York: Harper & Row (1964).
Hardcover, dustwrapper.
"FIRST EDITION"

THE BRIGADIER AND THE GOLF WIDOW. New York: Harper & Row (1964).
    Hardcover, dustwrapper; no priority:
        1). Trade edition.
        2). Unknown number of copies, signed by the author on sheet tipped in before
           title page.
    "FIRST EDITION"

MIMI BOYER. New York: Bodley Gallery, 1964.
    Folded sheet.
    NOTE: Exhibition brochure, with all text by Cheever.

HOMAGE TO SHAKESPEARE. Stevenson, Conn.: Country Squires Books (1968).
    Hardcover, dustwrapper.
    150 copies, numbered, signed by the author.
    NOTE: Uncorrected proofs in printed wrappers preceded publication.

BULLET PARK. New York: Knopf, 1969.
    Hardcover, dustwrapper.
    "FIRST EDITION"
    NOTE: Uncorrected proofs in printed wrappers preceded publication.

THE WORLD OF APPLES. New York: Knopf, 1973.
    Hardcover, dustwrapper.
    "FIRST EDITION"
    NOTE: Uncorrected proofs in printed wrappers preceded publication.

Tom Clark

AIRPLANES. (London): Once Book, 1966.
　　Wrappers, no priority:
　　　　1). Trade edition.
　　　　2). 4 copies, numbered, signed by the author.

THE SAND BURG. (London: Ferry Press, 1966).
　　Wrappers, no priority:
　　　　1). 440 copies, numbered, signed by the author.
　　　　2). 60 copies, numbered, signed, with holograph poem by the author.

PARIS REVIEW REJECTION BOOK. (N.p., 1966).*
　　Wrappers.
　　5 copies, numbered, signed by the author.

BIJOUX. New York: Adventures In Poetry, 1967.*
　　Wrappers.
　　50 copies (approximately).
　　NOTE: An offprint from the magazine *Adventures In Poetry*.

THE EMPEROR OF THE ANIMALS. (London): Goliard Press (1967).
　　Wrappers, no priority:
　　　　1). 265 copies.
　　　　2). 35 copies, numbered, signed by the author and all members of the original
　　　　production.

BUN. (New York): Angel Hair Books (1968).
　　Wrappers, no priority:
　　　　1). 500 copies.
　　　　2). 19 copies, numbered, signed by both authors, with a page of manuscript
　　　　included.
　　NOTE: With Ron Padgett.

SONNET. New York: Angel Hair Books, 1968.*
 Broadside.
 50 copies, signed by the author.

CHICAGO: FOR EDWIN DENBY. Bolinas, Calif.: Angel Hair Books, 1969.
 Wrappers, no priority:
  1). 196 copies.
  2). 4 copies, lettered.
 NOTE: With Lewis Warsh.
 ALSO: Los Angeles: Black Sparrow Press, 1974.
  NOTE: 1). Revised text.
   2). Retitled *Chicago*.
 Sparrow 27.

STONES. New York: Harper & Row (1969).
 Two issues, no priority:
  1). Hardcover, dustwrapper.
  2). Wrappers.
 "FIRST EDITION"

ODE TO NEGATIVITY. (Detroit: Alternative Press) 1970.
 Postcard.
 NOTE: With Lewis Warsh.

AIR. New York: Harper & Row (1970).
 Two issues, no priority:
  1). Hardcover, dustwrapper.
  2). Wrappers.
 "FIRST EDITION"

NEIL YOUNG. (Bolinas, Calif.): Angel Hair Books (1970).
 Wrappers.
 200 copies, signed by the author.
 ALSO: (Toronto: Coach House Press, 1971).
  Wrappers.
  1500 copies.
  NOTE: Expanded edition.

CAR WASH. (Bolinas, Calif.: Privately published, ca. 1970).
 Wrappers.
 NOTE: Photographs, photocopied without text.

CAPTAIN AMERICA. (N.p.): Blue Suede Shoes, 1971.
 Broadside.
 Blue Suede Shoes Free Poem.

THE NO BOOK. Wivenhoe Park, Essex, England: Ant's Forefoot Eleventh Finger Voiceprint Edition, 1971.
   Wrappers.

GREEN. Los Angeles: Black Sparrow Press, 1971.
   Two issues, no priority:
      1). Hardcover, acetate dustwrapper; no priority:
         a). 200 copies, numbered, signed by the author.
         b). 26 copies, lettered, signed, with an original drawing by the author.
         c). 4 special copies, for the publisher, author, printer and binder.
      2). Wrappers.
         1000 copies.

SCENES ALONG THE ROAD. Seattle: (Michael Wiater) 1971.
   Broadside, no priority:
      1). Trade edition.
      2). 25 copies (approximately), signed by the author.

JOHN'S HEART. New York: Goliard/Santa Fe, 1972.
   Two issues, no priority:
      1). Hardcover, dustwrapper; no priority:
         a). Trade edition.
         b). 100 copies, numbered, signed by the author.
      2). Wrappers.

SMACK. Los Angeles: Black Sparrow Press, 1972.
   Two issues, no priority:
      1). Hardcover, dustwrapper; no priority:
         a). 175 copies, numbered, signed by the author.
         b). 26 copies, lettered, signed, with an original illustration by the author.
      2). Wrappers.
         1000 copies.
   NOTE: A flyer, printing one poem from the book, preceded publication.

BACK IN TULSA. Detroit: Alternative Press (ca. 1972).
   Broadside.

MORE HAIR EVERY DAY. (Detroit: Alternative Press, ca. 1972).
   Bumper-sticker.

BACK IN BOSTON AGAIN. (New York): Telegraph Books (1972).
   Two issues, no priority:
      1). Library binding.
      2). Wrappers, no priority:
         a). Trade edition.
         b). 50 copies, numbered, signed by the authors.
   "FIRST EDITION"
   NOTE: With Ron Padgett and Ted Berrigan.

SUITE. (Los Angeles): Black Sparrow Press, 1974.
    Wrappers.
    Sparrow 17.

BLUE. Los Angeles: Black Sparrow Press, 1974.
    Two issues, no priority:
        1). Hardcover, acetate dustwrapper; no priority:
            a). 200 copies, numbered, signed by the author.
            b). 26 copies, lettered, signed, with an original drawing by the author.
        2). Wrappers.
            1530 copies.

I WAS BORN TO SPEAK YOUR NAME. (Boulder, Colo.: Lodestar, ca. 1974).
    Broadside.
    NOTE: Laid in portfolio entitled *The Lodestar Broadside Portfolio*, which is
        numbered; 150 copies.

AT MALIBU. (New York): Kulchur Foundation (1975).
    Wrappers.

Robert Coover

THE ORIGIN OF THE BRUNISTS. New York: Putnam (1966).
Hardcover, dustwrapper.
No statement of first edition.
NOTE: Uncorrected proofs in printed wrappers preceded publication.

THE UNIVERSAL BASEBALL ASSOCIATION, INC. J. HENRY WAUGH, PROP.
New York: Random House (1968).
Hardcover, dustwrapper.
"First Printing"
ALSO: London: Rupert Hart-Davis, 1970.
Hardcover, dustwrapper.
No statement of first edition.
NOTE: Contains a *Glossary* not in the American edition.

PRICKSONGS & DESCANTS. New York: Dutton, 1969.
Hardcover, dustwrapper.
"First Edition"

THE WATER POURER. Bloomfield Hills, Mich.: Bruccoli-Clark, 1972.
Hardcover, glassine dustwrapper.
350 copies, numbered, signed by the author.

A THEOLOGICAL POSITION. New York: Dutton, 1972.
Hardcover, dustwrapper.
"First Edition"

THE FALLGUY'S FAITH. Chicago: No Mountains Poetry Project, 1975.
Broadside.
150 copies, numbered, signed by the author.
Broadside Number 3.

Cid Corman

SUBLUNA. (Dorchester, Mass.: Privately published, 1944).
    Wrappers.
    400 copies.

A THANKSGIVING ECLOGUE FROM THEOCRITUS. Corona, N.Y.: Sparrow Magazine
    (1954).
    Wrappers.
    Vagrom Chapbook 2.

THE PRECISIONS. (Corona, N.Y.): Sparrow Press, 1955.
    Wrappers, no priority:
        1). 200 copies.
        2). 25 copies, numbered, signed by the author.

THE RESPONSES. (Ashland, Mass.): Origin Press, 1956.
    Wrappers.

THE MARCHES. (Ashland, Mass.): Origin Press, 1957.
    Wrappers.
    200 copies.

STANCES AND DISTANCES. (Ashland, Mass.): Origin Press, 1957.
    Wrappers.

A TABLE IN PROVENCE. (Ashland, Mass.): Origin Press, 1959.
    Hardcover.
    200 copies, numbered, signed by the author.

THE DESCENT FROM DAIMONJI. (Ashland, Mass.): Origin Press, 1959.
    Wrappers.

COOL MELON. (Ashland, Mass.): Origin Press, 1959.
    Wrappers.

COOL GONG. (Ashland, Mass.): Origin Press, 1959.
    Wrappers.

CLOCKED STONE. (Ashland, Mass.): Origin Press, 1959.
    Hardcover, boxed.
    210 copies, numbered, signed by the author and illustrator.
    Illustrated by Hidetaka Ohno.

FOR SURE. (Ashland, Mass.): Origin Press, 1959.
    Wrappers.

FOR INSTANCE. (Ashland, Mass.): Origin Press, 1962.
    Wrappers.

SUN ROCK MAN. (Kyoto: Origin Press, 1962).
    Hardcover, no priority:
        1). Trade edition, no known priority:
            a). Striped boards.
            b). Plain colored boards.
        2). 250 copies, signed by the author.
   "first edition"

IN NO TIME. (Kyoto: Origin Press, 1963).
    Hardcover, no known priority:
        1). 100 copies, numbered.
        2). Unknown number of copies, signed by the author, with special watercolor
           frontispiece by the illustrator.
    Illustrated by Will Peterson.

IN GOOD TIME. (Kyoto: Origin Press, 1964).
    Wrappers.
    300 copies.

ALL IN ALL. (Kyoto: Origin Press, 1964).
    Hardcover, dustwrapper.
    300 copies, numbered, signed by the author and illustrator.
    Illustrated by Hidetaka Ohno.

FOR GOOD. (Kyoto): Origin Press, 1964.
    Wrappers.

NONCE. (New Rochelle, N.Y.: Elizabeth Press, 1965).
    Wrappers.
    500 copies.

STEAD. (New Rochelle, N.Y.: Elizabeth Press, 1966).
    Wrappers.
    500 copies.

AT : BOTTOM. (Bloomington, Ind. : Caterpillar, 1966).
   Wrappers.

FOR YOU. (Kyoto) : Origin Press, 1966.
   Wrappers.
   100 copies, numbered, signed by the author.

FOR GRANTED. (New Rochelle, N.Y.) : Elizabeth Press, 1967.
   Wrappers.
   500 copies.

WORDS FOR EACH OTHER. London : Rapp & Carroll (1967).
   Hardcover, dustwrapper ; no priority :
      1). Trade edition.
      2). 100 copies, numbered, signed by the author.
   No statement of first edition.
   NOTE : Uncorrected proofs in printed wrappers preceded publication.

& WITHOUT END. (New Rochelle, N.Y. : Elizabeth Press, 1968).
   Hardcover, dustwrapper.

HEARTH. (Kyoto : Origin Press, 1968).
   Hardcover, dustwrapper, boxed.
   100 copies, numbered, signed by the author ; etchings numbered, signed by the
   illustrator.
   Illustrated by Ryohei.

NO LESS. (New Rochelle, N.Y.) : Elizabeth Press, 1968.
   Wrappers.
   500 copies.

THE WORLD AS UNIVERSITY. (Kyoto : Origin Press, ca. 1968).*
   Wrappers.
   Origin Memo #1.
   NOTE : Anonymous.

NO MORE. (New Rochelle, N.Y.) : Elizabeth Press, 1969.
   Wrappers.
   1000 copies.

PLIGHT. (New Rochelle, N.Y. : ELizabeth Press, 1970).
   Hardcover, dustwrapper.

FOR KEEPS. (Kyoto) : Origin Press, 1970.
   Wrappers.
   300 copies.

NIGH. (New Rochelle, N.Y.): Elizabeth Press, 1970.
  Wrappers.
  500 copies.

LIVINGDYING. (New York): New Directions (1970).
  Two issues, no priority:
      1). Hardcover, no priority:
          a). Trade edition, dustwrapper.
          b). 150 copies, signed by the author, glassine dustwrapper, boxed.
      2). Wrappers.
  NOTE: Review copies in printed wrappers preceded publication.

OF THE BREATH OF. (San Francisco): Maya (1970).
  Wrappers, no priority:
      1). 250 copies.
      2). 50 copies, numbered, signed by the author.
  Maya Quarto Twelve.

FOR NOW. (Kyoto): Origin Press, 1971.
  Wrappers.
  300 copies.

CICADAS. (Amherst, N.Y.: Slow Loris Press, 1971).
  Broadside, no priority:
      1). 175 copies.
      2). 25 copies, numbered, signed by the author.

OUT & OUT. New Rochelle, N.Y.: Elizabeth Press (1972).
  Two issues, no priority:
      1). Hardcover.
          200 copies.
      2). Wrappers.
          200 copies.

BE QUEST. (New Rochelle, N.Y.): Elizabeth Press, 1972.
  Wrappers, no priority:
      1). 250 copies.
      2). 50 copies, signed by the author.

A LANGUAGE WITHOUT WORDS. (Arkesden, Saffron Walden, Essex: Hedda's Cottage, 1972).
  Wrappers, no priority:
      1). Trade edition.
      2). 30 copies, signed by the author.
  Byways 6.

POEMS: THANKS TO ZUCKERKANDL. Rushden, Northamptonshire, England:
Sceptre Press (1973).
Wrappers, no priority:
1). 100 copies, numbered.
2). 50 copies, numbered, signed by the author.

SO FAR. (New Rochelle, N.Y.): Elizabeth Press, 1973.
Wrappers, no priority:
1). 250 copies.
2). 50 copies, signed by the author.

THREE POEMS. Rushden, Northamptonshire, England: Sceptre Press (1973).
Wrappers, no priority:
1). 100 copies, numbered.
2). 50 copies, numbered, signed by the author.
NOTE: There were an unknown number of copies unnumbered, unsigned.

RSVP. Knotting, Bedfordshire, England: Sceptre Press (1974).
Wrappers, no priority:
1). 100 copies, numbered.
2). 50 copies, numbered, signed by the author.

YET. (New Rochelle, N.Y.): Elizabeth Press, 1974.
Wrappers, no priority:
1). 450 copies.
2). 50 copies, signed by the author.

O/I. New Rochelle, N.Y.: Elizabeth Press (1974).
Two issues, no priority:
1). Hardcover, boxed.
2). Wrappers.
400 copies.

FOR DEAR LIFE. (Los Angeles): Black Sparrow Press, 1975.
Wrappers.
Sparrow 33.

ONCE AND FOR ALL. New Rochelle, N.Y.: Elizabeth Press (1975).
Two issues, no priority:
1). Hardcover, boxed.
100 copies.
2). Wrappers, dustwrapper.
400 copies.

TRANSLATIONS.

Kusano Shimpei.
SELECTED FROGS. (Kyoto: Origin Press, ca. 1963).
    Wrappers.
    NOTE: Translated with Kamaike Susumu.

TRANSLATIONS FROM THE SPANISH. (Reno: Richard Morris) 1967.
    Wrappers.
    Quark I.
    NOTE: Cesar Vallejo translated by Clayton Eshleman; Jose Hierro translated by
        Eshleman and Corman.

Basho.
BACK ROADS TO FAR TOWNS. (New York): Grossman (1968).
    Hardcover, dustwrapper.
    "First edition, 1968"
    NOTE: Translated with Kamaike Susumu.

Kusano Shimpei.
FROGS & OTHERS. (New York): Grossman (1969).
    Hardcover, dustwrapper, boxed.
    "First edition"

Francis Ponge.
THINGS. (New York): Grossman (1971).
    Hardcover, dustwrapper.
    "First Edition"

Rene Char.
LEAVES OF HYPNOS. (New York): Grossman (1973).
    Hardcover.
    "First Edition"

Philippe Jaccottet.
BREATHINGS. (New York): Grossman (1974).
    Hardcover.
    "First Edition"

Robert Creeley

LE FOU. Columbus, Ohio: Golden Goose Press, 1952.
    Wrappers, tissue dustwrapper.
    "This first edition. . ." noted in colophon.

PRINTING IS CHEAP IN MALLORCA. (Palma de Mallorca: Divers Press, ca. 1953).
    Single sheet.
    NOTE: 1). Anonymous.
        2). A prospectus for Divers Press.

THE KIND OF ACT OF. (Palma de Mallorca): Divers Press, 1953.
    Wrappers.

THE IMMORAL PROPOSITION. (Baden, Germany: Jonathan Williams, 1953).
    Wrappers.
    200 copies.
    Jargon 8.

THE GOLD DIGGERS. (Palma de Mallorca): Divers Press, 1954.
    Wrappers.
    ALSO: (Frankfurt am Main): Insel, 1964.
        Hardcover.
        NOTE: 1). Titled *Mister Blue; Sechzehn Geschichten.*
            2). Expanded edition.
            3). This expanded edition was later published in hardcover and dust-
               wrapper by John Calder in London, 1965; and subsequently in
               wrappers by Scribner's in New York (1965).

MAYAN LETTERS. Palma de Mallorca: Divers Press, 1954.
    Single sheet.
    NOTE: 1). Anonymous.
        2). An advance notice for the publication of Charles Olson's *Mayan Letters.*

A SNARLING GARLAND OF XMAS VERSES. (Palma de Mallorca: Divers Press, 1954).
    Wrappers.
    NOTE: Written as "Anonymous."

ALL THAT IS LOVELY IN MEN. Asheville, N.C.: Jonathan Williams, 1955.
Wrappers.
200 copies, signed by the author and illustrator.
Jargon 10.
Illustrated by Dan Rice.

IF YOU. San Francisco: Porpoise Bookshop, 1956.
Sheets in portfolio.
200 copies.
Poems and Pictures: Number Eight.

THE WHIP. (Worcester, England): Migrant Books, 1957.
Two issues, no priority:
    1). Hardcover.
        100 copies.
    2). Wrappers.
        500 copies.

TWO WAYS OF LOOKING IN A MIRROR. (N.p: Privately published, 1957).
Broadside.
2 copies.

A FORM OF WOMEN. New York: Jargon Books/Corinth Books (1959).
Wrappers.
2000 copies.
Jargon 33.
ALSO: FOUR POEMS FROM "A FORM OF WOMEN." New York: Friends of the
Eighth Street Bookshop, 1959.
Wrappers.

READING AND COMMENTING ON HIS POEMS. San Francisco: Poetry Center, 1959.
Mechanically reproduced sheets.
NOTE: With Robert Duncan.

FOR LOVE. New York: Scribner's, 1962.
Two issues, no priority:
    1). Hardcover, dustwrapper.
    2). Wrappers, priority as listed:
        a). Perfect-bound sheets.
        b). Sewn sheets.
"A" on copyright page.

AN AMERICAN SENSE. (London): Sigma (ca. 1963).
Mechanically reproduced sheets, varying color stock; no priority:
    1). Trade edition.
    2). 20 copies (approximately), signed by the author.
Sigma Portfolio 26.

THE ISLAND. New York: Scribner's (1963).
    Priority as listed:
        1). Wrappers.
        Perfect-bound sheets.
        Page 145 has lines 20, 21 and 22 transposed.
        2). Hardcover, dustwrapper.
        Error corrected on tipped-in sheet.
        3). Wrappers.
        Error corrected on integral sheet.
        4). Hardcover, dustwrapper.
        Perfect-bound sheets.
        Error as in 1).
   "A" on copyright page.

DISTANCE. Lawrence, Kan.: Terence Williams, 1964.
    Broadside.
    500 copies.
    "Special first printing"
    Broadside Poem #6.
    NOTE: An unknown number of copies were signed by the author.

TWO POEMS. (Berkeley): Oyez, 1964.
    Broadside, priority as listed:
        1). White showing around the gold diamonds in the "T."
        2). Yellow hand-colored around the gold diamonds.
    350 copies.
    Oyez 5.
    NOTE: 27 copies, numbered, signed by the author in 1964 but published in 1965 in
        portfolio entitled *Poems in Broadside. Oyez. First Series.*

HI THERE! Urbana, Ill.: Finial Press, 1965.*
    Broadside.
    9 copies.

WORDS. (Rochester, Mich.: W.S. Hamady) 1965.
    Hardcover, tissue dustwrapper; no priority:
        1). 30 copies, signed by the author.
        2). 5 copies, described as "variant proofs."

WORDS. (La Grande, Ore.): Eastern Oregon College (ca. 1966).
    Broadside.

ABOUT WOMEN. Los Angeles: Gemini, 1966.
    Sheets in portfolio.
    NOTE: These five sheets consituted the introduction to John Altoon's *Ten Original
        Lithographs in Color* and a few extra sets of the introduction were published
        separately.

POEMS 1950-1965. London: Calder and Boyars (1966).
>   Hardcover, glassine dustwrapper; priority as listed:
>   >   1). 100 copies, numbered, signed by the author, "hors commerce in advance of the first edition," boxed.
>   >   2). Trade edition.
>   No statement of first edition.

FOR JOEL. (Rochester, Mich.): Perishable Press, 1966.
>   Broadside, no priority:
>   >   1). 60 copies.
>   >   2). 25 copies, hors commerce.

WORDS. New York: Scribner's (1967).
>   Two issues, no priority:
>   >   1). Hardcover, dustwrapper.
>   >   2). Wrappers.
>   "A" on copyright page.
>   NOTE: Much expanded from the 1965 book of the same title.

A SIGHT. (London): Cape Goliard (1967).
>   Sheets in portfolio, no priority:
>   >   1). 50 copies.
>   >   2). 50 copies, signed by the author and illustrator.
>   Illustrated by R. B. Kitaj.

ROBERT CREELEY READS. (London): Turret Books/Calder & Boyars (1967).
>   Wrappers.
>   350 copies.

THE CHARM. (Mt. Horeb, Wisc.): Perishable Press, 1967.
>   Hardcover.
>   250 copies, numbered, signed by the author (reportedly, only 235 copies were actually published).
>   "This is the first edition..." noted in the colophon.
>   NOTE: 1). An unknown number of copies had variant proofs for the title page.
>   >   2). Although the title page states "1967," this book was not published until 1968.
>   ALSO: San Francisco: Four Seasons Foundation, 1969.
>   >   Two issues, no priority:
>   >   >   1). Hardcover, no priority:
>   >   >   >   a). Trade edition.
>   >   >   >   b). 100 copies, numbered, signed by the author.
>   >   >   2). Wrappers.
>   >   Writing 23.
>   >   NOTE: Expanded edition.

KATE'S. (New York): Indianakatz, 1967.
    Broadside.
    225 copies.
    NOTE: Laid in portfolio entitled *Stamped Indelibly*, numbered.

THE FINGER. Los Angeles: Black Sparrow Press, 1968.
    Two issues, priority as listed:
        1). Wrappers, priority as listed:
            a). 200 copies (approximately), correctly printed.
            b). 50 copies (approximately), with lines transposed on page 13.
        2). Hardcover, no priority:
            a). 50 copies, numbered, signed by the author, with an original drawing signed by the illustrator.
            b). 5 special copies, for the publisher, author, illustrator, printer & binder.
    Illustrated by Bobbie Creeley.
    ALSO: London: Calder & Boyars (1970).
    Two issues, no priority:
        1). Hardcover, dustwrapper; no priority:
            a). Trade edition.
            b). 100 copies, numbered, signed by the author.
        2). Wrappers.

DIVISIONS. (Madison, Wisc.): Perishable Press, 1968.
    Wrappers, no priority:
        1). 100 copies, numbered in Arabic.
        2). 10 copies, numbered in Roman.

5 NUMBERS. (New York: Poets Press, 1968).
    Wrappers, no priority:
        1). 150 copies, numbered, signed by the author.
        2). 20 copies, starred, signed by the author.
    ALSO: Stuttgart: Edition Domberger (1968).
    Three issues, no priority:
        1). Hardcover.
            275 copies, numbered, signed by the author and illustrator.
        2). Sheets in portfolio; no priority:
            a). 125 copies, numbered in Arabic, signed by the author and illustrator.
            b). 35 copies, numbered in Roman, signed by the author and illustrator.
        3). Wrappers, boxed.
            2500 copies.
    Illustrated by Robert Indiana.
    NOTE: 1). Entitled *Numbers*.
           2). Expanded edition.

THE BOY. Buffalo, N.Y.: Gallery Upstairs Press, 1968.
    Broadside, no priority:
        1). Trade edition.
        2). 50 copies, signed by the author.

IF YOU. (London: Lion and Unicorn Press, 1968).
    Broadside.
    400 copies.

PIECES. Los Angeles: Black Sparrow Press, 1968.
    Two issues, no priority:
        1). Hardcover, acetate dustwrapper; no priority:
            a). 150 copies, numbered, signed by the author and illustrator.
            b). 26 copies, lettered, signed by the author and illustrator, with an
                original drawing by the illustrator tipped in.
            c). 5 special copies, for the publisher, author, illustrator, printer & binder.
        2). Wrappers.
           250 copies, numbered, signed by the author.
    Illustrated by Bobbie Creeley.
    ALSO: New York: Scribner's (1969).
        Two issues, no priority:
        1). Hardcover, dustwrapper.
        2). Wrappers.
    "A" on copyright page.
    NOTE: Expanded edition.

WHAT IT SAYS IS THAT ONE. (New York: Brownstone Press, 1968).
    Broadside, no priority:
        1). 200 copies.
        2). 50 copies, signed by the author.
    NOTE: Also referred to as *Gemini*; it is one of a set of broadsides laid in portfolio
        entitled *The Zodiac*. 250 numbered copies of *The Zodiac* were published.

CONTEXTS OF POETRY. (Buffalo: Audit/Poetry) 1968.
    Wrappers.
    NOTE: 1). Issued as *Audit*, Vol. 5, No. 1.
           2). With Allen Ginsberg.

MAZATLAN: SEA. (San Francisco): Poets Press, 1969.
    Wrappers, no priority:
        1). 50 copies, numbered, signed by the author.
        2). 10 copies, lettered, signed by the author.
        3). 20 copies, hors commerce.

HERO. (New York: Indianakatz, 1969).
    Wrappers.
    1000 copies.

PATERSON SOCIETY. Cambridge, Mass.: Paterson Society (ca. 1969).*
    Broadside.

A WALL. New York/Stuttgart: Bouwerie Editions/Edition Domberger (1969).
    Wrappers, in portfolio, no priority:
        1). 125 copies, numbered 1-125, signed by the author and illustrator.
        2). 25 copies, numbered P1-P25, for the use of the author.
        3). 25 copies, numbered, A1-A25, for the use of the illustrator.
        4). 25 copies, numbered I-XXV, for the use of the publisher.
        5). 10 copies, numbered D1-D10, for the use of the printer.
    Illustrated by William Katz.

MARY'S FANCY. (New York): Bouwerie Editions, 1970.
    Wrappers, no priority:
        1). 250 copies.
        2). 100 copies, numbered, signed by the author.
    NOTE: There were 52 uncorrected proofs, divided into two sets, each set lettered A-Z.

AMERICA. (Miami: Press of the Black Flag, 1970).
    Broadside.

AFTER LORCA. (Brockport, N.Y.: Department of English, State University College, 1970).
    Wrappers.
    NOTE: Cover title is *Department of English, State University College, Brockport.*

IN LONDON. Bolinas, Calif.: Angel Hair Books, 1970.
    Wrappers, no priority:
        1). 200 copies.
        2). 10 copies, numbered, signed by the author.
        3). 4 copies with the "L" on the title page inked in, hors commerce.

FOR BETSY AND TOM. Detroit: Alternative Press (1970).
    Broadside.

FOR BENNY & SABINA. (Brooklyn): Samuel Charters (1970).
    Broadside.
    100 copies.
    Portents 18.

AS NOW IT WOULD BE SNOW. Los Angeles: Black Sparrow Press, 1970.
   Two issues, no priority:
         1). Hardcover, acetate dustwrapper; no priority:
               a). 50 copies, numbered, signed by the author.
               b). 4 special copies, for the publisher, author, printer and binder.
         2). Wrappers, priority unknown:
               a). Untrimmed wrappers.
               b). Trimmed wrappers.
                    525 copies.

CHRISTMAS: MAY 10, 1970. (Buffalo: Friends of the Lockwood Memorial Library) 1970.
   Broadside, no priority:
         1). 1940 copies.
         2). 35 copies, signed by the author.
         3). 25 copies, numbered, signed by the author.

A QUICK GRAPH. San Francisco: Four Seasons Foundation, 1970.
   Two issues, no priority:
         1). Hardcover.
         2). Wrappers.
   Writing 22.

SEA. (Bolinas, Calif.: Privately published, 1970).
   Broadside.

ST. MARTIN'S. Los Angeles: Black Sparrow Press, 1971.
   Two issues, no priority:
         1). Hardcover, acetate dustwrapper; no priority:
               a). 250 copies, numbered, signed by the author.
               b). 50 copies, numbered, signed by the author and illustrator, with an
                    original drawing by the illustrator.
               c). 5 special copies, for the publisher, author, illustrator, printer & binder.
         2). Wrappers.
               1000 copies.
   Illustrated by Bobbie Creeley.
   NOTE: A flyer, printing a poem from the book, preceded publication; no known
         priority:
               1). Line 5: "and, as I am welcome. . ."
               2). Line 5: "and, as I am. . ."

THE CHARM. (Berkeley): Book People/Mudra (1971).
   Broadside.

THE BIRDS. (Berkeley: Arif Press, 1971).
   Broadside.
   125 copies.

1.2.3.4.5.6.7.8.9.0. Berkeley/San Francisco: Shambala/Mudra, 1971.
  Two issues, no priority:
      1). Hardcover, acetate dustwrapper.
      200 copies, numbered, signed by the author and illustrator.
      2). Wrappers.
  Illustrated by Arthur Okamura.

FOR THE GRADUATION: BOLINAS SCHOOL, JUNE 11, 1971. Bolinas, Calif.:
  (Privately published) 1971.
  Two issues, no priority:
      1). Broadside.
      2). Broadside, glued in wrappers.
  Wrappers illustrated by Arthur Okamura.
  NOTE: 1). Anonymous.
      2). An unknown number of copies in wrappers were signed by both author and
      illustrator.

ONE DAY AFTER ANOTHER. (Detroit: Alternative Press, 1972).
  Postcard.

LISTEN. Los Angeles: Black Sparrow Press, 1972.
  Two issues, no priority:
      1). Hardcover, acetate dustwrapper; no priority:
          a). 250 copies, numbered, signed by the author.
          b). 50 copies, numbered, signed by the author, with an original drawing
              by the illustrator.
          c). 5 special copies, for the publisher, author, illustrator, printer & binder.
      2). Wrappers.
      1500 copies.
  Illustrated by Bobbie Creeley.

A DAY BOOK. Berlin: Graphics (1972).
  Three issues, no priority:
      1). 25 copies in leather, numbered in Roman, signed by the author and illustrator,
      with 14 original graphics; the *Edition de Tete.*
      2). The *Standard Edition*; no priority:
          a). 175 copies, in portfolio, numbered in Arabic, signed by the author and
              illustrator, with 13 original graphics.
          b). 25 copies in linen, numbered in Arabic, signed by the author and illus-
              trator, with 13 original graphics.
      3). Hardcover, boxed.
      70 copies, signed by the author; hors commerce.
  "This first edition. . ." noted in the colophon.
  Illustrated by R. B. Kitaj.
  NOTE: Precedes the American edition (Scribner's), which adds no new text.

FOR THE GRADUATION: JUNE 15, 1972. Bolinas, Calif.: (Privately published) 1972.
    Two issues, no priority:
        1). Broadside.
        2). Broadside, glued in wrappers.
    Wrappers illustrated by Arthur Okamura.
    NOTE: 1). Anonymous.
        2). An unknown number of copies in wrappers were signed by both author and
        illustrator.

CHARACTERISTICALLY. Cambridge, Mass.: Pomegranate Press, 1972.
    Broadside, no priority:
        1). 350 copies, numbered.
        2). 150 copies, numbered, signed by the author and illustrator.
    Illustrated by Karyl Klopp.

KITCHEN. (Chicago: Wine Press, 1972).
    Broadside.
    500 copies.
    Letters, Number 2.

CHANGE. (San Francisco: Cranium Press, 1972).*
    Postcard.

NOTEBOOK. New York: Bouwerie Editions, 1972.
    Wrappers, no priority:
        1). 300 copies.
        2). 50 copies, numbered, signed by the author.

A SENSE OF MEASURE. (London): Calder and Boyars (1972).
    Two issues, no priority:
        1). Hardcover, dustwrapper.
        2). Wrappers.
    No statement of first edition.
    Signature 16.

FOR MY MOTHER. Rushden, Northamptonshire, England: Sceptre Press (1973).
    Wrappers, no priority:
        1). 100 copies, numbered.
        2). 50 copies, numbered, signed by the author.

CONTEXTS OF POETRY. Bolinas, Calif.: Four Seasons Foundation, 1973.
    Wrappers.
    Writing 30.

THE LANGUAGE. (Brockport, N.Y.: Department of English, State University College,
    1973).
    Wrappers.
    NOTE: Cover title is *Writer's Forum.*

THE CREATIVE. (Los Angeles): Black Sparrow Press, 1973.
    Wrappers.
    Sparrow 6.

HIS IDEA. (Toronto: Coach House Press, 1973).
    Wrappers, priority as listed:
        1). Gold unprinted wrappers; beige printed dustwrapper.
        2). Gold printed wrappers.

INSIDE OUT. (Los Angeles): Black Sparrow Press, 1973.
    Wrappers.
    Sparrow 14.

THE PLAN IS THE BODY. Philadelphia: Middle Earth Bookstore (1973).
    Broadside, no priority:
        1). 275 copies.
        2). 25 copies, numbered, signed by the author.
    NOTE: This is to be differentiated from the later broadside printing published by
    Prester John in Vancouver (1975).

THE CLASS OF '47. (New York: Bouwerie Editions, 1973).
    Wrappers, no priority:
        1). 200 copies, numbered.
        2). 100 copies, numbered, signed by the author and illustrator.
        3). 28 copies (approximately), for the use of the author, numbered, with the
        letter "A" preceding the number.
    Illustrated by Joe Brainard.

SITTING HERE. (Storrs, Conn.): University of Connecticut Library, 1974.
    Broadside.
    350 copies.

THIRTY THINGS. Los Angeles: Black Sparrow Press, 1974.
    Two issues, no priority:
        1). Hardcover, acetate dustwrapper; no priority:
            a). 250 copies, numbered, signed by the author.
            b). 50 copies, numbered, signed by the author and illustrator, with an
            original drawing by the illustrator.
        2). Wrappers.
            2038 copies.
    Illustrated by Bobbie Creeley.

NIGHT IN NYC: FOR ANGUS. (Boulder, Colo.: Lodestar, ca. 1974).
    Broadside.
    NOTE: Laid in portfolio entitled *The Lodestar Broadside Portfolio*. 150 numbered
    copies of the portfolio were published.

BACKWARDS. Knotting, Bedfordshire, England: Sceptre Press (1975).
    Wrappers, no priority:
        1). 100 copies, numbered.
        2). 50 copies, numbered, signed by the author.

KORE. (Oakland: Native Dancer Press, 1975).
    Broadside, no priority:
        1). 13 copies.
        2). 13 copies, numbered, signed by the author.
    NOTE: According to a separate colophon, there were "about 4 proofs on Tovil paper."

BUT. (Buffalo: Just Buffalo, 1975).
    Broadside, no priority:
        1). Trade edition.
        2). 50 copies, numbered, signed by the author.

James Dickey

POETS OF TODAY VII. New York: Scribner's (1960).
 Hardcover, dustwrapper.
 "A" on copyright page.
 NOTE: Paris Leary and Jon Swan also contributed.

DROWNING WITH OTHERS. Middletown, Conn.: Wesleyan University (1962).
 Two issues, no priority:
  1). Hardcover, dustwrapper.
  2). Wrappers.
 "First Edition"

TWO POEMS OF THE AIR. Portland, Ore.: Centicore Press (1964).
 Hardcover, boxed.
 300 copies, numbered, signed by the author and illustrator.
 Illustrated by Monica Moseley Pincus.

HELMETS. Middletown, Conn.: Wesleyan University Press (1964).
 Two issues, no priority:
  1). Hardcover, dustwrapper.
  2). Wrappers.
 "First Edition"

THE SUSPECT IN POETRY. (Madison, Minn.): Sixties Press, 1964.
 Two issues, no priority:
  1). Hardcover, dustwrapper.
  2). Wrappers, dustwrapper.

BUCKDANCER'S CHOICE. Middletown, Conn.: Wesleyan University Press (1965).
 Two issues, no priority:
  1). Hardcover, dustwrapper.
  2). Wrappers.
 "FIRST EDITION"

A PRIVATE BRINKMANSHIP. (Claremont, Calif.: Pitzer College, 1965).
    Wrappers.
    1000 copies.

NATIONAL BOOK AWARD IN POETRY 1966 ACCEPTANCE SPEECH. (New York:
    Privately published) 1966.*
    Mechanically reproduced sheets.

POEMS 1957-1967. Middletown, Conn.: Wesleyan University Press (1967).
    Hardcover, dustwrapper.
    "FIRST EDITION"
    NOTE: 500 miniature copies, in wrappers identical in appearance to the later
        dustwrapper, preceded publication and contained one poem from the book.
    ALSO: London: Rapp and Carroll (1967).
        Hardcover, dustwrapper; no priority:
            1). Trade edition.
            2). 50 copies, numbered, signed by the author.

SPINNING THE CRYSTAL BALL. Washington, D.C.: Library of Congress, 1967.
    Wrappers.
    NOTE: Not actually published until 1968.

BABEL TO BYZANTIUM. New York: Farrar, Straus & Giroux (1968).
    Hardcover, dustwrapper.
    "First printing, 1968"

METAPHOR AS PURE ADVENTURE. Washington, D.C.: Library of Congress, 1968.
    Wrappers.

THE EYE-BEATERS, BLOOD, VICTORY, MADNESS, BUCKHEAD AND MERCY.
    Garden City, N.Y.: Doubleday, 1970.
    Hardcover, priority as listed:
            1). 250 copies, numbered, signed by the author.
            2). Trade edition, dustwrapper.
                "FIRST EDITION AFTER A LIMITED EDITION OF 250 COPIES"

DELIVERANCE. Boston: Houghton Mifflin, 1970.
    Hardcover, dustwrapper.
    "First Printing"
    NOTE: 1). An advance prospectus in wrappers preceded publication and contained 19
        facsimile manuscript pages with facsimiles of the author's corrections.
        2). A Formosan piracy of the first edition, in reduced format, has been examined.

SELF-INTERVIEWS. Garden City, N.Y.: Doubleday, 1970.
    Hardcover, dustwrapper.
    "First Edition"
    NOTE: A Formosan piracy of the first edition, in reduced format, has been examined.

THE FLASH. (Brockport, N.Y.: Department of English, State University College, 1970).
    Wrappers.
    NOTE: Cover title is *Department of English State University College Brockport.*

EXCHANGES. (Bloomfield Hills, Mich.: Bruccoli-Clark, 1971).
    Wrappers.
    200 copies, numbered, signed by the author.

SORTIES. Garden City, N.Y.: Doubleday, 1971.
    Hardcover, dustwrapper.
    "First Edition"

FIRING LINE. (Columbia, S.C.): Southern Educational Communications Association, 1971.*
    Wrappers.
    NOTE: Transcript of the television interview of Dickey by William F. Buckley, Jr.

JERICHO. Birmingham, Ala.: Oxmoor House (1974).
    Hardcover, dustwrapper.
    "First Edition"

Diane DiPrima

THIS KIND OF BIRD FLIES BACKWARD. (New York: Totem Press, 1958).
Wrappers.
ALSO: New York: Cooper Union Art School (ca. 1960).
Sheets in portfolio.
NOTE: Six poems from *This Kind of Bird Flies Backward*, silkscreened.

MURDER CAKE. New York: Living Theatre, 1960.*
Mechanically reproduced sheets.
NOTE: This is to be differentiated from the mimeographed edition by the Judson Poets
Theatre (1963), the mimeographed edition by the New York Theatre for Poets
(1964) and the dittoed edition by an unknown publisher (ca. 1965).

PAIDEUMA. New York: Living Theatre, 1960.*
Mechanically reproduced sheets.

DINNERS AND NIGHTMARES. New York: Corinth Books, 1961.
Wrappers.
"$1.25" on cover.
ALSO: New York: Corinth Books, 1974.
Wrappers.
"Third Printing, New Enlarged Edition"

THE MONSTER. New Haven, Conn.: Penny Poems, 1961.
Broadside.
Penny Poems No. 136.

THE NEW HANDBOOK OF HEAVEN. San Francisco: Auerhahn Press, 1963.
Two issues, no priority:
1). Hardcover.
30 copies, signed by the author.
2). Wrappers.
1000 copies.

LIKE. New York: American Theatre For Poets (ca. 1964).
  Mimeographed sheets.

POETS VAUDEVILLE. New York: Feed Folly Press (1964).
  Wrappers, priority as listed:
      1). Stapled in wrappers, without credit to illustrator.
      2). Stapled in wrappers, with credit to illustrator.
  200 copies, numbered.
  Illustrated by Jeanne Marlowe.

COMBINATION THEATRE POEM & BIRTHDAY POEM FOR TEN PEOPLE. New York:
  Brownstone Press, 1965.
  Sheets in portfolio.
  100 copies, numbered, signed by the author.
  "First Edition"

HAIKU. (Topanga, Calif.: Love Press, 1966).
  Sheets in leather pouch, no priority:
      1). 100 copies, the poems printed.
      2). 12 copies, the poems in manuscript.

HYMN. Pleasant Valley, N.Y.: Kriya Press, 1967.
  Broadside.
  100 copies, numbered.
  NOTE: There were an unknown number of unnumbered copies.

NEW MEXICO POEM. (New York: Poets Press, 1968).
  Wrappers, varying cover stock, no priority:
      1). 50 copies, numbered, signed by the author.
      2). 12 copies, lettered, signed by the author.

HOTEL ALBERT. (New York: Poets Press, 1968).
  Wrappers, no priority:
      1). 150 copies, numbered, signed by the author.
      2). 12 copies, lettered, for the use of the author.

EARTHSONG. New York: Poets Press, 1968.
  Wrappers.

LOVE ON A TRAMPOLINE. (New York: Maurice Girodias, 1968).
  Wrappers.
  No statement of first edition.
  Traveller's Companion Series TC-431.
  NOTE: The author is "Sybah Darrich"; however, the sex scenes were written by
      DiPrima.

OF SHEEP AND GIRLS. (New York: Traveller's Companion Inc., 1968).
>   Wrappers.
>   No statement of first edition.
>   Traveller's Companion Series T C-2222.
>   NOTE: The author is "Robert M. Duffy"; however, the sex scenes were written by
>   DiPrima and Alice Malloy.

REVOLUTIONARY LETTERS.
>   No known priority:
>   1). New York: Communication Company, 1968.
>   Mimeographed sheets.
>   2). Ann Arbor, Mich.: Artists Workshop Press, ca. 1968.
>   Mechanically reproduced sheets.
>   NOTE: Both editions print *Letters 1-15.*
>   ALSO: (New York: Privately published) 1968.
>   Wrappers.
>   NOTE: Prints *Letters 1-34.*
>   ALSO: (Ann Arbor, Mich.: White Panther Party, 1969).
>   Wrappers.
>   NOTE: Prints *Letters 1-34*, an additional poem and an autobiographical
>   statement.
>   ALSO: (Santa Fe, N.M.: Noose and Earth Read Out-Southwest, 1971).
>   Wrappers.
>   NOTE: Prints *Letters 1-43.*
>   ALSO: (San Francisco): City Lights Books (1971).
>   Wrappers.
>   No statement of first edition.
>   Pocket Poets No. 27.
>   NOTE: 1). Expanded edition.
>   2). The second and third printings, both of which are so identified on the
>   copyright page, each have additional *Letters.*

THE STAR, THE CHILD, THE LIGHT. (Privately published) 1968.
>   Two issues, no known priority:
>   1). Narrow brown card, illustrated.
>   2). Folded red card, with illustration pasted on.

MONUMENTS. New York: Cafe Cino, 1968.
>   Single sheet, folded.

A POEM FOR SCORPIOS. (New York: Brownstone Press, 1968).
>   Broadside, no priority:
>   1). 200 copies.
>   2). 50 copies, signed by the author.
>   NOTE: Also referred to as *Scorpio*; it appeared as one of a set of broadsides, laid in
>   portfolio entitled *The Zodiac*. 250 numbered copies of *The Zodiac* were
>   published.

NOTES ON THE SUMMER SOLSTICE. (San Francisco: Privately published) 1969.
    Mimeographed sheets.
    NOTE: Anonymous.

NEW AS. (San Francisco: Privately published) 1969.
    Postcard.

L. A. ODYSSEY. (San Francisco: Poets Press, 1969).
    Wrappers.
    100 copies, numbered, signed by the author.
    NOTE: There were an unknown number of out-of-series copies, signed by the author.

MEMOIRS OF A BEATNIK. (New York: Olympia Press, 1969).
    Wrappers.
    No statement of first edition.

I FEEL MYSELF FADE. Denver: Croupier Press, 1969.
    Postcard.
    Poetry Card Series #3.

THE BOOK OF HOURS. San Francisco: Brownstone Press, 1970.
    Sheets in box, no priority:
        1). 150 copies, numbered.
        2). 50 copies, numbered, signed by the author and illustrator.
    Illustrated by Bret Rohmer.

PRAYER TO THE MOTHERS. (San Francisco: Privately published) 1971.
    Broadside.

XV DEDICATIONS. (Santa Barbara, Calif.: Unicorn Press) 1971.
    Broadside.
    Unicorn Broadsheet Series II No. 7.

KERHONKSON JOURNAL. Berkeley: Oyez, 1971.
    Wrappers.

I AM NO. San Francisco: Tenth Muse (1971).
    Broadside.

FOR BLAKE. (Santa Barbara, Calif.: Unicorn Press, 1971).
    Postcard, no priority:
        1). Trade edition.
        2). 30 copies, signed by the author.
    Unicorn Press Poetry Post Card Series Three, Number Four.

SO FINE. Portland, Ore.: Yes! Press, 1971.
    Broadside.

THE CALCULUS OF VARIATION. San Francisco: (Privately published) 1972.
    Wrappers, no priority:
        1). 1950 copies.
        2). 50 copies, numbered, signed by the author.

AFTER COMPLETION. (San Francisco): Mongrel Press (1972).
    Broadside.

TO TARA. (San Francisco): Panjandrum Press, 1972.
    Broadside.
    Panjandrum Broadside #2.

FRIEND. (Detroit): Alternative Press (1972).
    Bookmark.

LIKE WIND, DISPERSING, LIKE SOME HUGE. (Detroit: Alternative Press, ca. 1972).
    Postcard.

DISCOVERY OF AMERICA. New York: Theatre For the New City (ca. 1972).
    Wrappers.

APRIL FOOL BIRTHDAY POEM FOR GRANDPA. (San Francisco): San Francisco Art
    Institute (ca. 1973).
    Mimeographed sheet.

LOBA: PART 1. Santa Barbara, Calif.: Capra Press, 1973.
    Two issues, no priority:
        1). Hardcover.
            100 copies, numbered, signed by the author.
        2). Wrappers.
    Yes! Capra Chapbook Number Ten.

NORTH COUNTRY MEDICINE. Canton, N.Y.: (Privately published, ca. 1974).
    Wrappers.
    Bulletin 3.

FROM LOBA, PART 5. (San Francisco: Naropa Institute, 1974).
    Broadside.
    50 copies, numbered, signed by the author.
    NOTE: Laid in portfolio entitled 8 From Naropa, numbered.

FREDDIE POEMS. Point Reyes, Calif.: Eidolon Editions, 1974.
    Wrappers, no priority:
        1). 500 copies.
        2). 500 copies, numbered, signed by the author.

TRAJECTORY. Detroit: Alternative Press (1974).
> Broadside.

12 WISHES FOR ANY SEASON. (San Francisco: Privately published, 1975).
> Wrappers.
> NOTE: With Grant Fisher, whose poem is entitled *12 Wishes For Any Season*; DiPrima's poem is untitled.

WHALE HONEY. San Francisco: Poets Institute, 1975.
> Photocopied sheets.

SELECTED POEMS 1956-1975. (Plainfield, Vt.): North Atlantic Books (1975).
> Wrappers.

BRASS FURNACE GOING OUT. (Syracuse, N.Y.: Pulpartforms/Intrepid Press, 1975).
> Wrappers.
> Beau Fleuve Series, Number Nine.

TRANSLATIONS.

Jean Genet.
THE MAN CONDEMNED TO DEATH. (New York: Privately published, ca. 1965).
Two issues, no priority:
1). Hardcover.
12 copies.
2). Wrappers.
300 copies.
NOTE: Translated with Alan Marlowe, Harriet & Bret Rohmer.

SEVEN LOVE POEMS FROM THE MIDDLE LATIN. New York: Poets Press, 1965.
Two issues, no priority:
1). Hardcover.
12 copies, signed by the translator.
2). Wrappers, priority as listed:
a). Laid paper covers.
b). Wove paper covers.

Edward Dorn

WHAT I SEE IN THE MAXIMUS POEMS. (Ventura, Calif.): Migrant Press, 1960.
Wrappers.

PATERSON SOCIETY. Cambridge, Mass.: Paterson Society, 1960.
Mimeographed sheet.

THE NEWLY FALLEN. New York: Totem Press (1961).
Wrappers.
NOTE: An advertising flyer, printing the author's statement of purpose and philosophy, preceded publication of the book.

THE LANDSCAPES BELOW. New York: Floating Bear, 1961.
Mimeographed sheets.
NOTE: Comprises the whole of *The Floating Bear: a newsletter*, issue 3.

PROSE 1. (San Francisco: Four Seasons Foundation, 1964).
Wrappers.
Writing 2.
NOTE: With Michael Rumaker and Warren Tallman.

HANDS UP! New York: Totem Press/Corinth Books (1964).
Wrappers.
"$1.25" on cover.

FROM GLOUCESTER OUT. (London): Matrix Press (1964).
Wrappers, no priority:
1). 335 copies.
2). 15 copies, numbered, signed by the author, artist and printer (Tom Raworth).
Illustrated by Barry Hall.

GEOGRAPHY. London: Fulcrum Press (1965).
    Hardcover, dustwrapper; no priority:
        1). 950 copies.
        2). 50 copies, numbered, signed by the author.
    ALSO: London: Fulcrum Press (1968).
        Hardcover, dustwrapper.
        No statement of first edition.
        NOTE: Expanded edition.

IDAHO OUT. London: Fulcrum Press (1965).
    Wrappers, no priority:
        1). 224 copies, numbered.
        2). 26 copies, lettered, signed by the author.

THE RITES OF PASSAGE. (Buffalo, N.Y.: Frontier Press, 1965).
    Wrappers.
    ALSO: Mt. Vernon, Wash.: Frontier Press, 1971.
        Wrappers.
        NOTE: 1). Retitled *By the Sound*.
             2). Revised edition.

THE SHOSHONEANS. New York: Morrow, 1966.
    Hardcover, dustwrapper.
    No statement of first edition.

THE NORTH ATLANTIC TURBINE. London: Fulcrum Press (1967).
    Two issues, no priority:
        1). Hardcover, dustwrapper; no priority:
            a). Trade edition.
            b). 100 copies, numbered, signed by the author.
        2). Wrappers.
   "First edition 1967"
    NOTE: An advertising brochure, in wrappers, preceded publication. The text of the
        brochure later appeared on the flaps of the dustwrapper of the book; however,
        the brochure contained one additional sentence.

GUNSLINGER. BOOK I. Los Angeles: Black Sparrow Press, 1968.
    Two issues, no priority:
        1). Hardcover, no priority:
            a). 100 copies, numbered, signed by the author; half-cloth.
            b). 26 copies, lettered, signed by the author; chapskin.
            c). 7 copies, numbered, "For Presentation"; chapskin.
            d). 4 special copies, for the publisher, author, printer & binder; chapskin.
        2). Wrappers.
            600 copies (according to the publisher, only 531 were published).
    NOTE: An advertising flyer, printing an extract from the book, preceded publication.

THE MIDWEST IS THAT SPACE BETWEEN THE BUFFALO STATLER AND THE LAW-
RENCE ELDRIDGE. Lawrence, Kan.: T(erence) Williams, 1968.
Broadside.

SONG. (Newcastle upon Tyne, England: Barry McSweeney) 1968.
Broadside.

ED DORN SPORTCASTS COLONIALISM. (N.p.: Free Poems/Among Friends,
ca. 1969).
Wrappers.
NOTE: Comprises the whole of *Free Poems/Among Friends Special Booklet,*
vol. 5, no. 3.

GUNSLINGER. BOOK II. Los Angeles: Black Sparrow Press, 1969.
Two issues, no priority:
1). Hardcover, acetate dustwrapper; no priority:
a). 250 copies, numbered, signed by the author; half-cloth.
b). 26 copies, lettered, signed by the author; chapskin.
c). 4 special copies, for the publisher, author, printer & binder; chapskin.
2). Wrappers.
1000 copies.
NOTE: An advertising flyer, printing a poem in an earlier version than that which
appears in the book, preceded publication.

TWENTY-FOUR LOVE SONGS. (Buffalo, N.Y.): Frontier Press, 1969.
Wrappers, no known priority:
1). Wrappers measure 6 x 8¼".
2). Wrappers measure 6 x 9¼".

THE COSMOLOGY OF FINDING YOUR SPOT. (Lawrence, Kan.): Cottonwood, 1969.
Broadside.

INAUGURATION POEM 2. (Toronto: Coach House/NTO Press, 1969).
Broadside.

SONGS: SET TWO. (Buffalo, N.Y.): Frontier Press, 1970.
Wrappers.

THE POEM CALLED ALEXANDER HAMILTON. Lawrence, Kan.: Tansy/Peg Leg Press,
1971.
Broadside, no priority:
1). 1000 copies.
2). 50 copies on finer stock.

THE KULTCHURAL EXCHANGE. (Lisbon: Toothpick, 1971).
Wrappers.

THE CYCLE. West Newbury, Mass.: Frontier Press, 1971.
    Wrappers.

SOME BUSINESS RECENTLY TRANSACTED IN THE WHITE WORLD. (West Newbury,
    Mass.): Frontier Press, 1971.
    Wrappers.

SPECTRUM BREAKDOWN. (LeRoy, N.Y.): Athanor Books, 1971.
    Wrappers.
    NOTE: Laid in *Athanor 1*, Winter/Spring 1971.

BEAN NEWS. San Francisco: Hermes Free Press, 1972.
    Wrappers, no priority:
        1). White paper.
        2). Newsprint.
    NOTE: 1). Anonymous.
        2). With Jeremy Prynne.

GUNSLINGER BOOK III. West Newbury, Mass.: Frontier Press, 1972.
    Wrappers.

OLD NEW YORKERS REALLY GET MY HEAD. Lawrence, Kan.: Cottonwood Review,
    1972.
    Broadside, no priority:
        1). Trade edition, no priority:
          a). Yellow stock.
          b). White stock.
        400 copies.
        2). 600 copies, numbered, signed by the author; no priority:
          a). Yellow stock.
          b). White stock.
    NOTE: In total there were 900 copies on yellow stock and 100 copies on white.

THE HAMADRYAS BABOON AT THE LINCOLN PARK ZOO. (Chicago: Wine Press,
    1972).
    Broadside.
    500 copies.
    Letters, Number 3.

THE CONTRACT. (Allendale, Mich.): National Poetry Festival, Thomas Jefferson College,
    1973.
    Broadside.

THE OCTOPUS THINKS WITH ITS THIRD ARM (AFTER YOUNG. (San Francisco:
    Zephyrus Image, 1973).
    Broadside, no known priority:
        1). Illustration printed in orange.
        2). Illustration printed in blue.
    Illustrated by Michael Myers.
    NOTE: An unknown number of copies were signed by the author, illustrator and
        printer (Holbrook Teter).

GREEN POEMS. (Kent, Ohio: Kent State Arts Festival, 1974).
    Broadside.

MESOZOIC LANDSCAPE. (Kent, Ohio: Kent State Arts Festival, 1974).
    Broadside.

RECOLLECTIONS OF GRAN APACHERIA. (San Francisco): Turtle Island (1974).
    Two issues, no priority:
        1). Hardcover.
        2). Wrappers.

SEMI-HARD. (San Francisco: Privately published, 1974).
    Wrappers.
    NOTE: With George Kimball.

THE COLLECTED POEMS 1956-1974. Bolinas, Calif.: Four Seasons Foundation (1975).
    Two issues, priority as listed:
        1). Wrappers.
        2). Hardcover.
    "First Edition"
    Writing 34.

SLINGER. Berkeley: Wingbow Press, 1975.
    Two issues, priority as listed:
        1). Wrappers.
          4500 copies.
        2). Hardcover, no priority:
          a). 450 copies, lettered dustwrapper.
          b). 50 copies, numbered, signed by the author, unlettered dustwrapper.
    "FIRST Edition"
    NOTE: The title on the spine of the book is *Gunslinger*.

SHUFFLIN OFF TO BUFFALO. (Buffalo: Just Buffalo, 1975).
    Broadside, no priority:
        1). 500 copies.
        2). 50 copies, numbered, signed by the author.

MANCHESTER SQUARE. London : Permanent Press, 1975.
>   Wrappers, no priority :
>> 1). 500 copies.
>> 2). 100 copies, numbered, signed by the authors ; glassine dustwrapper.
>   Permanent Press series number six.
>   NOTE : With Jennifer Dunbar.

Translations.

OUR WORD: GUERILLA POEMS FROM LATIN AMERICA. New York: Grossman, 1968.
    Two issues, no priority:
        1). Hardcover, dustwrapper.
        2). Wrappers.
    No statement of first edition.
    NOTE: Translated with Gordon Brotherston.

Jose Emilio Pacheco.
ARBOL ENTRE DOS MUROS: TREE BETWEEN TWO WALLS. Los Angeles:
    Black Sparrow Press, 1969.
    Two issues, no priority:
        1). Hardcover, acetate dustwrapper; no priority:
            a). 100 copies, numbered, signed by the author and translators.
            b). 6 special copies, for the publisher, author, translators, printer & binder.
        2). Wrappers, no priority:
            a). 250 copies.
            b). 250 copies, numbered, signed by the author and translators.
    NOTE: Translated with Gordon Brotherston.

Robert Duncan

HEAVENLY CITY, EARTHLY CITY. (Berkeley: Bern Porter) 1947.
> Hardcover, no priority:
>> 1). Trade edition, dustwrapper.
>> 2). 100 copies, signed by the author and illustrator, with a manuscript poem added.
>
> Illustrated by Mary Fabilli.

POEMS 1948-49. (Berkeley): Berkeley Miscellany Editions (1949).
> Wrappers, priority as listed:
>> 1). Lines on pages 31-32 expurgated; 400 copies.
>> 2). Lines on pages 31-32 unexpurgated; 100 copies.

MEDIEVAL SCENES. San Francisco: Centaur Press (1950).
> Wrappers.
> 250 copies, signed by the author.

FRAGMENTS OF A DISORDERED DEVOTION. (San Francisco: Privately published) 1952.
> Wrappers.
> 50 copies (approximately), numbered, signed by the author.
> NOTE: Copies were signed and dated when given away by the author. Consequently, all signatures are not contemporaneous.
> ALSO: (Toronto/San Francisco: Island Press/Gnomen Press, 1966).
>> Wrappers, priority as listed:
>>> 1). Two profiles on cover.
>>> 2). Cover title in facsimile of the author's holograph.

WHOSE THIS LIDDL BOOB COMING? (San Francisco: Privately published, 1952).
> Broadside.
> NOTE: This is sometimes referred to as *Boob 2*. It was preceded by *Boob Number One: A Dada Derivative: Lovely Lovely Lovely: Boob Number One!* (San Francisco: Privately published, 1952), which is also a broadside, the images for which were selected by Duncan, but the paste-up and all text was by Jess (Collins).

THE SONG OF THE BORDER-GUARD. Black Mountain, N.C. : Nicola Cernovich
(ca. 1952).
Broadside.

FAUST FOUTU. (San Francisco : Privately published, 1953).
Mimeographed sheets.
100 copies.
ALSO : FAUST FOUTU ACT ONE. San Francisco : (White Rabbit Press, 1958).
Wrappers, no priority :
1). 278 copies.
2). 22 copies, "to be reserved for a limited edition of the complete work
bound and decorated by the author."
ALSO : FAUST FOUTU, AN ENTERTAINMENT. (Stinson Beach, Calif. : Enkidu
Surrogate, 1959).
Wrappers, no priority :
1). 700 copies.
2). 50 copies, numbered, signed by the author.
NOTE : First complete edition.

PAGES FROM A NOTEBOOK. San Francisco : Artist's View, 1953.
Wrappers.
Artist's View #5.

CAESAR'S GATE. (Palma de Mallorca) : Divers Press, 1955.
Wrappers, no priority :
1). 200 copies.
2). 10 copies, numbered, signed by the author and illustrator.
3). 3 copies, lettered, signed by the author and illustrator.
Illustrated by Jess(Collins).
ALSO : (San Francisco) : Sand Dollar, 1972.
Two issues, no priority :
1). Hardcover, dustwrapper ; priority as listed :
a). With headband (approximately 7 copies).
b). Without headband.
600 copies.
2). Wrappers, priority as listed :
a). Signatures not sewn.
b). Signatures sewn.
2000 copies.
NOTE : Expanded edition.

CHARLES OLSON : NOTES. San Francisco : Poetry Center, 1957.
Mimeographed sheets.

SPICER WORKSHOP. San Francisco : Privately published (ca. 1957).
Mimeographed sheet.
NOTE : The title is misleading, in that this is work by the author which was used in a
class taught by Jack Spicer.

A GROUP READING OF "THE WILL". San Francisco: Poetry Center (1957).
Mimeographed sheet.
NOTE: Issued as an announcement for the reading, it consists mainly of the author's
Notes On the Writing of the Play.

A WORKSHOP READING/POETRY AS MAGIC. San Francisco: Poetry Center, 1957.
Mimeographed sheet.

NOTES ON THE POETICS OF MARIANNE MOORE. San Francisco: Poetry Center, 1957.
Mimeographed sheets.
NOTE: Text of an announcement for a reading by Marianne Moore.

HELEN ADAM AND JESS COLLINS. San Francisco: Poetry Center, 1957.
Mechanically reproduced sheets.
NOTE: Issued as an announcement for a reading, it consists mainly of the author's
Notes: Memoirs Of Our Time and Place.

MEMOIRS OF OUR TIME AND PLACE. San Francisco: Poetry Center (ca. 1957).
Mechanically reproduced sheets.
NOTE: Text of an announcement for a reading by Madeline Gleason and Brother
Antoninus (William Everson).

LETTERS. (Highlands, N.C.: Jonathan Williams, 1958).
Two issues, no priority:
1). Hardcover.
60 copies, signed and decorated on endpaper by the author.
2). Wrappers, dustwrapper.
450 copies, numbered.
Jargon 14.
NOTE: An advertising flyer ("Regarding *Letters*"), with text by Duncan, preceded
publication.

SELECTED POEMS. San Francisco: City Lights Books (1959).
Wrappers, priority as listed:
1). Stapled on spine.
2). Square-backed.
No statement of first edition.
Pocket Poets Series: Number Ten.

ROBERT CREELEY: READING AND COMMENTING ON HIS POEMS. San Francisco:
Poetry Center, 1959.
Stapled sheets.
NOTE: With Robert Creeley.

ROBERT DUNCAN. San Francisco: Poetry Center, 1959.
Mechanically reproduced sheet.
NOTE: Autobiographical and self-critical notes by the author.

FROM THE MABINOGION. (Privately published, ca. 1959).
    Wrappers.
    NOTE: An offprint from *Quarterly Review of Literature,* vol. XII, no. 3.

THE OPENING OF THE FIELD. New York: Grove Press, 1960.
    Wrappers, priority as listed:
        1). "$1.45" on cover.
        2). "$1.75" on cover.
    "First Printing"

A PLAY WITH MASKS. (San Francisco: Paul Alexander, ca. 1962).
    Photocopied sheets.
    NOTE: Unconfirmed by textual comparison is the report that the author revised this
        work for the 1968 publication by Tenth Muse, San Francisco.

ADAM'S WAY. (San Francisco: Privately published, 1962).
    Mimeographed sheets.

UNKINGD BY AFFECTION. (San Francisco: San Francisco Arts Festival Commission,
    1963).
    Broadside.
    300 copies, signed by the author and illustrator.
    Illustrated by Jess (Collins).
    NOTE: Laid in portfolio entitled *San Francisco Arts Festival: A Poetry Folio: 1963.*

TOWARDS AN OPEN UNIVERSE. (New York): Voice of America Central Program
    Services Division (1964).
    Mechanically reproduced sheets.

AS TESTIMONY. San Francisco: White Rabbit Press (1964).
    Wrappers.
    No "1966" on copyright page.

WRITING, WRITING. A COMPOSITION BOOK. STEIN IMITATIONS. (Albuquerque,
    N.M.: Sumbooks, 1964).
    Wrappers, no priority:
        1). 350 copies.
        2). 25 copies, signed by the author.
    "First Printing"

ROOTS AND BRANCHES. New York: Scribner's (1964).
    Two issues, no priority:
        1). Hardcover, dustwrapper.
        2). Wrappers.
    "A" on copyright page.

WINE. (Berkeley): Oyez, 1964.
    Broadside.
    350 copies.
    Oyez 4.
    NOTE : 27 copies, numbered, signed by the author in 1964 but published in 1965 in
        portfolio entitled *Poems in Broadside. Oyez. First Series.*

THE SWEETNESS AND GREATNESS OF DANTE'S DIVINE COMEDY. San Francisco :
    Open Space (1965).
    Wrappers.
    Colophon on final recto.
    500 copies.

MEDEA AT KOLCHIS, THE MAIDEN HEAD. Berkeley : Oyez, 1965.
    Two issues, no priority :
        1). Hardcover.
            28 copies, numbered, signed by the author.
        2). Wrappers.
            500 copies.

UP RISING. Berkeley : Oyez, 1965.
    Broadside, no priority :
        1). Orange paper.
            6 copies (approximately).
        2). White paper.
            1954 copies (approximately).
    NOTE : There is no first state; all copies have the misprint, "milllions."

THE YEARS AS CATCHES. Berkeley : Oyez, 1966.
    Two issues, no priority :
        1). Hardcover, dustwrapper; no priority :
            a). 172 copies.
            b). 28 copies, numbered, signed by the author.
        2). Wrappers.
            1800 copies.

PASSAGES 22-27 OF THE WAR. (Berkeley): Oyez (1966).
    Priority as listed :
        1). Sheets in portfolio.
            100 copies, numbered, signed by the author.
        2). Photo offset edition, no priority :
            a). Hardcover.
                6 copies, numbered, signed by the author.
            b). Wrappers.

PASSAGES 26: THE SOLDIERS. (San Francisco: Privately published, ca. 1966).
    Mimeographed sheets.
    NOTE: This is most likely the result of the rewriting of this Passage in preparation for
        the Oyez publication and thereafter distributed privately.

SIX PROSE PIECES. (Madison, Wisc.): Perishable Press, 1966.
    Two issues, no priority:
        1). Hardcover, dustwrapper.
           70 copies.
        2). Unbound signatures, boxed.
           Unknown number of copies, signed and illustrated by the author.

A BOOK OF RESEMBLANCES. New Haven, Conn.: Henry W. Wenning, 1966.
    Hardcover, no priority:
        1). 200 copies, numbered, signed by the author and illustrator.
        2). 3 copies, for the publisher, author and illustrator.
    Illustrated by Jess (Collins).
    NOTE: 1). There were a few copies, unbound, from over-run sheets.
         2). A folded broadside flyer from Auerhahn Press printed an excerpt poem in
            advance of what was then (1962) to have been the Auerhahn Press
            publication of the book.

THE CAT AND THE BLACKBIRD. (San Francisco: White Rabbit, 1967).
    Hardcover, ring-bound.
    500 copies.

EPILOGOS. (Los Angeles: Black Sparrow Press, 1967).
    Two issues, priority as listed:
        1). Wrappers.
           100 copies, numbered, signed, with an original drawing by the author.
        2). Hardcover, no priority:
           a). 15 copies, lettered, signed, with an original drawing by the author.
           b). 4 special copies, for the publisher, author, printer and binder.

CHRISTMAS PRESENT, CHRISTMAS PRESENCE! (Los Angeles: Black Sparrow Press,
    1967).
    Broadside, loosely matted on green stock, no priority:
        1). 241 copies.
        2). 59 copies, signed by the author.
        3). 4 special copies, for the publisher, author, printer and binder.

MY MOTHER WOULD BE A FALCONRESS. (Berkeley): Oyez, 1968.
    Broadside, no priority:
        1). 75 copies, numbered, signed by the author.
        2). 15 copies, for the use of the author.
    NOTE: There were 5 copies, lettered, signed and decorated by the author in 1973.

THE STRUCTURE OF RIME XXVII. (San Francisco: San Francisco Museum of Art, 1968).
Broadside.
NOTE: Laid in a catalogue-folder for a showing of the works of Jess (Collins).

NAMES OF PEOPLE. Los Angeles: Black Sparrow Press, 1968.
Hardcover, acetate dustwrapper; no priority:
1). 250 copies, numbered, signed by the author and illustrator.
2). 26 copies, lettered, signed by the author and illustrator.
3). 5 special copies, for the publisher, author, illustrator, printer and binder.
Illustrated by Jess (Collins).

BENDING THE BOW. (New York): New Directions, 1968.
Two issues, no priority:
1). Hardcover, dustwrapper.
2). Wrappers.
No statement of first edition.
NOTE: Text which should continue from page 91 is missing on page 92 and *Golden Lines* starts there instead; the second printing has an unnumbered page inserted which continues the poem & is therefore a first edition, of sorts; wrappers only.

THE TRUTH AND LIFE OF MYTH. New York: House of Books, Ltd., 1968.
Hardcover, glassine dustwrapper; no priority:
1). 300 copies, numbered, signed by the author.
2). 26 copies, lettered, signed by the author.
Crown Octavo Series #16.

THE FIRST DECADE. (London): Fulcrum Press (1968).
Hardcover, dustwrapper; no priority:
1). Trade edition.
2). 150 copies, numbered, signed by the author.

DERIVATIONS. London: Fulcrum Press (1968).
Hardcover, dustwrapper; no priority:
1). Trade edition.
2). 150 copies, numbered, signed by the author.
3). 12 copies, numbered out-of-series, signed by the author.

FRAGMENTS OF PASSAGES 33. (Stony Brook, N.Y.: Stony Brook Poetics Foundation, 1968).
Broadside.
10 copies, signed by the author.
NOTE: Laid in portfolio entitled *Stony Brook Holographs 1968.*

ACHILLES' SONG. New York: Phoenix Book Shop, 1969.
Wrappers, no priority:
1). 100 copies, numbered, signed by the author.
2). 26 copies, lettered, signed, with an original drawing by the author.
3). 50 copies, signed by the author, hors commerce.
Oblong Octavo Series Number 7.

PLAYTIME PSEUDO STEIN. 1942: A STORY. FROM THE LABORATORY RECORDS
OF 1953. A FAIRY PLAY. HOW EXCITED WE GET. A TRIBUTE TO MOTHER
CAREY'S CHICKENS. (San Francisco): Poets Press, 1969.
Wrappers, no priority:
1). 35 copies, numbered, signed by Diane DiPrima.
2). 15 copies, lettered, for the use of the author.
ALSO: PLAYTIME PSEUDO STEIN. FROM THE LABORATORY RECORDS
NOTEBOOK. 1942: A STORY. SMOKING THE CIGARETTE. A FAIRY
PLAY. A BUTTER MACHINE. HOW EXCITED WE GET. (San Francisco):
Tenth Muse (1969).
Wrappers.
NOTE: First authorized edition, with different contents and a new preface
by the author.

NOTES ON GROSSINGER'S "SOLAR JOURNAL: OECOLOGICAL SECTIONS."
(Los Angeles: Black Sparrow Press, 1970).
Wrappers, no priority:
1). Grey stock.
2). White stock.

POETIC DISTURBANCES. (San Francisco): Maya (1970).
Wrappers, no priority:
1). 300 copies.
2). 50 copies, numbered, signed by the author.
Maya Quarto Eight.

A SELECTION OF 65 DRAWINGS FROM ONE DRAWING BOOK 1952-1956.
Los Angeles: Black Sparrow Press, 1970.
Sheets in portfolio, boxed; no priority:
1). 300 copies, numbered, signed by the author.
2). 26 copies, lettered, signed, with an original drawing by the author.
3). 4 special copies, for the publisher, author, printer and binder.

BRING IT UP FROM THE DARK. (Berkeley): Cody's Books, 1970.
Broadside.

TRIBUNALS. Los Angeles: Black Sparrow Press, 1970.
Two issues, no priority:
1). Hardcover, acetate dustwrapper; no priority:
a). 250 copies, numbered, signed by the author.
b). 26 copies, lettered, signed by the author.
c). 4 special copies, for the publisher, author, printer and binder.
2). Wrappers, no priority:
a). 950 copies, stapled in wrappers.
b). 50 copies, sewn in wrappers.
NOTE: A pamphlet, containing a note by the author and facsimiles of the holograph
notebook and of the final typescript of *Passages 34*, was inserted in a pocket in
the rear of each hardcover copy.

FROM A SUITE OF METAPHYSICAL POEMS. San Francisco: Privately published
(ca. 1971).*
Photo-offset sheet.

GROUND WORK. (San Francisco: Privately published , 1971).
Multilithed sheets.

AN INTERVIEW. (Toronto: Coach House Press, 1971).
Wrappers.

POEMS FROM THE MARGINS OF THOM GUNN'S MOLY. (San Francisco: Privately
published, ca. 1972).
Wrappers.
250 copies.

THE BALLAD OF ELECTION DAY. (San Francisco: Privately published, 1972).
Mechanically reproduced sheets.

IN MEMORIAM WALLACE STEVENS. Storrs, Conn.: University of Connecticut,
1972.
Wrappers.

PROSPECTUS FOR "STUDIES IN IDEAS OF THE POETIC IMAGINATION".
San Francisco: (Privately published) 1972.
Mechanically reproduced sheet.

GEORGE HERMS: SELECTED WORKS 1960-1973. Davis, Calif.: University of California
Memorial Union Art Gallery, 1973.
Wrappers.
NOTE: A catalogue of Herms' art, with text by Duncan and Michael McClure.

A SEVENTEENTH CENTURY SUITE IN HARMONY TO THE METAPHYSICAL GENIUS
IN ENGLISH POETRY (1590-1690). (San Francisco: Privately published, 1973).
Wrappers, no priority:
1). 150 copies, numbered.
2). 100 copies, numbered, initialed by the author.

FEB. 22, 1973. Berkeley: Arif Press, 1973.
Broadside.
5 copies.

MEMOIRS OF OUR TIME AND PLACE. (San Francisco): Poetry Center, 1974.
Broadside.

DANTE. (Canton, N.Y.): Institute of Further Studies (1974).
Wrappers.
A Curriculum of the Soul 8.

AN ODE AND ARCADIA. Berkeley: Ark Press, 1974.
    Wrappers.
    1000 copies.
    NOTE: With Jack Spicer.

THE VENICE POEM. (Sydney, Australia): Prism (1975).
    Wrappers.
    500 copies.

George P. Elliott

PARKTILDEN VILLAGE. Boston: Beacon Press (1958).
Hardcover, dustwrapper.
No statement of first edition.

AMONG THE DANGS. New York: Holt, Rinehart & Winston (1961).
Hardcover, dustwrapper.
"First Edition"

FEVER AND CHILLS. Iowa City, Iowa: Stone Wall Press (1961).
Hardcover.
220 copies, numbered.

DAVID KNUDSEN. New York: Random House (1962).
Hardcover, dustwrapper.
"FIRST PRINTING"

A PIECE OF LETTUCE. New York: Random House (1964).
Hardcover, dustwrapper.
"FIRST PRINTING"

FOURTEEN POEMS. Lanham, Md.: Goosetree Press (1964).
Wrappers.

IN THE WORLD. New York: Viking Press (1965).
Hardcover, dustwrapper.
No statement of first edition.
NOTE: Uncorrected proofs in spiral-bound wrappers preceded publication.

AN HOUR OF LAST THINGS. New York: Harper & Row (1968).
Hardcover, dustwrapper.
"FIRST EDITION"

FROM THE PERSON OF THE MAKER. (Brockport, N.Y.: Department of English,
State University College, 1968).
Wrappers.
NOTE: Cover title is *Department of English State University College Brockport.*

FROM THE BERKELEY HILLS. New York: Harper & Row (1969).
    Hardcover, dustwrapper.
    "FIRST EDITION"

CONVERSIONS. New York: Dutton, 1971.
    Hardcover, dustwrapper.
    "FIRST EDITION"

MURIEL. New York: Dutton, 1972.
    Hardcover, dustwrapper.
    "First Edition"

Clayton Eshleman

MEXICO & NORTH. (Tokyo: Privately published, 1961).
    Wrappers.

THE CHAVIN ILLUMINATION. Lima, Peru: (Ediciones de La Rams Florida) 1965.
    Wrappers.
    100 copies, numbered, signed by the author.

THE CROCUS BUD. (Reno): Camels Hump (ca. 1965).
    Wrappers.
    The Camels Hump 4.

LACHRYMAE MATEO. (New York): Caterpillar, 1966.
    Wrappers.
    Colophon calls for 100 copies; dark blue wrappers with title and author's name each on one line; unexposed staples.
    Caterpillar III.

WALKS. (New York): Caterpillar (1967).
    Hardcover, no priority:
        1). 300 copies, numbered; priority as listed:
            a). Red backstrip.
            b). Black backstrip.
        2). 26 copies, lettered, signed by the author.
    Caterpillar X.

BROTHER STONES. Kyoto: Caterpillar, 1968.
    Sheets in box.
    250 copies, numbered, signed by the author and illustrator.
    Illustrated by William Paden.

CANTALOUPS & SPLENDOR. Los Angeles: Black Sparrow Press, 1968.
   Two issues, no priority:
      1). Hardcover, no priority:
         a). 75 copies, numbered, signed by the author.
         b). 4 special copies for the publisher, author, printer and binder.
      2). Wrappers.
         250 copies, numbered, signed by the author.

THE HOUSE OF OKUMURA. Toronto: Weed/Flower Press, 1969.
   Wrappers.
   500 copies.

A PITCHBLENDE. (San Francisco): Maya (1969).
   Wrappers, priority as listed:
      1). 250 copies.
      2). 50 copies, numbered, signed by the author.
   Maya Quarto Three.

INDIANA. Los Angeles: Black Sparrow Press, 1969.
   Two issues, no priority:
      1). Hardcover, acetate dustwrapper; no priority:
         a). 250 copies, numbered, signed by the author.
         b). 26 copies, lettered, signed, with holograph poem by the author.
         c). 4 special copies for the publisher, author, binder and printer.
      2). Wrappers.
         1000 copies.
   NOTE: An advertising flyer, with a poem from the book, preceded publication.

T'AI. Cambridge, Mass.: Sans Souci Press (1969).
   Hardcover, glassine dustwrapper.
   99 copies, numbered, signed by the author.
   "First edition"
   NOTE: There were an unknown number of unnumbered copies.

THE HOUSE OF IBUKI. (Fremont, Mich.): Sumac Press (1969).
   Two issues, no priority:
      1). Hardcover, no priority:
         a). 100 copies, numbered.
         b). 26 copies, numbered, signed by the author.
      2). Wrappers.
         1000 copies.

YELLOW RIVER RECORD. (London): Big Venus (1969).
   Wrappers.

A BRINGING OF RILKE INTO MY OWN ROAD AND THOUGHT. Sherman Oaks,
    Calif. : (Privately published) 1970.
    Photocopied sheets.
    10 copies (approximately).

THE WAND. Sherman Oaks, Calif. : (Privately published) 1970.
    Broadside.
    50 copies, signed by the author.

THE BRIDGE AT THE MAYAN PASS. (Valencia, Calif. : California Institute of the Arts,
    1971).
    Broadside.

ALTARS. Los Angeles : Black Sparrow Press, 1971.
    Two issues, no priority :
        1). Hardcover, acetate dustwrapper ; no priority :
            a). 200 copies, numbered, signed by the author.
            b). 26 copies, lettered, signed by the author.
            c). 4 special copies for the publisher, author, printer and binder.
        2). Wrappers.
            1000 copies.

BEARINGS.. Santa Barbara, Calif. : Capricorn, 1971.
    Two issues, no priority :
        1). Hardcover.
            100 copies, numbered.
        2). Wrappers.
            900 copies.

ONE OF THE OLDEST DREAMS. (Detroit : Alternative Press, ca. 1971).
    Postcard.

COMPOSITION FOR CARYL. (Sherman Oaks, Calif. : Privately published) 1971.
    Hardcover.
    2 copies.

THE SANJO BRIDGE. (Los Angeles) : Black Sparrow Press, 1972.
    Wrappers.
    Sparrow 2.

CLAYTON ESHLEMAN LITERARY MATERIALS. Sherman Oaks, Calif. : (Privately
    published, 1972).
    Mimeographed sheets in folder.
    12 copies (approximately).
    NOTE : The author's description of his life, writings and archives.

COILS. Los Angeles: Black Sparrow Press, 1973.
    Two issues, no priority:
        1). Hardcover, acetate dustwrapper; no priority:
            a). 200 copies, numbered, signed by the author.
            b). 26 copies, lettered, signed by the author.
            c). 4 special copies for the publisher, author, printer and binder.
        2). Wrappers.
            1491 copies.
    NOTE: An advertising flyer (*Broadside/Flyer No. 5*), printing a poem from the book, preceded publication; 100 copies were numbered, signed by the author.

ADHESIVE LOVE. (Sherman Oaks, Calif.: Privately published) 1973.
    Mimeographed sheets.

THE LAST JUDGMENT. Sherman Oaks, Calif.: (Privately published) 1973.
    Broadside.
    100 copies, numbered, signed by the author.

HUMAN WEDDING. Los Angeles: Black Sparrow Press, 1973.
    Wrappers, no priority:
        1). 200 copies, numbered, signed by the author.
        2). 26 copies, lettered, signed by the author.

AUX MORTS. (Los Angeles): Black Sparrow Press, 1974.
    Wrappers.
    Sparrow 18.

REALIGNMENT. (Providence, R.I.): Treacle Press, 1974.
    Two issues, no priority:
        1). Hardcover.
            20 copies, numbered, signed by the author and illustrator.
        2). Wrappers.
            430 copies, numbered.
    "First Edition"
    Illustrated by Nora Jaffe.
    NOTE: An advertising broadside, printing a poem from the book, preceded publication.

PORTRAIT OF FRANCIS BACON. Sheffield, England: Rivelin Press (1975).
    Wrappers, no priority:
        1). 225 copies.
        2). 25 copies, numbered, signed by the author.

THE GULL WALL. Los Angeles: Black Sparrow Press, 1975.
        Two issues, no priority:
                1). Hardcover, acetate dustwrapper; no priority:
                        a). 200 copies, numbered, signed by the author.
                        b). 26 copies, lettered, signed, with holograph poem by the author.
                2). Wrappers.
                        1502 copies.

Translations.

Pablo Neruda.
RESIDENCE ON EARTH. (San Francisco): Amber House Press, 1962.
    Wrappers.
    "first edition"

Aime Cesaire.
STATE OF THE UNION. (Bloomington, Ind.): Caterpillar, 1966.
    Wrappers.
    NOTE: Translated with Denis Kelly.

TRANSLATIONS FROM THE SPANISH. (Reno: Richard Morris) 1967.
    Wrappers.
    Quark I.
    NOTE: Contains translations of Cesar Vallejo and Jose Hierro, the latter translated
        with Cid Corman.

Cesar Vallejo.
POEMAS HUMANOS/HUMAN POEMS. New York: Grove Press (1968).
    Hardcover, dustwrapper.
    "First Printing"

Antonin Artaud.
LETTER TO ANDRE BRETON. (Los Angeles): Black Sparrow Press, 1974.
    Wrappers.
    Sparrow 23.

Cesar Vallejo.
SPAIN, TAKE THIS CUP FROM ME. New York: Grove Press (1974).
    Wrappers.
    "First Printing"
    NOTE: Translated with Jose Rubia Barcia.

Antonin Artaud.
TO HAVE DONE WITH THE JUDGMENT OF GOD. (Los Angeles): Black Sparrow Press,
    1975.
    Sparrow 34.
    NOTE: Translated with Norman Glass.

William Everson (Brother Antoninus)

THESE ARE THE RAVENS. San Leandro, Calif.: Greater West Publishing Co., 1935.
   Wrappers.
   NOTE: Written as "Bill Everson."

SAN JOAQUIN. Los Angeles: Ward Ritchie Press, 1939.
   Hardcover.
   100 copies.

THE MASCULINE DEAD. Prairie City, Ill.: Press of James A. Decker (1942).
   Hardcover, no priority:
      1). Green cloth.
      2). Maroon cloth.

X WAR ELEGIES. Waldport, Ore.: Untide Press, 1943.
   Wrappers, priority as listed:
      1). Black and yellow lettering.
      2). Black and red lettering.
   ALSO: Waldport, Ore.: Untide Press, 1944.
      Wrappers.
      975 copies.
      NOTE: 1). Retitled *War Elegies*.
            2). Expanded edition.

WALDPORT POEMS. Waldport, Ore.: Untide Press, 1944.
   Wrappers.
   975 copies.

THE RESIDUAL YEARS. (Waldport, Ore.): Untide Press (1944).
   Wrappers.
   330 copies, signed by the author.

POEMS: MCMXLII. (Waldport, Ore.: William Everson/Untide Press, 1945).
   Wrappers.
   500 copies.

THE EQUINOX PRESS. (Berkeley): Equinox Press, 1947.
  Broadside.
  500 copies.

THE RESIDUAL YEARS. (New York): New Directions (1948).
  Hardcover, dustwrapper.
  No statement of first edition.
  NOTE: Collects four prior books.
  ALSO: (New York): New Directions (1968).
      Two issues, no priority:
          1). Hardcover, dustwrapper.
          2). Wrappers.
      No statement of first edition.
  NOTE: Expanded edition.

A PRIVACY OF SPEECH. Berkeley: Equinox Press, 1949.
  Hardcover.
  100 copies.

TRIPTYCH FOR THE LIVING. (Oakland): Seraphim Press, 1951.
  Wrappers.
  200 copies.

A FRAGMENT FOR THE BIRTH OF GOD. Oakland: Albertus Magnus Press, 1958.
  Wrappers.
  "Deus" on cover, in addition to the title.
  NOTE: 1). Anonymous.
      2). There are two later printings of this title (1959 and 1963), but neither has
          "Deus" on the cover.

AT THE EDGE. (Oakland: Albertus Magnus Press, 1958).
  Broadside.
  NOTE: 1). Written as Brother Antoninus.
      2). An advertising flyer, *At the Edge: A Poem*, was written by Everson and pre-
          ceded publication of the broadside.

AN AGE INSURGENT. San Francisco: Blackfriars Publications (1959).
  Wrappers.
  NOTE: 1). Written as Brother Antoninus.
      2). 500 copies (approximately) were printed and, reportedly, 400-440 were
          destroyed.

THE CROOKED LINES OF GOD. (Detroit): University of Detroit Press, 1959.
  Hardcover, dustwrapper.
  1000 copies.
  "FIRST EDITION"
  NOTE: 1). Written as Brother Antoninus.
      2). The second and third printings were each revised by the author.

THE CATHOLIC AND CREATIVITY. Collegeville, Minn.: American Benedictine Review
    (1960).*
    Wrappers.
    NOTE: An offprint from the *American Benedictine Review.*

THERE WILL BE HARVEST. (Berkeley: University of California General Library, 1960).
    Wrappers.
    200 copies.

THE YEAR'S DECLENSION. Berkeley: (University of California General Library) 1961.
    Hardcover.
    100 copies, signed by the author.

THE HAZARDS OF HOLINESS. Garden City, N.Y.: Doubleday, 1962.
    Hardcover, dustwrapper.
    "First Edition"
    NOTE: Written as Brother Antoninus.

THE TONGS OF JEOPARDY. (Oakland: Privately published, 1963).
    Mimeographed sheets.
    50 copies (approximately).
    NOTE: 1). Written as Brother Antoninus.
          2). This is to be differentiated from the broadside (Los Angeles: Memorare Rec-
          ordings, ca. 1967) which prints an excerpt from the speech to advertise the
          forthcoming recording of the entire speech.

THE POET IS DEAD. San Francisco: Auerhahn Press, 1964.
    Hardcover, dustwrapper; no priority:
          1). 200 copies, signed by the author.
          2). 5 copies, signed by the author, boxed.
    NOTE: 1). Written as Brother Antoninus.
          2). An advertising brochure, containing an excerpt from the author's intro-
          duction to the book, preceded publication.

THE ROSE OF SOLITUDE. (Berkeley): Oyez, 1964.
    Broadside.
    350 copies.
    Oyez Number Two.
    NOTE: 1). 27 copies, numbered, signed by the author in 1964 but published in 1965 in
          portfolio entitled *Poems in Broadside. Oyez. First Series.*
          2). Written as Brother Antoninus.
    ALSO: (Berkeley: Oyez, ca. 1965).
          Broadside.
          NOTE: Bilingual (Spanish and English) edition.

THE DOMINICAN BROTHER. (San Francisco: Brother's Vocation, ca. 1965).
    Wrappers.
    NOTE: Anonymous.

THE BLOWING OF THE SEED. New Haven, Conn.: Henry W. Wenning, 1966.
    Hardcover, no priority:
        1). 200 copies, numbered in Arabic, signed by the author.
        2). 15 copies, numbered in Roman, signed by the author.
        3). 3 copies, lettered, for the author, publisher and printer.

SINGLE SOURCE. Berkeley: Oyez (1966).
    Hardcover, dustwrapper; no priority:
        1). Trade edition, priority as listed:
            a). "Langauge" on page ix, line 17.
            b). Spelling corrected, but the "u," the second "a" and/or the "e" float
               variously above or below the line.
            c). Spelling and positioning of the letters corrected.
        2). 25 copies, numbered, signed by the author.
        3). 5 copies, lettered, signed by the author.

THE ROSE OF SOLITUDE. Garden City, N.Y.: Doubleday, 1967.
    Hardcover, dustwrapper.
    "First Edition"

IN THE FICTIVE WISH. (Berkeley): Oyez (1967).
    Hardcover, dustwrapper; no priority:
        1). 200 copies, numbered, signed by the author.
        2). 20 copies, lettered, signed by the author.

A CANTICLE TO THE WATERBIRDS. Berkeley: Eizo, 1968.
    Two issues, no priority:
        1). Hardcover.
          200 copies, numbered, signed by the author and illustrator.
        2). Wrappers.
          2000 copies.
    Illustrated by Allen Say.
    NOTE: Written as Brother Antoninus.

THE SPRINGING OF THE BLADE. (Reno, Nev.: Black Rock Press, 1968).
    Hardcover.
    180 copies, signed by the author.

IF I SPEAK TRUTH. (San Francisco: Goliards Press, ca. 1968).
    Wrappers.

ROBINSON JEFFERS: FRAGMENTS OF AN OLDER FURY. (Berkeley): Oyez, 1968.
    Hardcover, dustwrapper.
    NOTE: 1). Written as Brother Antoninus.
        2). Review copies in wrappers preceded publication, priority as listed:
            a). Stapled in red printed wrappers.
            b). Glued in white printed wrappers.
            c). Glued in red unprinted wrappers.

THE LAST CRUSADE. (Berkeley): Oyez (1969).
 Hardcover, glassine dustwrapper.
 165 copies, numbered, signed by the author.
 NOTE: Written as Brother Antoninus.

THE CITY DOES NOT DIE. (Berkeley: Oyez, 1969).
 Wrappers.
 NOTE: Written as Brother Antoninus.

FOR IMMEDIATE RELEASE. (Berkeley): Oyez, 1969.
 Stapled sheets.
 NOTE: A press release announcing the author's return to secular life and his imminent marriage.

BROTHER ANTONINUS — MYSTIC OF THE FLESH. (Kentfield, Calif.:
 Privately published, ca. 1969).
 Wrappers.
 NOTE: 1). Written as "Virginia Spanner."
 2). A publicity item to be sent out before readings.

BIRTH OF A POET. Santa Cruz, Calif.: Kresge College, University of California (1971).
 Broadside.

EARTH POETRY. (Berkeley: Oyez, 1971).
 Wrappers.

WHO IS SHE THAT LOOKETH FORTH AS THE MORNING. Santa Barbara, Calif.:
 Capricorn Press, 1972.
 Hardcover, acetate dustwrapper.
 250 copies, numbered, signed by the author.
 NOTE: Written as Brother Antoninus.

GALE AT DAWN. (Santa Cruz, Calif.: Lime Kiln Press, 1972).
 Broadside.
 200 copies, signed by the author.
 NOTE: Laid in portfolio entitled *West to the Water*, which is numbered and signed by Everson.

TENDRIL IN THE MESH. (San Francisco): Cayucos Books, 1973.
 Hardcover.
 250 copies, numbered, signed by the author.

BLACK HILLS. (San Francisco): Didymus Press (1973).
 Hardcover, no priority:
 1). 285 copies, numbered, signed by the author.
 2). Unknown number of copies, lettered.

ROBINSON JEFFERS TRAGEDY HAS OBLIGATIONS. Santa Cruz, Calif.: Lime Kiln
      Press (1973).
      Broadside.
      NOTE: An over-sized advertising flyer, which consists of text by Everson regarding the
          forthcoming Jeffers book to which Everson contributed an afterword.

I AM LONG WEANED. (Brockport, N. Y.: Department of English, State University College,
      1973).
      Wrappers.
      NOTE: Cover title is *Writer's Forum.*

MAN-FATE. (New York): New Directions (1974).
      Two issues, no priority:
              1). Hardcover, dustwrapper.
              2). Wrappers.
      No statement of first edition.

Lawrence Ferlinghetti

PICTURES OF THE GONE WORLD. San Francisco: City Lights Pocket Bookshop (1955).
Two issues, no priority:
1). Hardcover.
25 copies, signed by the author.
2). Wrappers.
500 copies.
No statement of first edition.
Pocket Poets Series: Number One.

TENTATIVE DESCRIPTION OF A DINNER GIVEN TO PROMOTE THE IMPEACH-
MENT OF PRESIDENT EISENHOWER. (San Francisco: Golden Mountain Press,
1958).
Wrappers, priority as listed:
1). Publisher's logogram in gold.
2). Publisher's logogram in black.
1000 copies.
NOTE: There were covers with black lettering and covers with red; priority unknown.

A CONEY ISLAND OF THE MIND. (Norfolk, Conn.): New Directions (1958).
Wrappers.
No statement of first edition.
ALSO: London: Hutchinson (1959).
Hardcover, dustwrapper.
No statement of first edition.
NOTE: Expanded edition.
ALSO: (New York): New Directions (1968).
Hardcover, boxed.
No statement of first edition.
NOTE: Further expanded edition.

HER. (Norfolk, Conn.): New Directions (1960).
Two issues, no priority:
1). Hardcover, dustwrapper.
2). Wrappers.
No statement of first edition.

ONE THOUSAND FEARFUL WORDS FOR FIDEL CASTRO. San Francisco: City Lights
      Publications, 1961.
      Broadside.

BERLIN. (San Francisco: Golden Mountain Press, 1961).
      Wrappers.
      1000 copies.

STARTING FROM SAN FRANCISCO. (Norfolk, Conn.): New Directions (1961).
      Two issues, priority as listed:
            1). Hardcover, dustwrapper.
            2). Wrappers.
      No statement of first edition.
      ALSO: (New York: New Directions, 1967).
            Wrappers.
            No statement of first edition.
      NOTE: Expanded edition.

DEAR FERLINGHETTI. (San Francisco): White Rabbit Press (1962).
      Wrappers.
      NOTE: With Jack Spicer.

THOUGHTS OF A CONCERTO OF TELEMANN. (San Francisco: San Francisco Arts
      Festival Commission) 1963.
      Broadside.
      300 copies, signed by the author and illustrator.
      Illustrated by Eleanor Dickinson.
      NOTE: Laid in portfolio entitled *San Francisco Arts Festival: A Poetry Folio: 1963.*

UNFAIR ARGUMENTS WITH EXISTENCE. (New York): New Directions (1963).
      Wrappers.
      "$1.50" on rear cover.

ROUTINES. (New York): New Directions (1964).
      Wrappers.
      No statement of first edition.

WHERE IS VIETNAM? (San Francisco: City Lights Books, 1965).
      Broadside.
      1000 copies.

TO FUCK IS TO LOVE AGAIN. New York: Fuck You Press, 1965.
      Wrappers.

LAWRENCE FERLINGHETTI. (Spoleto, Italy: Spoleto Festival, 1965).*
    Mimeographed sheets, no priority:
        1). English language edition.
           200 copies.
        2). Italian language edition.
           200 copies.

CHRIST CLIMBED DOWN. (Syracuse, N.Y.): Syracuse University, 1965.*
    Broadside.

AFTER THE CRIES OF THE BIRDS. San Francisco: Dave Haselwood Books, 1967.
    Wrappers.

MOSCOW IN THE WILDERNESS, SEGOVIA IN THE SNOW. (San Francisco: Beach
    Books, 1967).
    Broadside.

AN EYE ON THE WORLD. (London): MacGibbon & Kee (1967).
    Hardcover, dustwrapper.
    No statement of first edition.

REPEAT AFTER ME. (Boston: Impressions Workshop, ca. 1967).
    Broadside.
    200 copies, signed by the author and illustrator.
    Illustrated by Hershon.

FUCLOCK. (London: Fire Publication, 1968).
    Broadside.

THE SECRET MEANING OF THINGS. (New York): New Directions (1969).
    Two issues, no priority:
        1). Hardcover, no priority:
           a). Trade edition, dustwrapper.
           b). 150 copies, numbered, signed by the author, boxed.
        2). Wrappers.
    No statement of first edition.

TYRANNUS NIX? (New York: New Directions, 1969).
    Wrappers.
    No statement of first edition.
    NOTE: An advertising flyer, printing an excerpt from the book, preceded publication.

THE MEXICAN NIGHT. (New York): New Directions (1970).
    Wrappers.
    No statement of first edition.

SOMETIME DURING ETERNITY. Conshohocken: Poster Prints (ca. 1970).
    Broadside.

THE WORLD IS A BEAUTIFUL PLACE. Conshohocken: Poster Prints (ca. 1970).
    Broadside.

BACK ROADS TO FAR TOWNS AFTER BASHO. (San Francisco: Privately published,
    1970).
    Wrappers.
    NOTE: This is to be differentiated from *Back Roads to Far Places* (New York):
       New Directions (1971). Wrappers.

LOVE IS NO STONE ON THE MOON. (Berkeley: Arif Press) 1971.
    Wrappers.

THE ILLUSTRATED WILFRED FUNK. (San Francisco): City Lights Books (1971).
    Wrappers.

A WORLD AWASH WITH FASCISM & FEAR. (San Francisco: Cranium Press, 1971).
    Broadside.
    White stock.
    NOTE: This is to be differentiated from the edition on red stock (Saturn Island, British
       Columbia: Free School Press, 1971).

OPEN EYE. Melbourne, Australia: Sun Books (1972).
    Wrappers.
    NOTE: Bound back-to-back with *Open Head* by Allen Ginsberg.

OPEN EYE. Cambridge, Mass.: Pomegranate Press (1973).
    Broadside, no priority:
        1). 150 copies, numbered.
        2). 100 copies, numbered, signed by the author and illustrator.
    Illustrated by Karyl Klopp.

OPEN EYE, OPEN HEART. (New York): New Directions (1973).
    Two issues, no priority:
        1). Hardcover, dustwrapper.
        2). Wrappers.
    No statement of first edition.

WATERGATE RAP 1969-1973. (San Francisco: City Lights Books, 1973).
    Broadside.
    NOTE: More accurately, this is a detachable wrap-around band for a later printing of
       Tyrannus Nix.

CONSTANTLY RISKING ABSURDITY. (Brockport, N.Y.: Department of English, State
    University College, 1973).
    Wrappers.
    NOTE: Cover title is *Writer's Forum.*

SOON IT WILL BE NIGHT. (N.p.: Privately published, ca. 1975).
    Broadside.
    NOTE: An advertising flyer for a book of the same title by Alexis De Vilar, but the
        only text is a poem by Ferlinghetti.

POPULIST MANIFESTO. (San Francisco: Privately published, 1975).*
    Broadside.

Translations.

Jacques Prevert.
SELECTIONS FROM PAROLES. San Francisco: City Lights Books (1958).
    Wrappers.
    No statement of first edition.

Yevgeny Yevtushenko.
FLOWERS AND BULLETS: FREEDOM TO KILL. (San Francisco): City Lights Books
    (1970).
    Wrappers.
    No statement of first edition.
    NOTE: With Anthony Kahn.

Andrei Voznesensky.
DOGALYPSE: SAN FRANCISCO POETRY READING. (San Francisco): City Lights
    Books (1972).
    Wrappers.
    Pocket Poets Series Number 29.
    No statement of first edition.
    NOTE: Translated with Maureen Sager, Catherine Leech, Vera Reck, Vera Dunham
        and Robert Bly.

Jacques Prevert.
TO PAINT THE PORTRAIT OF A BIRD. Garden City, N.Y.: Doubleday, 1973.
    Hardcover, dustwrapper.
    "First Edition"

Bruce Jay Friedman

STERN. New York: Simon & Schuster, 1962.
    Hardcover, dustwrapper.
    "FIRST PRINTING"

FAR FROM THE CITY OF CLASS. New York: Frommer-Pasmantier, 1963.
    Hardcover, dustwrapper.
    "First Edition"

23 PAT O'BRIEN MOVIES: A ONE ACT PLAY. (New York: American Place Theatre,
    ca. 1963).
    Mimeographed sheets in folder.

A MOTHER'S KISSES. New York: Simon & Schuster, 1964.
    Hardcover, dustwrapper.
    "First Printing"
    ALSO: New York: Osterman Productions (ca. 1965).
        Mechanically reproduced sheets in folder.
        NOTE: Acting script for *A Mother's Kisses: A New Musical.*

BLACK ANGELS. New York: Simon & Schuster, 1966.
    Hardcover, dustwrapper.
    "FIRST PRINTING"

SCUBA DUBA. New York: Simon & Schuster (1967).
    Hardcover, dustwrapper.
    "First Printing"
    NOTE: Unconfirmed is the reported priority of the playscript: New York: Establish-
        ment Theatre Company (N.d.), wrappers.

THE DICK. New York: Knopf, 1970.
    Hardcover, dustwrapper.
    "First Edition"

STEAMBATH. New York: Knopf, 1971.
    Hardcover, dustwrapper.
    "FIRST EDITION"

ABOUT HARRY TOWNS. New York: Knopf, 1974.
    Hardcover, dustwrapper.
    "First Edition"
    NOTE: Uncorrected proofs in printed wrappers preceded publication.

John Gardner

THE RESURRECTION. (New York): New American Library (1966).
  Hardcover, dustwrapper.
  "First Printing"

THE GAWAIN-POET. Lincoln, Neb.: Cliff's Notes (1967).
  Wrappers.
  Bethany Station, Lincoln, Nebraska 68505 on cover.

LE MORTE DARTHUR. Lincoln, Neb.: Cliff's Notes (1967).
  Wrappers.
  Bethany Station, Lincoln, Nebraska 68505 on cover.

SIR GAWAIN AND THE GREEN KNIGHT. Lincoln, Neb.: Cliff's Notes (1967).
  Wrappers.
  Bethany Station, Lincoln, Nebraska 68505 on cover.

THE WRECKAGE OF AGATHON. New York: Harper & Row (1970).
  Hardcover, dustwrapper.
  "FIRST EDITION"
  NOTE: Uncorrected proofs in printed wrappers, ringbound, preceded publication.

GRENDEL. New York: Knopf, 1971.
  Hardcover, dustwrapper.
  "FIRST EDITION"

THE SUNLIGHT DIALOGUES. New York: Knopf, 1972.
  Hardcover, dustwrapper.
  "First Edition"
  NOTE: Uncorrected proofs in printed wrappers preceded publication.

JASON AND MEDEIA. New York: Knopf, 1973.
  Hardcover, dustwrapper.
  "FIRST EDITION"
  NOTE: Uncorrected proofs in printed wrappers preceded publication.

NICKEL MOUNTAIN. New York: Knopf, 1973.
    Hardcover, dustwrapper; no known priority:
        1). Dark orange background on title page.
        2). Light orange background on title page.
    "First Edition"
    NOTE: Uncorrected proofs in printed wrappers preceded publication.

THE KING'S INDIAN. New York: Knopf, 1974.
    Hardcover, dustwrapper.
    "First Edition"
    NOTE: Uncorrected proofs in printed wrappers preceded publication.

THE CONSTRUCTION OF THE WAKEFIELD CYCLE. Carbondale, Ill.: Southern Illinois
    University Press (1974).
    Hardcover, dustwrapper.
    No statement of first edition.

THE OLD MEN. (Ann Arbor, Mich.: University Microfilms, 1974).
    Two issues (in either single or double volume), no priority:
        1). Hardcover.
        2). Wrappers.
    NOTE: Published as "John C. Gardner, Jr.," this is a xerox copy of his Ph. D. thesis,
        a novel, at State University of Iowa, submitted August 1958; however,
        the date of reproduction ("publication") is noted on the page preceding the
        title page.

THE CONSTRUCTION OF CHRISTIAN POETRY IN OLD ENGLISH. Carbondale/
    London: Southern Illinios University Press/Feffer & Simons (1975).
    Hardcover, dustwrapper.
    No statement of first edition.

DRAGON, DRAGON. New York: Knopf (1975).
    Hardcover, no known priority:
        1). Blue paper boards, blue cloth back, dustwrapper.
        2). Glazed illustrated paper boards.
    No statement of first edition.

Translations.

THE COMPLETE WORKS OF THE GAWAIN-POET. Chicago: University of Chicago
Press (1965).
Hardcover, dustwrapper.
No statement of first edition.
NOTE: The author's first published book is an anthology, *The Forms of Fiction*, New
York: Random House (1962), hardcover, no dustwrapper. The planned
companion volume, *Poetry: Form and Substance* (1965), is advertised on the
rear flap of *The Complete Works of the Gawain-Poet*, but was never published.

THE ALLITERATIVE MORTE ARTHURE, THE OWL AND THE NIGHTINGALE AND
FIVE OTHER MIDDLE ENGLISH POEMS. Carbondale, Ill./London: Southern Ill-
inois University Press/Feffer & Simons (1971).
Hardcover, dustwrapper.
No statement of first edition.

William H. Gass

OMENSETTER'S LUCK. (New York): New American Library (1966).
  Hardcover, dustwrapper.
  "FIRST PRINTING"

IN THE HEART OF THE HEART OF THE COUNTRY. New York: Harper & Row (1968).
  Hardcover, dustwrapper.
  "FIRST EDITION"

WILLIE MASTERS' LONESOME WIFE. (Evanston, Ill.: Northwestern University Press, 1968).
  Two issues, no known priority:
      1). Hardcover, no priority:
          a). 300 copies.
          b). 100 copies, numbered, signed by the author.
      2). Wrappers.

FICTION AND THE FIGURES OF LIFE. New York: Knopf, 1970.
  Hardcover, dustwrapper.
  "First Edition"
  NOTE: Uncorrected proofs in printed wrappers preceded publication; priority as listed:
      1). Printed by Harper & Row.
      2). Printed by Knopf.

Herbert Gold

BIRTH OF A HERO. New York: Viking Press, 1951.
    Hardcover, dustwrapper.
    No statement of first edition.

THE PROSPECT BEFORE US. Cleveland: World (1954).
    Hardcover, dustwrapper.
    "FIRST EDITION"
    NOTE: Later published as *Room Clerk*. (New York): Signet (1955).
    Wrappers.

THE MAN WHO WAS NOT WITH IT. Boston: Little, Brown (1956).
    Hardcover, dustwrapper.
    "FIRST EDITION"

THE OPTIMIST. Boston: Little, Brown (1959).
    Hardcover, dustwrapper.
    "FIRST EDITION"

THEREFORE BE BOLD. New York: Dial Press, 1960.
    Hardcover, dustwrapper.
    No statement of first edition.

LOVE & LIKE. New York: Dial Press, 1960.
    Hardcover, dustwrapper.
    No statement of first edition.
    ALSO: New York: Studio Duplicating Service (ca. 1961).
    Wrappers.
    NOTE: Entitled *Love & Like: A Play In Two Acts*.

THE AGE OF HAPPY PROBLEMS. New York: Dial Press, 1962.
    Hardcover, dustwrapper.
    No statement of first edition.

SALT. New York: Dial Press, 1963.
    Hardcover, dustwrapper.
    No statement of first edition.

FATHERS. New York: Random House (1966).
    Hardcover, dustwrapper.
    "First Printing"

THE GREAT AMERICAN JACKPOT. New York: Random House (1969).
    Hardcover, dustwrapper.
    "First Printing"

BIAFRA GOODBYE. San Francisco: Twowindows Press (1970).
    Two issues, no priority:
            1). Leather wrappers.
                100 copies, numbered, signed by the author.
            2). Wrappers.
                1000 copies.

THE MAGIC WILL. New York: Random House (1971).
    Hardcover, dustwrapper.
    "First Edition"

MY LAST TWO THOUSAND YEARS. New York: Random House (1972).
    Hardcover, dustwrapper.
    "First Edition"

THE PRINCE AND THE MAGIC CONE. Garden City, N.Y.: Doubleday (1973).
    Hardcover, dustwrapper; no priority:
            1). Trade edition.
            2). Library edition.
    "First Edition"

SWIFTIE THE MAGICIAN. New York: McGraw-Hill (1974).
    Hardcover, dustwrapper.
    "1 2 3 4 5 6 7 8 9" on copyright page.
    NOTE: Uncorrected proofs in printed wrappers preceded publication.

Paul Goodman

TEN LYRIC POEMS. (New York: 5x8 Press, 1934).
   Wrappers.

12 ETHICAL SONNETS. (New York: 5x8 Press, 1935).
   Wrappers.

15 POEMS WITH TIME EXPRESSIONS. (New York: 5x8 Press, 1936).
   Wrappers.

HOMECOMING AND DEPARTURE. (New York: 5x8 Press, 1937).
   Wrappers.

CHILDISH JOKES. (New York: 5x8 Press, 1938).
   Wrappers.

A WARNING AT MY LEISURE. (Harrington Park, N.J.: 5x8 Press, 1939).
   Wrappers.

FIVE YOUNG AMERICAN POETS. Norfolk, Conn.: New Directions, 1941.*
   Hardcover, dustwrapper.
   No statement of first edition.
   NOTE: With Mills, Shapiro, Schubert and McGahey.

STOP-LIGHT. Harrington Park, N.J.: 5x8 Press, 1941.
   Hardcover, dustwrapper; priority as listed:
      1). Dustwrapper has all lettering in red above the illustration.
      2). Unlettered brown dustwrapper and lettered cream dustwrapper issued
         together on each copy of the book.

THE GRAND PIANO. (San Francisco): Colt Press, 1942.
   Hardcover, dustwrapper.
   No statement of first edition.

PIECES OF THREE. (Harrington Park, N.J.: 5x8 Press, 1942).
    Wrappers, priority as listed:
        1). Cream wrappers.
        2). Grey wrappers.
    NOTE: With Meyer Liben and Edouard Roditi.

THE FACTS OF LIFE. New York: Vanguard Press (1945).
    Hardcover, dustwrapper.
    No statement of first edition.

ART AND SOCIAL NATURE. (New York): Vinco Publishing Co. (1946).
    Hardcover, dustwrapper.
    No statement of first edition.

THE STATE OF NATURE. New York: Vanguard Press (1946).
    Hardcover, dustwrapper.
    No statement of first edition.

THE COPERNICAN REVOLUTION. (Saugatuck, Conn.: 5x8 Press, 1946).
    Green wrappers.
    ALSO: (Saugatuck, Conn.: 5x8 Press, 1947).
        Grey wrappers.
        NOTE: Expanded edition.

COMMUNITAS. Chicago: University of Chicago Press (1947).
    Hardcover, dustwrapper.
    No statement of first edition.
    NOTE: With Percival Goodman.
    ALSO: New York: Vintage Books (1960).
        Wrappers, priority as listed:
            1). Grey, orange-cream and black on white background.
            2). Light blue, dark blue and yellow on white background.
        No statement of first edition.
        NOTE: Expanded edition.

KAFKA'S PRAYER. New York: Vanguard Press (1947).
    Hardcover, dustwrapper.
    No statement of first edition.

THE BREAK-UP OF OUR CAMP. (Norfolk, Conn.: New Directions, 1949).
    Hardcover, dustwrapper.
    No statement of first edition.

TUBES AND TELESCOPES. New York: Hugo Gallery (1949).
    Folded sheet.
    NOTE: Exhibition catalogue on bihk piston Petrov.

MARIE MENKEN. New York: Betty Parsons Gallery, 1949.
    Broadside.

THE DEAD OF SPRING. Glen Gardner, N.J.: Libertarian Press, 1950.
    Wrappers.
    2000 copies.

THE DRAMA OF AWARENESS. (N.p., ca. 1950).
    Wrappers.

GESTALT THERAPY. New York: Julian Press (1951).
    Hardcover, dustwrapper.
    No statement of first edition.
    NOTE: With Frederick S. Perls and Ralph F. Hefferline.

PARENTS' DAY. Saugatuck, Conn.: 5x8 Press, 1951.
    Hardcover, no priority:
        1). Trade edition, dustwrapper.
        2). 100 copies, numbered, signed by the author, boxed.

THE STRUCTURE OF LITERATURE. (Chicago): University of Chicago Press (1954).
    Hardcover, dustwrapper.
    No statement of first edition.

DAY AND OTHER POEMS. (New York: Privately published, ca. 1954).
    Wrappers.

PAINTINGS: 1955. New York: Bernard-Ganymede Gallery, 1955.
    Single sheet.
    NOTE: Exhibition catalogue on Julian Beck.

RED JACKET. (New York: Privately published, 1955).
    Wrappers.

JOAN TANSIK. New York: Lynn Kottler Galleries, 1957.
    Single sheet.

PROGRAM/PROGRAM NOTES. New York: Alfred Scott, 1957.
    Wrappers.
    NOTE: For a production of The American Concert Choir and Orchestra, Town Hall, February 15, 1957; contains *The Poets' Requiem*, first published in *The Dead of Spring*.

THE WELL OF BETHLEHEM. (New York: Privately published, ca. 1957).
    Wrappers.

THE EMPIRE CITY. Indianapolis: Bobbs-Merrill (1959).
    Hardcover, dustwrapper.
    No statement of first edition.

CENSORSHIP AND PORNOGRAPHY ON THE STAGE and ARE WRITERS SHIRKING
    THEIR POLITICAL DUTY? New York: Living Theatre, 1959.
    Mimeographed sheets.

GROWING UP ABSURD. New York: Random House (1960).
    Hardcover, dustwrapper.
    "FIRST PRINTING"

OUR VISIT TO NIAGARA. New York: Horizon Press, 1960.
    Hardcover, dustwrapper.
    No statement of first edition.

YOUTH IN THE ORGANIZED SOCIETY. (Privately published, 1960).*
    Wrappers.
    NOTE: An offprint from *Commentary*, February, 1960.

THE SEASONS OF MAN. (Privately published, ca. 1960).
    Mimeographed sheets.

TEN POEMS. (Fieldston, N.Y.: Rachel Goodman, 1961).
    Wrappers.

UTOPIAN ESSAYS AND PRACTICAL PROPOSALS. New York: Random House (1962).
    Hardcover, dustwrapper.
    "First Printing"

DRAWING THE LINE. New York: Random House (1962).
    Wrappers.
    "FIRST PRINTING"

THE UNIVERSAL TRAP. Washington, D.C.: National Education Association, 1962.*
    Mimeographed sheet.

THE SOCIETY I LIVE IN IS MINE. New York: Horizon Press (1962).
    Hardcover, dustwrapper.
    No statement of first edition.

THE LORDLY HUDSON. New York: Macmillan (1962).
    Two issues, priority as listed:
            1). Hardcover, dustwrapper.
            2). Wrappers.
    "First Printing"

THE COMMUNITY OF SCHOLARS. New York: Random House (1962).
    Hardcover, dustwrapper.
    "FIRST PRINTING"

THE WAITING ONES. New York: Waverly Gallery (1962).
    Wrappers.
    NOTE: Exhibition catalogue on Percival Goodman.

MAKING DO. New York: Macmillan (1963).
    Hardcover, dustwrapper.
    "First Printing"

COMPULSORY MIS-EDUCATION. New York: Horizon Press (1964).
    Hardcover, dustwrapper.
    No statement of first edition.

HOW TO MAKE A COLLEGE. (San Francisco: Privately published, 1965).*
    Wrappers.
    1000 copies.
    NOTE: This is to be differentiated from the reprint in wrappers by the
        Cunningham Press (1973).

PEOPLE OR PERSONNEL. New York: Random House (1965).
    Hardcover, dustwrapper.
    "FIRST PRINTING"

THREE PLAYS: THE YOUNG DISCIPLE, FAUSTINA, JONAH. New York: Random
    House (1965).
    Hardcover, dustwrapper.
    "FIRST PRINTING"

VERY SMALL URBAN SCHOOLS. Washington: Institute For Policy Studies (ca. 1965).
    Mimeographed sheets.

THE MORAL AMBIGUITY OF AMERICA. (Toronto): Canadian Broadcasting Co.
    Publications (1966).
    Wrappers.
    NOTE: The Massey Lectures for 1966.
    ALSO: LIKE A CONQUERED PROVINCE: THE MORAL AMBIGUITY OF
        AMERICA. New York: Random House (1967).
        Hardcover, dustwrapper.
        "First American Edition"
        NOTE: Revised edition.

FIVE YEARS. New York: Brussel & Brussel, 1966.
    Hardcover, dustwrapper; priority as listed:
        1). Dustwrapper printed in blue, black and white.
        2). Dustwrapper printed in blue, white, green and grey.
    No statement of first edition.

MASS EDUCATION IN SCIENCE. (Los Angeles: University of California, 1966).
    Wrappers.

HAWKWEED. New York: Random House (1967).
    Hardcover, dustwrapper.
    "First Printing"

TO SIGNATORIES OF ADS IN THE TIMES PROTESTING AGAINST THE VIETNAM
    WAR. (Privately published) 1967.*
    Mimeographed sheet.

THE HIP OF INDUSTRIAL TRIBALISM. (New York: Union Theological Seminary, 1967).*
    Mimeographed sheets.
    NOTE: An interview laid in a periodical, *The Plastic Bag* (which is just that), along
      with material by others.

A MESSAGE TO THE MILITARY-INDUSTRIAL COMPLEX. (London: Freedom Press/
    Peace News, ca. 1967).
    Wrappers.
    NOTE: 1). From *Peace News,* December 15, 1967.
          2). Reprinted as *A Causerie at the Military-Industrial,* Palo Alto, Calif.:
            Institute fot the Study of Violence (ca. 1972).

ADAM AND HIS WORKS. New York: Vintage Books (1968).
    Wrappers.
    "VINTAGE BOOKS EDITION, September, 1968"

NORTH PERCY. Los Angeles: Black Sparrow Press, 1968.
    Two issues, no priority:
        1). Hardcover, no priority:
          a). 250 copies, numbered, signed by the author.
          b). 4 special copies, for the publisher, author, printer and binder.
        2). Wrappers.
          1000 copies.

REFLECTIONS ON RACISM, SPITE, GUILT AND VIOLENCE. (Nyack, N.J.:
    Fellowship Publications, ca. 1968).
    Wrappers.
    NOTE: Offprint from *Fellowship,* July 1968.

TWO POINTS OF PHILOSOPHY AND AN EXAMPLE. (Washington, D.C.: Smithsonian
    Institution Press, 1968).
    Wrappers.
    NOTE: Offprint from *The Fitness of Man's Environment,* Washington, D.C.: Smith-
      sonian Institution Press, 1968.

THE OPEN LOOK. New York: Funk & Wagnalls (1969).
    Hardcover, dustwrapper.
    No statement of first edition.

TRAGEDY & COMEDY. Los Angeles: Black Sparrow Press, 1970.
>   Two issues, no priority:
>>   1). Hardcover, no priority:
>>>   a). 200 copies, numbered, signed by the author.
>>>   b). 4 special copies, for the publisher, author, printer and binder.
>>   2). Wrappers.
>>   750 copies.
>   NOTE: A flyer, printing an extract from one of the plays, preceded publication.

NEW REFORMATION. New York: Random House (1970).
>   Hardcover, dustwrapper.
>   "FIRST PRINTING"
>   NOTE: Uncorrected proofs in printed wrappers preceded publication.

TWO SENTENCES. (Toronto: Coach House Press, 1970).
>   Broadside, in envelope.
>   500 copies.
>   Orange Bear Reader Number One.

ANARCHISM AND REVOLUTION. (Chicago: Encyclopedia Brittanica, 1970).
>   Wrappers.
>   NOTE: Offprint from *The Great Ideas Today 1970*.

THE PRESENT MOMENT IN EDUCATION. (South Bend, Ind.: Journal of Education,
>   ca. 1970).
>   Wrappers.
>   NOTE: Offprint from *Journal of Education*, Spring 1970.

HIGH SCHOOL IS TOO MUCH. (New York: Psychology Today, ca. 1970).
>   Wrappers.
>   NOTE: Offprint from *Psychology Today*, October 1970.

HOMESPUN OF OATMEAL GRAY. Two issues, no priority:
>   1). New York: Random House (1970).
>   Hardcover, dustwrapper.
>   "FIRST EDITION" and "9 8 7 6 5 4 3 2"
>   2). New York: Vintage Books (1970).
>   Wrappers.
>   "First Vintage Books Edition, November 1970."

SPEAKING AND LANGUAGE: DEFENCE OF POETRY. New York: Random House
>   (1971).
>   Hardcover, dustwrapper.
>   "First Edition" and "9 8 7 6 5 4 3 2"

FATHER. New York: Theatre For Ideas, 1971.
>   Mimeographed sheets.
>   NOTE: One scene, *On the Way Back from Mount Moriah,* was not produced but was
>   distributed separately with original pagination and may have been included in
>   some copies of the final playscript (the copy examined did not have it included).

LITTLE PRAYERS & FINITE EXPERIENCE. New York: Harper & Row (1972).
>   Hardcover, dustwrapper.
>   "FIRST EDITION" and, on page 124, "72 73 74 75 10 9 8 7 6 5 4 3 2 1."
>   *Religious Perspectives, Volume Twenty-Four.*

THE BLACK FLAG OF ANARCHISM. (Corinth, Vt.: Black Mountain Press, ca. 1972).
>   Wrappers.

POEMS OF PAUL GOODMAN. (Privately published, 1972).
>   Wrappers, no priority:
>   1). Blue wrappers.
>   2). Olive wrappers.
>   NOTE: Laid in program, *A Memorial for Paul Goodman at the Community Church
>   of New York, October 22nd, 1972.*

COLLECTED POEMS. New York: Random House (1973).
>   Hardcover, dustwrapper.
>   "First Edition" and "9 8 7 6 5 4 3 2"

TRANSLATION.

Aloysius Bertrand.
UNDINE, LE GIBET, SCARBO. New York: Alfred Scott, 1948.
    Wrappers.
    NOTE: This is actually a program for a concert by Eugene Istomin at Carnegie Hall,
        February 20, 1948, but all text is by Goodman.

William Goyen

THE HOUSE OF BREATH. New York: Random House (1950).
    Hardcover, dustwrapper.
    "FIRST PRINTING"
    NOTE: Review copies in printed wrappers preceded publication.

GHOST AND FLESH. New York: Random House (1952).
    Hardcover, dustwrapper.
    "FIRST PRINTING"

IN A FARTHER COUNTRY. New York: Random House (1955).
    Hardcover, dustwrapper.
    No statement of first edition.

THE FACES OF BLOOD KINDRED. (New York): Random House (1960).
    Hardcover, dustwrapper.
    "First Printing"

THE FAIR SISTER. Garden City, N.Y.: Doubleday, 1963.
    Hardcover, dustwrapper.
    "FIRST EDITION"
    NOTE: Published in England as *Savata, My Fair Sister*.

RALPH ELLISON'S INVISIBLE MAN: A CRITICAL COMMENTARY. New York:
    American R.D.M. Corporation (1966).
    Wrappers.

MY ANTONIA: A CRITICAL COMMENTARY. New York: American R.D.M. Corporation
    (1966).
    Wrappers.

A BOOK OF JESUS. Garden City, N.Y.: Doubleday, 1973.
    Hardcover, dustwrapper.
    "FIRST EDITION"
    NOTE: Uncorrected proofs in printed wrappers preceded publication.

THE SELECTED WRITINGS OF WILLIAM GOYEN. (New York/Berkeley): Random
    House/Bookworks (1974).
    Two issues, no priority:
        1). Hardcover, dustwrapper.
        2). Wrappers.
    "First printing, February 1974"

COME, THE RESTORER. Garden City, N.Y.: Doubleday, 1974.
    Hardcover, dustwrapper.
    "FIRST EDITION"

TRANSLATION.

Albert Cossery.
THE LAZY ONES. New York: New Directions (1949).*

Shirley Ann Grau

THE BLACK PRINCE. New York: Knopf, 1955.
    Hardcover, dustwrapper.
    "FIRST EDITION"

THE HARD BLUE SKY. New York: Knopf, 1958.
    Hardcover, dustwrapper.
    "FIRST EDITION"

THE HOUSE ON COLISEUM STREET. New York: Knopf, 1961.
    Hardcover, dustwrapper.
    "FIRST EDITION"

THE KEEPERS OF THE HOUSE. New York: Knopf, 1964.
    Hardcover, dustwrapper.
    "FIRST EDITION"

THE CONDOR PASSES. New York: Knopf, 1971.
    Hardcover, dustwrapper.
    "FIRST EDITION"
    NOTE: Review copies in printed wrappers preceded publication.

THE WIND SHIFTING WEST. New York: Knopf, 1973.
    Hardcover, dustwrapper.
    "FIRST EDITION"

Donald Hall

(POEMS). Swinford, Eynsham (England): Fantasy Press (1952).
    Wrappers.
    Fantasy Poets Number Four.
    NOTE: There is no formal title.

EXILE. Swinford, Eynsham: (Fantasy Press, 1952).
    Wrappers.

TO THE LOUD WIND. Cambridge, Mass.: Harvard Advocate, 1955.
    Wrappers, dustwrapper.
    Pegasus Publications Series, Vol. 1, No. 1.

EXILES & MARRIAGE. New York: Viking Press, 1955.
    Hardcover, dustwrapper.
    No statement of first edition.

THE DARK HOUSES. New York: Viking Press, 1958.
    Hardcover, dustwrapper.
    No statement of first edition.

ANDREW THE LION FARMER. New York: Franklin Watts (1959).
    Hardcover, dustwrapper.
    "FIRST PRINTING"

STRING TOO SHORT TO BE SAVED. New York: Viking Press, 1961.
    Hardcover, dustwrapper.
    No statement of first edition.

A ROOF OF TIGER LILIES. New York: Viking Press (1964).
    Hardcover, dustwrapper.
    No statement of first edition.

HENRY MOORE: THE LIFE AND WORK OF A GREAT SCULPTOR. New York:
    Harper & Row (1966).
    Hardcover, dustwrapper.
    "FIRST EDITION"

THE ALLIGATOR BRIDE. (Menomonie, Wisc.): Ox Head Press, 1968.
　　Wrappers, priority as listed:
　　　　1). Title at top of cover; author's name at bottom.
　　　　2). Title and author's name at top of cover; bottom blank.
　　350 copies.
　　ALSO: New York: Harper & Row (1969).
　　　　Hardcover, dustwrapper.
　　　　"FIRST EDITION"
　　　　NOTE: Expanded edition.

MARIANNE MOORE: THE CAGE AND THE ANIMAL. New York: Pegasus (1970).
　　Hardcover, dustwrapper.
　　No statement of first edition.
　　NOTE: Uncorrected proofs in printed wrappers preceded publication.

THE YELLOW ROOM. New York: Harper & Row (1971).
　　Two issues, no priority:
　　　　1). Hardcover, dustwrapper.
　　　　2). Wrappers.
　　"FIRST EDITION"

WHEN I THINK OF. (Brockport, N.Y.: Department of English, State University College,
　　1972).
　　Wrappers.
　　NOTE: Cover title is *Department of English State University College Brockport.*

THE GENTLEMEN'S ALPHABET BOOK. New York: Dutton, 1972.
　　Hardcover, dustwrapper.
　　"First Edition"

JANE AT PIGALL'S. (Highland Park, Mich.: Red Hanrahan Press, 1973).
　　Broadside.

BREASTS. Highland Park, Mich.: Red Hanrahan Press (ca. 1973).
　　Postcard.

"OH," SAID KATE, "I DO." (Austin: Cold Mountain Press, 1973).
　　Postcard.

AS THE EYE MOVES. New York: Harry N. Abrams. (1973).
　　Hardcover, dustwrapper.
　　No statement of first edition.

WRITING WELL. Boston: Little, Brown (1973).*
　　Hardcover, dustwrapper.
　　NOTE: It is the practice of this publisher to indicate first edition.

THE TOWN OF THE HILL. Boston: David R. Godine (1975).
   Hardcover.

John Hawkes

FIASCO HALL. Cambridge, Mass.: Privately published, 1943.
    Wrappers.
    150 copies, of which 60 were reportedly destroyed.
    NOTE: Written as "J.C.B.Hawkes, Jr."

THE CANNIBAL. (Norfolk, Conn.): New Directions (1949).
    Grey cloth, dustwrapper.
    No statement of first edition.
    NOTE: The second printing is so designated only on the dustwrapper, not the copy-
        right page; it is bound in rust cloth.
    ALSO: (New York): New Directions (1971).
        Hardcover, dustwrapper.
        "FIFTH PAPERBOOK PRINTING" and "FIRST REVISED CLOTHBOUND PRINTING"
        NOTE: Revised edition.

THE BEETLE LEG. (New York): New Directions (1951).
    Hardcover, dustwrapper; priority as listed:
        1). Orange cloth binding.
        2). Red cloth binding.
    No statement of first edition.

THE GOOSE ON THE GRAVE and THE OWL. (New York): New Directions (1954).
    Hardcover, dustwrapper.
    No statement of first edition.

THE LIME TWIG. (New York): New Directions (1961).
    Hardcover, priority as listed:
        1). Trade edition, dustwrapper.
        2). 100 copies, numbered, signed by the author, boxed.
    No statement of first edition.
    NOTE: The trade preceded the signed edition by two years.

SECOND SKIN. (New York): New Directions (1964).
    Two issues, no priority:
        1). Hardcover, no priority:
            a). Trade edition, dustwrapper.
            b). 100 copies, numbered, signed by the author, boxed.
        2). Wrappers.
    No statement of first edition.

THE INNOCENT PARTY. (New York): New Directions (1966).
    Hardcover, dustwrapper.
    No statement of first edition.

LUNAR LANDSCAPES. (New York): New Directions (1969).
    Hardcover, no priority:
        1). Trade edition, dustwrapper.
        2). 150 copies, numbered, signed by the author, boxed.
    No statement of first edition.

THE BLOOD ORANGES. (New York): New Directions (1971).
    Hardcover, dustwrapper.
    No statement of first edition.

THE AUTHOR RESPONDS. (Baltimore, Md.: Privately published, 1973).
    Mechanically reproduced sheets.
    50 copies (approximately).

DEATH, SLEEP & THE TRAVELER. (New York): New Directions (1974).
    Hardcover, dustwrapper.
    No statement of first edition.

Joseph Heller

CATCH-22. New York: Simon & Schuster, 1961.
   Hardcover, dustwrapper.
   "FIRST PRINTING"
   NOTE: 1). Review copies in printed wrappers preceded publication.
         2). Formosan piracies, in reduced format, of an unidentified American printing,
             as well as the sixth printing, have been examined.

WE BOMBED IN NEW HAVEN. (New York: Privately published) 1968.
   Wrappers.
   NOTE: Mechanically reproduced sheets for the production of the play "in a theatre
         in New York."
   ALSO: New York: Knopf, 1968.
         Hardcover, dustwrapper.
         "FIRST PRINTING"
         NOTE: 1). Revised edition.
               2). A Formosan piracy of the first printing, in reduced format, has been
                   examined.

CATCH-22: A DRAMATIZATION. New York: Samuel French (1971).
   Wrappers.
   No statement of first edition.
   ALSO: New York: Delacorte Press (1973).
         Hardcover, dustwrapper.
         "First Delacorte printing"
         NOTE: New preface by the author.

SOMETHING HAPPENED. New York: Knopf, 1974.
   Hardcover, no priority:
         1). Trade edition, yellow dustwrapper.
         2). 350 copies, numbered, signed by the author, cream dustwrapper, boxed.
   "First Edition"
   NOTE: Uncorrected proofs in printed wrappers preceded publication.

Jack Hirschman

FRAGMENTS. (New York: Privately published, 1952).*
    Wrappers.

A CORRESPONDENCE OF AMERICANS. Bloomington, Ind.: Indiana University Press,
    1960.
    Hardcover, tissue dustwrapper.
    No statement of first edition.

TWO. Los Angeles: Zora Gallery, 1964.
    Hardcover.
    100 copies, numbered.
    NOTE: Colophon specifies that there were six suites of artist's proofs, two suites of
        printer's proofs, and trial, state and artist's proofs.

INTERCHANGE. (Los Angeles: Zora Gallery, 1964).
    Sheets in box, no priority:
        1). 278 copies.
        2). 22 copies, signed by the author.
    NOTE: A radio version, 21 mimeographed pages, has been reported.

KLINE SKY. (Los Angeles: Privately published) 1965.*
    Sheets in portfolio.
    100 copies.

YOD. (London: Trigram Press, 1966).
    Bound signatures laid in covers, no priority:
        1). 200 copies, numbered.
        2). 60 copies, numbered, signed by the author.

LTD. (London: Privately published, 1967).
    Wrappers.
    100 copies, numbered.

JERUSALEM LTD. London: Trigram Press, 1967.*
    Broadside.

THE PEACE OF ME IN. (Los Angeles: Privately published, 1967).
    Broadside.
    26 copies, numbered, signed by the illustrator.
    Illustrated by Thomas Douglas.

WILLIAM BLAKE. (Topanga, Calif.: Love Press, 1967).
    Wrappers.
    300 copies, variously designated "Birthday edition" or "Student edition".

A WORD IN YOUR SEASON. (London: Trigram Press, 1967).
    Sheets in portfolio.
    100 copies, numbered.
    NOTE: With Asa Benveniste.

LONDON SEEN DIRECTLY. London: Cape Goliard Press (1967).
    Wrappers, no priority:
        1). 125 copies.
        2). 25 copies, numbered, signed by the author.

WASN'T IT LIKE. London: Cape Goliard Press, 1967.
    Broadside, no priority:
        1). 75 copies.
        2). 25 copies, numbered, signed by the author.

JERUSALEM. (Topanga, Calif.: Love Press, 1968).
    Hardcover.
    150 copies.

ALEPH, BENONI & ZADDIK. Los Angeles: Tenfingers Press (1968).
    Hardcover.
    150 copies, numbered.

EUROPE 1967. (Santa Barbara, Calif.: Unicorn Press, 1968).
    Broadside.
    350 copies.
    NOTE: Laid in portfolio entitled *Unicorn Folio: Series Two Number One*, numbered.

NEW YORK. (Santa Barbara, Calif.: Unicorn Press, 1968).
    Broadside.
    350 copies.
    NOTE: Laid in portfolio entitled *Unicorn Folio: Series Two, Number Four*, numbered.

WALLACE BERMAN. Los Angeles: Los Angeles County Museum, 1968.*
    Wrappers.

BLACK ALEPHS. London: Trigram Press, 1969.
    Two issues, no priority:
        1). Hardcover, no priority:
            a). Trade edition, dustwrapper.
            b). 100 copies, numbered, signed by the author, acetate dustwrapper.
        2). Wrappers.

SHEKINAH. (Berkeley): Maya, 1969.
    Wrappers, no priority:
        1). 250 copies.
        2). 50 copies, numbered, signed by the author.
    Maya Quarto One.

NHR. (Goleta, Calif.): Christopher's Books, 1970.
    Wrappers, no priority:
        1). 274 copies.
        2). 26 copies, numbered, signed by the author.

YOU EVOKE IN A FLASH. (Privately published, 1970).
    Broadside.

JOHN TREE HEAVY WITH ARCS. (Topanga, Calif.): Love Press, 1970.
    Broadside.

GOLEM. (Venice, Calif.: Privately published, ca. 1970).*
    Broadside.

SOLEDETH. (Venice, Calif.: Q Press, 1971).
    Sheets in folder.
    72 copies, numbered.

DT. Portland, Ore.: Yes! Press, 1971.
    Broadside.

SCINTILLA. (Bolinas, Calif.): Tree Books, 1971.
    Wrappers.
    400 copies.

THE BURNING OF LOS ANGELES. (Venice, Calif.: J'ose Press, 1971).
    Sheets in portfolio.
    150 copies, numbered.

HYNC. (Topanga, Calif.: R. Tamblyn/Skyline Press, 1971).
    Hardcover.
    200 copies.

ADAMNAN. (Santa Barbara, Calif.: Christopher's Books, 1972).
    Wrappers.
    450 copies, signed by the author.

LES VIDANGES. (Venice, Calif.: Privately published, 1972).
    Stapled sheets.

THE R OF THE ARI'S RAZIEL. Los Angeles: Press of the Pegacycle Lady, 1972.
    Wrappers.
    100 copies, numbered, signed by the author.

K'WAI SING. (Venice, Calif.: Beyond Baroque Foundation, 1973).
    Wrappers.
    650 copies.
    NOTE: Beyond Baroque Foundation Publication, Volume 4, Number 3.

K S. (Venice, Calif.: Beyond Baroque Foundation, 1973).
    Wrappers.
    600 copies.

CANTILLATIONS. Santa Barbara, Calif.: Capra Press, 1974.
        Two issues, no priority:
            1). Hardcover.
                75 copies, numbered, signed by the author.
            2). Wrappers.
    Yes! Capra Chapbook Number Fifteen.

AUR SEA. Berkeley: Tree, 1974.
    Wrappers, dustwrapper.

K. (Brattleboro, Vt.: Workshop/Jack Stage, 1974).
    Broadside.
    "Within 75 issues."
    Poets Who Sleep #3.

TIME OF THE PEOPLE CHANGED TO PRAYER. (Santa Barbara, Calif.): Lost Pleiade
    Press, 1974.
    Broadside.
    300 copies.

DJACKSON. (Salt Lake City: Rainbow Resin Press, 1974).
    Wrappers.

THE COOL BOYETZ CYCLE/AND. (San Francisco: Golden Mountain Press, 1975).
    Wrappers.

KASHTANIIA SEGODNIA (transliterated title). San Francisco: Beatitude Press, 1975.
   Wrappers, priority as listed:
      1). Black lettering only on cover.
      2). Black lettering with illustration in red on cover.

TRANSLATIONS.

Vladimir Mayakovsky.
ELECTRIC IRON. Berkeley: Maya, 1971.
    Wrappers.
    1000 copies.
    NOTE: With Victor Erlich.

Rene Depestre.
A RAINBOW FOR THE CHRISTIAN WEST. (Los Angeles): Red Hill Press, 1972.
    Wrappers.

Luisa Pasamanik.
THE EXILED ANGEL. Los Angeles: Red Hill Press, 1973.
    Wrappers.

Ait Djafer.
WAIL FOR THE ARAB BEGGARS OF THE CASBAH. West Los Angeles: Papa Bach
    Bookstore, 1973.
    Wrappers.

Stephane Mallarme.
IGITUR. Los Angeles: Press of the Pegacycle Lady, 1974.
    Two issues, no priority:
        1). Hardcover.
            100 copies, numbered, signed by the author.
        2). Wrappers.
            400 copies.

Louis Aragon.
ELEGIE A PABLO NERUDA. (Los Angeles: Red Hill Press, 1975).
    Wrappers.
    NOTE: 1). Translated with Josette Bryson.
        2). An offprint from the magazine *Invisible City*.

Eleazer of Worms.
THREE TRACTS. Berkeley: Tree, 1975.
    Wrappers, dustwrapper.
    NOTE: French translation by Hirschman; Hebrew translation by Alexander Altman.

BOOK OF NOAH. Berkeley: Tree, 1975.
    Wrappers, dustwrapper.
    NOTE: Translated from the *Sefer ha-Raziel*.

Robert Kelly

ARMED DESCENT. (New York): Hawk's Well Press (1961).
    Wrappers.

HER BODY AGAINST TIME. Mexico: El Corno Emplumado, 1963.
    Two issues, no priority:
        1). Hardcover.
           50 copies (approximately).
        2). Wrappers.

ROUND DANCES. New York: Trobar Press (1964).
    Wrappers, no priority:
        1). 150 copies, numbered.
        2). 30 copies, unnumbered.

TABULA. Lawrence, Kan.: Dialogue Press, 1964.
    Broadside.

ENSTASY. (Annandale-on-Hudson, N.Y.: Matter, 1964).
    Wrappers, no priority:
        1). 22 copies, numbered, signed by the author.
        2). 3 copies, numbered, signed by the author, hand-painted covers.

MATTER/FACT/SHEET/#1. (Buffalo, N.Y.: Matter) 1964.
    Broadside.

MATTER/FACT/SHEET 2. (Annandale-on-Hudson, N.Y.: Matter, 1964).
    Broadside.

LUNES. (New York: Hawk's Well Press, 1964).
    Wrappers.
    NOTE: With *Sightings* by Jerome Rothenberg.

LECTIONES. (Placitas, N.M.): Duende Press (1965).
    Wrappers.

WORDS IN SERVICE. (New Haven, Conn.: Robert Lamberton, 1965).
    Wrappers.
    100 copies.

WEEKS. (Mexico City): El Corno Emplumado (1966).
    Wrappers.
    1000 copies.
    NOTE: Although the book states 1000 copies, the printing of the book resulted in a
        mass of errors which caused the book to be suppressed by the author. Report-
        edly, only some 50 copies escaped.

THE SCORPIONS. Garden City, N.Y.: Doubleday, 1967.
    Hardcover, dustwrapper.
    "FIRST EDITION"

SONG XXIV. Cambridge, Mass.: Pym-Randall Press (1967).
    Wrappers, no priority:
        1). 100 copies, numbered, signed by the author.
        2). 26 copies, lettered, signed by the author.

TWENTY POEMS. (Annandale-on-Hudson, N.Y.): Matter, 1967.
    Wrappers.
    500 copies.

DEVOTIONS. (Annandale-on-Hudson, N.Y.: Matter, 1967).
    Wrappers.
    500 copies.
    Salitter 1.

AXON DENDRON TREE. Annandale-on-Hudson, N.Y.: Salitter Books, 1967.
    Wrappers.
    500 copies.
    Salitter 2.

CROOKED BRIDGE LOVE SOCIETY. (Annandale-on-Hudson, N.Y.: Salitter Books,
    1967).
    Wrappers.
    50 copies (according to the publisher, only 48 were actually published).
    Salitter 3.

CHRISTMAS. (Annandale-on-Hudson, N.Y.: Privately published, 1967).
    Broadside.

A JOINING. (Los Angeles: Black Sparrow Press, 1967).
    Two issues, priority as listed:
        1). Wrappers.
            115 copies, numbered, signed by the author.

2). Hardcover, no priority:
    a). 4 copies, lettered, signed by the author, blue cloth.
    b). 6 copies, lettered, signed by the author, brown cloth.
    c). 4 special copies, for the publisher, author, printer and binder.

ALPHA. (Gambier, Ohio: Joel Fisher, 1968).
    Wrappers, no priority:
        1). 300 copies.
        2). 26 copies, lettered, signed by the author.
    "First edition"
    NOTE: The 100 copies, numbered, signed by the author, as announced in the colophon, were never published.

FINDING THE MEASURE. Los Angeles: Black Sparrow Press, 1968.
    Two issues, priority as listed:
        1). Wrappers, priority as listed:
            a). Overlapping wrappers; black colophon.
                770 copies.
            b). Flush wrappers; black colophon.
                142 copies.
            c). Flush wrappers; blue colophon.
                20 copies.
        2). Hardcover, dustwrapper; no priority:
            a). 50 copies, numbered, signed by the author.
            b). 4 special copies, for the publisher, author, printer and binder.
    NOTE: An advertising flyer, printing part of a poem, preceded publication.

STATEMENT. Los Angeles: Black Sparrow Press, 1968.
    Two issues, priority as listed:
        1). Wrappers, priority as listed:
            a). 1000 copies with eight names in addition to the author's on the cover.
            b). Only the author's name on the cover; no priority:
                i). 428 copies.
                ii). 50 copies, signed by the author on the cover.
        2). Hardcover, no priority:
            a). 26 copies, lettered, signed by the author.
            b). 4 special copies, for the publisher, author, printer and binder.

SONGS I-XXX. Cambridge, Mass.: Pym-Randall Press, 1968.
    Two issues, no priority:
        1). Hardcover, dustwrapper; no priority:
            a). 310 copies.
            b). 90 copies, numbered, signed by the author.
        2). Wrappers.
            600 copies.

SONNETS. Los Angeles: Black Sparrow Press, 1968.
> Two issues, no priority:
>> 1). Hardcover, no priority:
>>> a). 65 copies, numbered, signed, with original drawing and/or holograph poem by the author; boards.
>>> b). 10 copies, numbered, with original drawing and/or holograph poem by the author; leather.
>>> c). 4 special copies, for the publisher, author, printer and binder.
>> 2). Wrappers.
>> 250 copies, numbered, signed by the author (according to the publisher, only 245 copies were actually published).

(FROM THE COMMON SHORE, BOOK 5). Great Neck, N.Y.: George Robert Minkoff, 1968.
> **Broadside, no priority:**
>> 1). 250 copies, numbered, signed by the author and illustrator.
>> 2). 200 copies, signed by the illustrator.
> Illustrated by M. Faunbach.

A PLAY AND TWO POEMS. Los Angeles: Black Sparrow Press, 1968.
> Wrappers, no priority:
>> 1). 300 copies (according to the publisher, only 224 were actually published).
>> 2). 100 copies, numbered, signed by the authors.
> NOTE: With Ron Loewinsohn and Diane Wakoski.

WE ARE THE ARBITERS. (Berkeley: MBVL Editions, 1969).
> **Broadside, photocopied.**
> 25 copies, numbered, signed by the author.

THE COMMON SHORE BOOKS I-V. Los Angeles: Black Sparrow Press, 1969.
> Two issues, no priority:
>> 1). Hardcover, acetate dustwrapper; no priority:
>>> a). 250 copies, numbered, signed by the author.
>>> b). **26 copies, lettered, signed, with holograph poem by the author.**
>>> c). 4 special copies, for the publisher, author, printer and binder.
>> 2). Wrappers.
>> 1000 copies.
> NOTE: An advertising flyer, printing part of a poem, preceded publication.

DEASIL & WIDDERSHINS. (Amherst, Mass.: Privately published) 1969.
> Wrappers.
> Poetry Signature V.
> NOTE: An offprint from *Massachusetts Review*, Autumn, 1969.

A CALIFORNIA JOURNAL. (London): Big Venus (1969).
> Wrappers.

KALI YUGA. (London): Cape Goliard Press (1970).
  Two issues, no priority:
    1). Hardcover, dustwrapper; no priority:
      a). Trade edition.
      b). 50 copies, numbered, signed by the author.
    2). Wrappers.
  NOTE: 1). The American edition has "Cape Goliard/Grossman" on the spine.
    2). An advertising flyer, printing a poem, preceded publication.

EROS AND PSYCHE. (New Paltz, N.Y.: State University of New York, 1971).
  Mimeographed sheets.

CITIES. (West Newbury, Mass.): Frontier Press, 1971.
  Wrappers.

IN TIME. West Newbury, Mass.: Frontier Press, 1971.
  Wrappers.

FLESH DREAM BOOK. Los Angeles: Black Sparrow Press, 1971.
  Two issues, no priority:
    1). Hardcover, acetate dustwrapper; no priority:
      a). 200 copies, numbered, signed by the author.
      b). 26 copies, lettered, signed, with holograph poem by the author.
      c). 4 special copies, for the publisher, author, printer and binder.
    2). Wrappers.
    1000 copies (according to the publisher, 1131 copies were actually published).

THE WISE MEN DRAWN TO KNEEL IN WONDER AT THE FACT SO OF ITSELF.
  Los Angeles: Black Sparrow Press, 1971.
  Two issues, no priority:
    1). Hardcover, acetate dustwrapper.
    100 copies, numbered, signed by the authors.
    2). Wrappers.
    525 copies.
  NOTE: With David Bromige and Diane Wakoski.

RALEGH. Los Angeles: Black Sparrow Press, 1972.
  Two issues, no priority:
    1). Hardcover, acetate dustwrapper.
    26 copies, lettered, signed, with holograph poem by the author.
    2). Wrappers.
    220 copies, numbered, signed by the author.

SULPHUR. (Los Angeles: Privately published, 1972).
  Broadside.
  10 copies (approximately).

THE PASTORALS. (Los Angeles): Black Sparrow Press, 1972.
    Wrappers.
    Sparrow 1.

READING HER NOTES. (Annandale-on-Hudson, N.Y.: Privately published, 1972).
    Wrappers.
    150 copies, numbered, signed by the author.

THE TEARS OF EDMUND BURKE. (Annandale-on-Hudson, N.Y.: Privately published) 1973.
    Wrappers.
    26 copies, lettered, signed by the author.

WHALER FRIGATE CLIPPERSHIP. (Lawrence, Kan.): Tansy, 1973.
    Broadside.

THE MILL OF PARTICULARS. Los Angeles: Black Sparrow Press, 1973.
    Two issues, no priority:
        1). Hardcover, acetate dustwrapper; no priority:
            a). 200 copies, numbered, signed by the author.
            b). 26 copies, lettered, signed, with an original drawing by the author.
        2). Wrappers.
            1500 copies.
    NOTE: There were 10 copies in advance of publication, in plain grey-brown wrappers, bearing a label which notes errors corrected for the published edition.

AITHERS. (Annandale-on-Hudson, N.Y.: Privately published, 1973).
    Broadside.
    5 copies.

WITH A SUN LIKE. (Annandale-on-Hudson, N.Y.: Privately published, 1973).
    Broadside.
    5 copies.

THE FOX WATCHED. (Annandale-on-Hudson, N.Y.: Privately published, 1973).
    Broadside.
    5 copies.

IDYLL. (Annandale-on-Hudson, N.Y.: Privately published, 1973).
    Broadside.
    5 copies.

DIE EVERY. (Annandale-on-Hudson, N.Y.: Privately published, 1973).
    Broadside.
    5 copies.

A PRAISE OF ORNAMENT. (Annandale-on-Hudson, N.Y.: Privately published, 1973).
Broadside.
5 copies.

READING NOVALIS. (Annandale-on-Hudson, N.Y.: Privately published, 1973).
Broadside.
5 copies.

ODE. (Annandale-on-Hudson, N.Y.: Privately published, 1973).
Broadside.
5 copies.

THE PERMISSION. (Annandale-on-Hudson, N.Y.: Privately published, 1973).
Broadside.
5 copies.

WHY WONT I LET THEM DIE. (Annandale-on-Hudson, N.Y.: Privately published, 1973).
Broadside.
5 copies.

LAMARCK ON BUGGERY / A MEETING WITH KHIDR / ESPALIER.
(Annandale-on-Hudson, N.Y.: Privately published, 1973).
Broadside.
5 copies.

ARE HER TRESSES MEASURED. (Annandale-on-Hudson, N.Y.: Privately published,
1973).
Broadside.

A LINE OF SIGHT. (Los Angeles): Black Sparrow Press, 1974.
Wrappers.
Sparrow 20.

FROM A NOTEBOOK AUGUST 74 and THE BELT. (Storrs, Conn.: University of
Connecticut Library, 1974).
Wrappers.
250 copies.

PREFIX TO FINDING THE MEASURE. (Port Townsend, Wash.): Copper Canyon Press,
1974.
Broadside.
100 copies.
Copperhead Broadside 7.
NOTE: Laid in box entitled *Copperhead: A Giftbox for Kenneth Rexroth*.

THE LOOM. Los Angeles: Black Sparrow Press, 1975.

    Two issues, no priority:

        1). Hardcover, acetate dustwrapper; no priority:

            a). 250 copies, numbered, signed by the author.

            b). 50 copies, numbered, signed, with holograph poem by the author.

        2). Wrappers.

          2015 copies.

John Oliver Killens

YOUNGBLOOD. New York: Dial Press, 1954.
    Hardcover, dustwrapper.
    No statement of first edition.

AND THEN WE HEARD THE THUNDER. New York: Knopf, 1963.
    Hardcover, dustwrapper.
    "FIRST EDITION"

BLACK MAN'S BURDEN. New York: Trident Press, 1965.
    Hardcover, dustwrapper.
    No statement of first edition.

'SIPPI. New York: Trident Press, 1967.
    Hardcover, dustwrapper.
    No statement of first edition.

SLAVES. New York: Pyramid Books (1969).
    Wrappers.
    "First Printing, May 1969"

THE COTILLION. New York: Trident Press (1971).
    Hardcover, dustwrapper.
    No statement of first edition.

GREAT GITTIN' UP MORNING. Garden City, N.Y.: Doubleday (1972).
    Hardcover, dustwrapper.
    "First Edition"

Kenneth Koch

POEMS. New York: Tibor de Nagy Gallery, 1953.
    Wrappers.
    300 copies.
    NOTE: With *Prints* by Nell Blaine, including four prints signed by her.

KO, OR A SEASON ON EARTH. New York: Grove Press (1959).
    Two issues, no priority:
        1). Hardcover, dustwrapper; no priority:
            a). Trade edition.
            b). 26 copies, lettered, signed by the author.
            c). 4 copies, numbered, hors commerce.
        2). Wrappers.
    "First Grove Press Edition 1959"

PERMANENTLY. New York: Tiber Press (1960).
    Hardcover, acetate dustwrapper; no priority:
        1). 200 copies, numbered in Arabic, signed by the author and illustrator.
        2). 25 copies, numbered in Roman, signed by the author and illustrator.
    Illustrated by Alfred Leslie.
    NOTE: Issued in box with *The Poems* by John Ashbery, *Odes* by Frank O'Hara and *Salute* by James Schuyler.

GUINEVERE, OR THE DEATH OF THE KANGAROO. New York: American Theatre For Poets, 1961.
    Mimeographed sheets.
    NOTE: Precedes the book of the same title by five years.

THANK YOU. New York: Grove Press (1962).
    Wrappers.
    "First Printing"

THE FUCK YOU QUOTE OF THE WEEK #3. New York: Fuck You Press, 1964.
    Broadside.

A CONVERSATION. Tucson, Ariz.: Interview Press (ca. 1965).
 Wrappers.
 NOTE: With John Ashbery.

BERTHA. New York: Grove Press (1966).
 Wrappers.
 "First Printing"

POEMS FROM 1952 AND 1953. Los Angeles: Black Sparrow Press, 1968.
 Two issues, no priority:
  1). Hardcover, dustwrapper; no priority:
   a). 50 copies, numbered, signed by the author (according to the
       publisher, only 47 were actually published).
   b). 4 special copies, for the publisher, author, printer and binder.
  2). Wrappers.
   a). 250 copies, numbered, signed by the author.
   b). 15 copies, numbered; for review.

WHEN THE SUN TRIES TO GO ON. Los Angeles: Black Sparrow Press, 1969.
 Three issues, no priority:
  1). Hardcover, acetate dustwrapper; no priority:
   a). 200 copies, numbered, signed by the author and illustrator.
   b). 5 special copies, for the publisher, author, illustrator, printer & binder.
  2). Leather.
   5 copies, numbered, signed by the author and illustrator, in portfolio in box,
   with illustration by the illustrator in shadow-box.
  3). Wrappers.
   1500 copies.
 Illustrated by Larry Rivers.

THE PLEASURES OF PEACE. New York: Grove Press (1969).
 Hardcover, dustwrapper.
 "First Printing"

SLEEPING WITH WOMEN. Los Angeles: Black Sparrow Press, 1969.
 Two issues, no priority:
  1). Hardcover, acetate dustwrapper; no priority:
   a). 150 copies, numbered, signed by the author.
   b). 4 special copies, for the publisher, author, printer and binder.
  2). Wrappers.
   300 copies, numbered, signed by the author.

INTERLOCKING LIVES. (New York: Kulchur Press, 1970).
 Two issues, no priority:
  1). Hardcover, dustwrapper.
  2). Wrappers.

WISHES, LIES AND DREAMS. New York: Chelsea House (1970).
    Hardcover, dustwrapper.
    No statement of first edition.

SCHWEITZERREICH. (New York: Museum of Modern Art, ca. 1971).
    Plastic sheet with raised letters.

ROSE, WHERE DID YOU GET THAT RED? New York: Random House (1973).
    Hardcover, dustwrapper.
    "First Edition"

A CHANGE OF HEARTS. New York: Random House (1973).
    Two issues, no priority:
        1). Hardcover, dustwrapper.
        2). Wrappers.
    "First Printing"

DIANA WITH POEM. West Islip: Universal Limited Art Editions (1974).*
    Broadside in portfolio.
    19 copies, numbered.

THE ART OF LOVE. New York: Random House (1975).
    Two issues, no priority:
        1). Hardcover, dustwrapper.
        2). Wrappers.
    "First Edition" and "9 8 7 6 5 4 3 2"

THE RED ROBINS. New York: Vintage Books (1975).
    Wrappers.
    "FIRST EDITION"

Philip Lamantia

EROTIC POEMS. (Berkeley): Bern Porter, 1946.
    Hardcover, white paper boards.
    No statement of first edition.
    NOTE: Reprinted by Bern Porter, ca. 1973. Buckram.

EKSTASIS. San Francisco: Auerhahn Press, 1959.
    Wrappers.
    950 copies.

NARCOTICA (I DEMAND EXTINCTION OF LAWS PROHIBITING NARCOTIC
    DRUGS!). (San Francisco): Auerhahn Press, 1959.
    Wrappers.

AH BLESSED VIRGIN MARY. (San Francisco: Wallace Berman, 1959).
    Broadside.
    NOTE: Laid in portfolio entitled *Semina 4*.

IT WILL CROWD. (San Francisco): Auerhahn Press (1959).
    Wrappers.
    NOTE: 1). Cover title of only *Auerhahn Press* for this folded broadside, which is also
        encountered without wrappers.
        2). With John Wieners, Philip Whalen and Michael McClure.
        3). Commonly referred to by Wieners' title, *Bag Dad By the Bay*.

MEMORIA. (Los Angeles: Wallace Berman, 1960).
    Broadside.
    NOTE: Laid in portfolio entitled *Semina 5*.

DESTROYED WORKS. (San Francisco): Auerhahn, 1962.
    Two issues, no priority:
        1). Hardcover.
            50 copies, signed by the author.
        2). Wrappers.
            1250 copies.

TOUCH OF THE MARVELOUS. (Berkeley): Oyez, 1966.
　　　Two issues, no priority:
　　　　　1). Hardcover.
　　　　　　　50 copies, numbered, signed by the author.
　　　　　2). Wrappers.
　　　　　　　1450 copies.
　　　ALSO: Bolinas, Calif.: Four Seasons Foundation, 1974.
　　　Wrappers.
　　　Writing 32.
　　　NOTE: Expanded edition.

SELECTED POEMS 1943-1966. (San Francisco): City Lights Books (1967).
　　　Wrappers.
　　　No statement of first edition.
　　　Pocket Poets Series Number 20.

THE BLOOD OF THE AIR. San Francisco: Four Seasons Foundation, 1970.
　　　Two issues, no priority:
　　　　　1). Hardcover, no priority:
　　　　　　　a). Trade edition.
　　　　　　　b). 50 copies, numbered, signed by the author.
　　　　　2). Wrappers.
　　　Writing 25.

Translation.

Sor Juana Ines De La Cruz.
SISTER JUANA INES OF THE CROSS. (Los Angeles: Wallace Berman, 1960).
  Broadside.
  NOTE: Laid in portfolio entitled *Semina 5*.

Denise Levertov

THE DOUBLE IMAGE. London: Cresset Press, 1946.
    Hardcover, dustwrapper.
    No statement of first edition.
    NOTE: Written as "Denise Levertoff."

HERE AND NOW. San Francisco: City Lights Pocket Bookshop (1957).
    Wrappers.
    No statement of first edition.
    Pocket Poets Series #6.

5 POEMS. (San Francisco: White Rabbit Press, 1958).
    Wrappers.
    200 copies.

OVERLAND TO THE ISLANDS. Highlands (N.C.): Jonathan Williams, 1958.
    Wrappers, dustwrapper; priority as listed:
        1). 450 copies.
        2). 50 copies, numbered, signed by the author (in 1964).
    Jargon Number Nineteen.

WITH EYES AT THE BACK OF OUR HEADS. (New York): New Directions (1959).
    Hardcover, dustwrapper.
    No statement of first edition.

THE JACOB'S LADDER. (New York): New Directions (1961).
    Wrappers.
    No statement of first edition.

PATERSON SOCIETY. Cambridge, Mass.: Paterson Society, 1961.*
    Broadside.

O TASTE AND SEE. (Norfolk, Conn.): New Directions (1964).
    Two issues, no priority:
        1). Hardcover, dustwrapper.
        2). Wrappers.
    No statement of first edition.

CITY PSALM. (Berkeley): Oyez, 1964.
    Broadside.
    350 copies.
    Oyez 7.
    NOTE: 27 copies, numbered, signed by the author in 1964 but published in 1965 in
        portfolio entitled *Poems in Broadside. Oyez. First Series.*

PSALM CONCERNING THE CASTLE. (Madison, Wisc.): W. S. Hamady (1966).
    Broadside.
    70 copies.

THE SORROW DANCE. (New York): New Directions (1967).
    Two issues, no priority:
        1). Hardcover, dustwrapper.
        2). Wrappers.
    No statement of first edition.
    NOTE: The last date on the copyright page is 1966.
    ALSO: London: Jonathan Cape (1968).
        Hardcover, dustwrapper.
        No statement of first edition.
        NOTE: 1). Uncorrected proofs in printed wrappers preceded publication.
                2). Errors in the American edition are corrected and a new poem is added.

A TREE TELLING OF ORPHEUS. Los Angeles: Black Sparrow Press, 1968.
    Two issues, priority as listed:
        1). Wrappers.
            250 copies, numbered, signed by the author (according to the publisher, only
            247 were actually published).
        2). Hardcover, no priority:
            a). 75 copies, numbered, signed by the author (according to the publisher,
                76 were published).
            b). 4 copies, lettered, signed, with an original drawing by the author.

IN THE NIGHT. New York: Albondocani Press, 1968.
    Wrappers.
    150 copies, numbered, signed by the author.
    Albondocani Press Publication Number One.

SWAN THAT SINGS AND. (Stony Brook, N.Y.: Stony Brook Poetics Foundation, 1968).
    Broadside.
    10 copies, signed by the author.
    NOTE: Laid in portfolio entitled *Stony Brook Holographs 1968.*

A MARIGOLD FROM NORTH VIETNAM. (New York: Albondocani Press, 1968).
    Wrappers, no priority:
        1). 100 copies with additional imprint of Albondocani Press on the greeting page.
        2). 200 copies without the additional imprint.

THREE POEMS. Mt. Horeb, Wisc.: Perishable Press, 1968.
    Wrappers.
    250 copies.

THE COLD SPRING. (New York): New Directions, 1968.
    Hardcover, dustwrapper; no priority:
        1). 100 copies, numbered, signed by the author.
        2). 8 copies, lettered, signed by the author, glassine dustwrapper.
    NOTE: Reportedly, the book was not actually published until 1969.

EMBROIDERIES. Los Angeles: Black Sparrow Press, 1969.
    Two issues, no priority:
        1). Hardcover, acetate dustwrapper; no priority:
            a). 150 copies, numbered, signed by the author.
            b). 4 special copies, for the publisher, author, printer and binder.
        2). Wrappers, no priority:
            a). 250 copies.
            b). 300 copies, numbered, signed by the author.

SUMMER POEMS/1969. Berkeley: Oyez (1970).
    Two issues, no priority:
        1). Hardcover.
            50 copies, numbered, signed by the author.
        2). Wrappers.
            300 copies.

RELEARNING THE ALPHABET. (New York): New Directions (1970).
    Two issues, no priority:
        1). Hardcover, dustwrapper.
        2). Wrappers.
    No statement of first edition.

A NEW YEAR'S GARLAND FOR MY STUDENTS. Mt. Horeb, Wisc.: Perishable Press, 1970.
    Wrappers, no priority:
        1). 125 copies, numbered.
        2). 100 copies, numbered, hors commerce, on pink stock.

TO STAY ALIVE. (New York): New Directions (1971).
    Two issues, no priority:
        1). Hardcover, dustwrapper.
        2). Wrappers.
    No statement of first edition.

THE DAY THE AUDIENCE WALKED OUT ON ME, AND WHY. (Kent, Ohio: Kent State
University Libraries, 1971).
Broadside.
500 copies.
NOTE: Laid in portfolio entitled *Six Poems/Seven Prints*, which is also *Occasional
Papers #6*.

THE ALTARS IN THE STREET. (Brockport, N.Y.: Department of English, State University
College, 1972).
Wrappers.
NOTE: Cover title is *Writer's Forum*.

FOOTPRINTS. (New York): New Directions (1972).
Two issues, no priority:
1). Hardcover, dustwrapper.
2). Wrappers.
No statement of first edition.

CONVERSATION IN MOSCOW. (Cambridge, Mass.): Hovey St. Press, 1973.
Wrappers, no priority:
1). 800 copies.
2). 200 copies, numbered, signed by the author.

APRIL IN OHIO. (Austin: Cold Mountain Press, 1973).
Postcard.

THE POET IN THE WORLD. (New York): New Directions (1973).
Two issues, no priority:
1). Hardcover, dustwrapper.
2). Wrappers.
No statement of first edition.

THERE IS AN ECHO YET, IT IS SAID. (New York: UNICEF, ca. 1973).
Wrappers.

A NOTE ON THE DEDICATION. (Port Townsend, Wash.: Copper Canyon Press, 1974).
Broadside.
100 copies.
NOTE: Laid in box entitled *Copperhead: A Giftbox for Kenneth Rexroth*.

VOYAGE. (Port Townsend, Wash.): Copper Canyon Press, 1974.
Broadside.
100 copies.
Copperhead Broadside 1.
NOTE: Laid in box entitled *Copperhead: A Giftbox for Kenneth Rexroth*.

THE FREEING OF THE DUST. (New York): New Directions (1975).
    Two issues, no priority:
        1). Hardcover, dustwrapper.
        2). Wrappers.
    No statement of first edition.

Translations.

Jules Supervielle.
SELECTED WRITINGS. (New York): New Directions (1967).
        Wrappers.
        No statement of first edition.
        NOTE: Translated with Kenneth Rexroth, James Kirkup, and Enid McLeod.

IN PRAISE OF KRISHNA: SONGS FROM THE BENGALI. Garden City, N.Y.:
        Doubleday, 1967.
        Wrappers.
        "First Edition"
        Illustrated by Anju Chaudhuri.
        NOTE: Translated with Edward C. Dimock.

Guillevic.
SELECTED POEMS. (New York): New Directions (1969).
        Two issues, no priority:
                1).Hardcover, dustwrapper.
                2). Wrappers.
        No statement of first edition.

Ron Loewinsohn

WATERMELONS. New York: Totem Press (1959).
   Wrappers.
   1000 copies.

THE PIECES OF WATERMELON. (San Francisco: Wallace Berman, 1959).
   Broadside.
   NOTE: Laid in portfolio entitled *Semina 4*.

THE WORLD OF THE LIE. San Francisco: Change Press (1963).
   Wrappers.

THE MENDACITY OF SCULPTURE. (San Francisco: San Francisco Arts Festival
   Commission, 1963).
   Broadside.
   300 copies, signed by the author.
   NOTE: Laid in portfolio entitled *San Francisco Arts Festival: A Poetry Folio: 1963*.

AGAINST THE SILENCES TO COME. San Francisco: Four Seasons Foundation, 1965.
   Wrappers, no priority:
       1). 1000 copies.
       2). 26 copies, lettered, signed by the author.
   Writing 4.

MY GREEN STREETCAR. (San Francisco: Don Carpenter, 1966).
   Broadside.
   125 copies.

3 BACKYARD DRAMAS, WITH MAMAS. (Santa Barbara, Calif.): Unicorn Press (1967).
   Wrappers, no priority:
       1). Trade edition, priority as listed:
           a). 5 copies, with "It has nothing to do with lakes" on page 3, line 3 and
           "cliffs hungs" on page 3, line 14.
           b). 95 copies, as a) but without "cliffs hungs".
           c). 270 copies, with "It has nothing to do with lakes" on page 3, line 5.
       2). 30 copies, numbered, signed by the author; all of the first state of the trade
           edition.

L'AUTRE. (Los Angeles): Black Sparrow Press, 1967.
    Two issues, priority as listed:
        1). Wrappers, priority as listed:
            a). 15 copies (approximately) have spine lettering with "Black Sparrow"
                equaling 1 7/16" and space between author's name and publisher's
                name equaling 1 3/16".
            b). 485 copies (approximately) have the above measurements 1/16" larger.
        2). Hardcover, no priority:
            a). 26 copies, lettered, signed by the author.
            b). 4 special copies, for the publisher, author, printer and binder.

LYING TOGETHER: TURNING THE HEAD & SHIFTING THE WEIGHT: THE PRODUCE
DISTRICT, & OTHER PLACES: MOVING —A SPRING POEM. (Los Angeles:
Black Sparrow Press, 1967).
    Wrappers, no priority:
        1). 122 copies, numbered, signed by the author; priority as listed:
            a). Numbers 1-113 have no errors; title in five lines.
            b). Numbers 114-122 have author's name misspelled; title in four lines.
        2). 3 copies, lettered, signed by the author.
        3). 4 special copies, for the publisher, author, printer and binder.

PAEAN. San Francisco: Cranium Press, 1967.
    Broadside.

THE SEA, AROUND US. Los Angeles: Black Sparrow Press, 1968.
    Two issues, no priority:
        1). Hardcover, no priority:
            a). 50 copies, numbered, signed by the author.
            b). 10 copies, signed by the author, labeled "Presentation Copy."
            c). 4 special copies, for the publisher, author, printer and binder.
        2). Wrappers.
        250 copies, numbered, signed by the author.

THE STEP. Los Angeles: Black Sparrow Press (1968).
    Two issues, no priority:
        1). Hardcover, no priority:
            a). 125 copies, numbered, signed by the author.
            b). Unknown number of copies, signed by the author, labeled
                "Presentation Copy."
            c). 4 special copies, for the publisher, author, printer and binder.
        2). Wrappers.
        750 copies.

A PLAY AND TWO POEMS. Los Angeles: Black Sparrow Press, 1968.
    Wrappers, no priority:
        1). 300 copies (according to the publisher, only 224 were actually published).
        2). 100 copies, numbered, signed by the authors.
    NOTE: With Robert Kelly and Diane Wakoski.

SONG. (Boston: Impressions Workshop, 1968).
    Broadside.

MEAT AIR. New York: Harcourt, Brace & World (1970).
    Two issues, no priority:
        1). Hardcover, dustwrapper.
        2). Wrappers.
    No statement of first edition.

COME IN, SIT DOWN. (Privately published) 1970.
    Broadside.

THE LEAVES. Los Angeles: Black Sparrow Press, 1973.
    Two issues, no priority:
        1). Hardcover, acetate dustwrapper; no priority:
            a). 26 copies, lettered, signed by the author.
            b). 4 special copies, for the publisher, author, printer and binder.
        2). Wrappers, no priority:
            a). 1000 copies.
            b). 200 copies, numbered, signed by the author.
    NOTE: An advertising flyer, printing one poem from the book, preceded publication.

EIGHT FAIRY TALES. (Los Angeles): Black Sparrow Press, 1975.
    Wrappers.
    Sparrow 38.

Norman Mailer

THE FOUNDATION. (Privately published, ca. 1947).
   Wrappers.

THE NAKED AND THE DEAD. New York: Rinehart (1948).
   Hardcover, dustwrapper.
   "R" within circle on copyright page.
   NOTE: Review copies in printed wrappers preceded publication.

BARBARY SHORE. New York: Rinehart (1951).
   Hardcover, dustwrapper; no known priority:
      1). Red and black dustwrapper.
      2). Green and black dustwrapper.
   "R" within circle on copyright page.
   NOTE: Review copies in printed wrappers, in either state of the dustwrapper, preceded
      publication.

THE DEER PARK. New York: Putnam (1955).
   Hardcover, no known priority:
      1). Dustwrapper with author's name in orange, title in green.
      2). Dustwrapper with author's name in green, title in orange.
   No statement of first edition.
   NOTE: Uncorrected proofs in printed wrappers preceded publication.

THE WHITE NEGRO. (San Francisco): City Lights Books (1957).
   Wrappers.
   35¢ printed on front cover.

ADVERTISEMENTS FOR MYSELF. New York: Putnam (1959).
   Hardcover, dustwrapper; presumed priority:
      1). Black and red cloth over boards.
      2). Pale green paper over boards.
   No statement of first edition.

DEATHS FOR THE LADIES. New York: Putnam (1962).
    Two issues, no priority:
        1). Hardcover, dustwrapper.
        2). Wrappers.
    No statement of first edition.
    ALSO: (New York): New American Library (1971).
        Wrappers.
        "FIRST PRINTING, DECEMBER 1971"
        NOTE: New introduction by the author.

THE PRESIDENTIAL PAPERS. New York: Putnam (1963).
    Hardcover, dustwrapper.
    No statement of first edition.
    NOTE: Issued with a wrap-around band which contains a statement by the author.
    ALSO: New York: Bantam Books (1964).*
        Wrappers.
        NOTE: New preface by the author.

GARGOYLE, GUIGNOL, FALSE CLOSET. (Palma de Mallorca: Anthony Kerrigan, 1964).
    Wrappers.
    100 copies.

AN AMERICAN DREAM. New York: Dial Press, 1965.
    Hardcover, dustwrapper.
    No statement of first edition.
    NOTE: 1). A chapter was issued in advance of publication in *Dial Souvenir Sampler*,
        New York: Dial Press, 1964; hardcover.
        2). Uncorrected proofs in printed wrappers, ringbound, preceded publication.

CANNIBALS AND CHRISTIANS. New York: Dial Press, 1966.
    Hardcover, dustwrapper.
    No statement of first edition.
    NOTE: Review copies, consisting of gathered signatures laid into the trade
        dustwrapper and held together by rivets, preceded publication.

THE DEER PARK, A PLAY. Priority as listed:
    1). (New York): Dell (1967).*
        Wrappers.
    2). New York: Dial Press, 1967.
        Hardcover, dustwrapper.
        "First printing, 1967"

THE BULLFIGHT. (New York): CBS Legacy Collection (1967).
    Hardcover, dustwrapper.
    No statement of first edition.

WHY ARE WE IN VIETNAM? New York: Putnam (1967).
    Hardcover, dustwrapper.
    "First Impression"

THE SHORT FICTION OF NORMAN MAILER. (New York): Dell (1967).
    Wrappers.
    "First Dell Printing — May, 1967"

THE IDOL AND THE OCTOPUS. (New York): Dell (1968).
    Wrappers.
    "First Printing — June 1968"

MIAMI AND THE SIEGE OF CHICAGO. Priority as listed:
    1). (New York): New American Library (1968).
        Wrappers.
        "First Printing, October, 1968"
    2). New York: World (1968).
        Hardcover, dustwrapper.
        "First Printing October, 1968"

THE ARMIES OF THE NIGHT. (New York): New American Library (1968).
    Two issues, priority as listed:
        1). Wrappers.
        2). Hardcover, dustwrapper.
    "First Printing"
    NOTE: Uncorrected proofs in printed wrappers, ringbound, entitled *Armies of the
        Dead*, preceded publication.

THE PROCEDURE WHEREBY NEW YORK CITY COULD BECOME A STATE.
    (New York: Privately published, 1969).
    Mimeographed sheets, stapled.
    Position Paper No. 4.
    NOTE: Presumably this campaign document was at least partially authored by Mailer,
        though no authorship is noted; there may have been three preceding Position
        Papers as well.

MAILER-BRESLIN AND THE 51st STATE. (New York: Privately published, 1969).
    Mechanically reproduced sheets.
    NOTE: A campaign document.

NATIONAL BOOK AWARD ACCEPTANCE SPEECH. (New York: Privately published,
    1969).*
    Mimeographed sheet.

OF A FIRE ON THE MOON. Boston: Little, Brown (1970).
>Hardcover, dustwrapper; no priority:
>>1). Trade edition.
>>2). 500 copies, signed by the author on sheet tipped in before the title page.
>"FIRST EDITION"
>NOTE: 1). Uncorrected proofs in printed wrappers preceded publication.
>>2). A Formosan piracy of the first printing, in reduced format, has been examined.

KING OF THE HILL. (New York): New American Library (1971).
>Wrappers.
>"First Printing, April, 1971"

MAIDSTONE. (New York): New American Library (1971).
>Wrappers.
>"FIRST PRINTING, OCTOBER, 1971"

THE PRISONER OF SEX. Boston: Little, Brown (1971).
>Hardcover, dustwrapper.
>"FIRST EDITION"
>NOTE: 1). Uncorrected proofs in printed wrappers preceded publication.
>>2). A Formosan piracy of the first edition, in reduced format, has been examined.

THE LONG PATROL. New York: World Publishing (1971).
>Hardcover, dustwrapper.
>"First printing—1971"

EXISTENTIAL ERRANDS. Boston: Little, Brown (1972).
>Hardcover, dustwrapper.
>"FIRST EDITION"

ST. GEORGE AND THE GODFATHER. (New York): New American Library (1972).
>Wrappers.
>"First Printing, September, 1972"

MARILYN. (New York: Grosset & Dunlap, 1973).
>Hardcover, dustwrapper; no priority:
>>1). Trade edition.
>>2). Unknown number of copies, numbered, signed by the author.
>"First printing"
>NOTE: A selection from the book in wrappers preceded publication.
>ALSO: New York: Grosset & Dunlap, 1973.*
>>Wrappers.
>NOTE: Expanded edition.

THE 1974 MARILYN MONROE DATEBOOK. Los Angeles: Alskog (1973).*
>Wrappers, no known priority:
>>1). Ringbound on the side.
>>2). Ringbound on the top.

THE FAITH OF GRAFFITI. (New York: Praeger, 1974).
    Hardcover, dustwrapper; no priority:
        1). Trade edition.
        2). 350 copies, numbered, signed by the author and photographers.
    "First Printing" on final recto.
    Photographs by Mervyn Kurlansky and Jon Naar.
    NOTE: 1). An advertising brochure, consisting of an illustrated, glossy-paged offprint
        from *Esquire* (May 1974), preceded publication.
        2). Retitled *Watching My Name Go By* for British publication: London:
        Matthews Miller Dunbar (1974), wrappers or hardcover, dustwrapper.

THE FIGHT. Boston: Little, Brown (1975).
    Hardcover, dustwrapper.
    "FIRST EDITION"

Bernard Malamud

THE NATURAL. New York: Harcourt, Brace & Co. (1952).
    Hardcover, dustwrapper; priority as listed:
        1). Priority unknown:
            a). Red cloth.
            b). Blue cloth.
        2). Gray cloth.
    "first edition"
    ALSO: London: Eyre & Spottiswoode, 1963.
        Hardcover, dustwrapper.
        No statement of first edition.
        NOTE: Includes, as an appendix, the author's explanation of baseball.

THE ASSISTANT. New York: Farrar, Straus & Cudahy (1957).
    Hardcover, dustwrapper; priority as listed:
        1). Reviews of *The Natural* on back panel of dustwrapper.
        2). Reviews of *The Assistant* on back panel of dustwrapper.
    "First Printing, 1957"

THE MAGIC BARREL. No known priority:
        1). New York: Farrar, Straus & Cudahy (1958).
        Hardcover, dustwrapper.
        "FIRST PRINTING, 1958"
        NOTE: A National Book Award sticker was later placed on the front of the
            dustwrapper.
        2). Philadelphia: Jewish Publication Society of America (1958).
        Hardcover, dustwrapper.
        "FIRST PRINTING, 1958"

NATIONAL BOOK AWARD ACCEPTANCE SPEECH. (New York: Privately published)
    1959.
    Mimeographed sheet.

A NEW LIFE. New York: Farrar, Straus & Cudahy (1961).
    Hardcover, dustwrapper.
    "FIRST PRINTING, 1961"
    NOTE: Sewn signatures, laid in finished dustwrapper, preceded publication.

IDIOTS FIRST. New York: Farrar, Straus & Co. (1963).
    Hardcover, dustwrapper.
    "FIRST PRINTING, 1963"

THE FIXER. New York: Farrar, Straus & Giroux (1966).
    Hardcover, dustwrapper.
    "First printing, 1966"

A MALAMUD READER. New York: Farrar, Straus & Giroux (1967).
    Hardcover, dustwrapper.
    No statement of first edition.

PICTURES OF FIDELMAN. New York: Farrar, Straus & Giroux (1969).
    Hardcover, dustwrapper.
    "First printing, 1969"

THE TENANTS. New York: Farrar, Straus & Giroux (1971).
    Hardcover, dustwrapper; no priority:
        1). Trade edition.
        2). 250 copies (approximately), signed by the author on sheet tipped in before
           the title page.
    "First printing, 1971"
    NOTE: Uncorrected proofs in printed wrappers preceded publication.

REMBRANDT'S HAT. New York: Farrar, Straus & Giroux (1973).
    Hardcover, dustwrapper.
    "First printing, 1973"
    NOTE: Uncorrected proofs in printed wrappers preceded publication.

Michael McClure

PASSAGE. Big Sur, Calif.: Jonathan Williams, 1956.
    Wrappers.
    200 copies.
    Jargon 20.

PEYOTE POEM. (San Francisco: Wallace Berman, 1958).
    Broadside.
    200 copies.
    NOTE: Tipped into printed wrappers, entitled *Semina 3.*

FOR ARTAUD. (New York: Totem Press, 1959).
    Wrappers.
    750 copies.
    Totem Blue Plate #2.

WE'RE IN THE MIDDLE OF A DEEP CLOUD. (San Francisco: Wallace Berman, 1959).
    Broadside.
    NOTE: Laid into portfolio entitled *Semina 4.*

HYMNS TO ST. GERYON. San Francisco: Auerhahn Press, 1959.
    Wrappers.

OH CHRIST GOD LOVE CRY OF LOVE STIFLED FURRED. (San Francisco): Auerhahn
    Press (1959).
    Wrappers.
    NOTE: 1). Cover title of only *Auerhahn Press* for this folded broadside, which is also
            encountered separately.
        2). With John Wieners, Philip Lamantia and Philip Whalen.
        3). Commonly referred to by Wieners' title, *Bag Dad By the Bay.*

!THE FEAST!. (San Francisco: Batman Gallery, 1960).
    Mimeographed sheets.
    NOTE: A playscript from which copies were made some years later (ca. 1966).

WE ARE IMPERVIOUS AS THE SKIN OF OUR DREAMS. (Los Angeles: Wallace Berman, 1960).
Broadside.
NOTE : Laid in portfolio entitled *Semina 5.*

FUCK DEATH. (San Francisco: Privately published, ca. 1960).
Broadside card.

THE NEW BOOK/THE BOOK OF TORTURE. New York: Grove Press (1961).
Wrappers.
"First Printing"

PATERSON SOCIETY. Cambridge, Mass.: Paterson Society (ca. 1961).*
Broadside.

PILLOW. New York: (New York Poets Theatre, ca. 1961).
Mechanically reproduced sheets.

DARK BROWN. San Francisco: Auerhahn Press, 1961.
Two issues, no priority:
1). Hardcover.
25 copies, signed by the author.
2). Wrappers.
725 copies.

MEAT SCIENCE ESSAYS. (San Francisco): City Lights Books (1963).
Wrappers.
$1.35 on cover.
ALSO: (London): Sigma Communications (ca. 1963).
Mechanically reproduced sheets.
Sigma Portfolio 9.
NOTE : Reprints an essay from *Meat Science Essays,* entitled *Revolt.*
ALSO: (San Francisco): City Lights Books (1966).*
Wrappers.
Second printing so indicated.
NOTE : Enlarged edition.

GRAHHR SHEET. (San Francisco: Auerhahn Press, 1963).*
Broadside.

GRAHHR APRIL GRHARRR APRIL. (Buffalo, N.Y.: Gallery Upstairs Press, ca. 1963).
Broadside.

TWO FOR BRUCE CONNER. (Berkeley): Oyez, 1964.
    Broadside.
    500 copies.
    Oyez 1.
    NOTE : 27 copies, numbered, signed by the author in 1964 but published in 1965
       in portfolio entitled *Poems in Broadside. Oyez. First Series.*

POETRY IS A MUSCULAR PRINCIPLE. (Los Angeles: Wallace Berman, 1964).
    Broadside.

BLUE-BLACK. (San Francisco: Privately published, 1964).*
    Broadside.

GHOST TANTRAS. San Francisco: (Privately published, 1964).
    Two issues, no priority:
        1). Hardcover, dustwrapper.
          20 copies, numbered, signed by the author on a tipped-in sheet.
        2). Wrappers.
          1480 copies.
    NOTE : A copy of *Blue-Black* was laid in the hardcover issue.

THE BLOSSOM; OR BILLY THE KID. (New York: American Theatre For Poets, 1964).
    Wrappers.
    NOTE : With *Pour En Finir avec le Jugement de Dieu* by Antonin Artaud.
    ALSO : (Milwaukee: Great Lakes Books, 1967).
        Wrappers, no priority:
          1). 500 copies, numbered.
          2). 10 copies, numbered, signed by the author.
          3). 15 copies, lettered, with a poem signed by the author.

DOUBLE MIRROR! VAHROOOOOOOHR!. (Los Angeles: Wallace Berman, 1964).
    Broadside.
    NOTE : Laid in portfolio entitled *Semina 9.*

LOVE LION, LIONESS. (Berkeley: Oyez, 1964).
    Broadside (approximately 22" x 28"), no priority:
        1). 300 copies.
        2). 5 copies, numbered, signed by the author.
    NOTE : 70 copies in identical format but much reduced in size were published later.

SPACE GRACE. (San Francisco: Auerhahn Press, 1964).*
    Broadside.

13 MAD SONNETS. Milan: (Privately published, 1965).
    Wrappers, dustwrapper; no priority:
        1). 299 copies, numbered.
        2). 16 copies, unnumbered, for the use of the author.

THE BEARD. (Berkeley: Oyez, 1965).
>   Wrappers.
>   330 copies.
>   ALSO: (San Francisco):Coyote, 1967.
>>   Wrappers, no priority:
>>>   1). 4960 copies.
>>>   2). 40 copies, signed by the author, special binding.
>>   "First Printing March 1967"

POISONED WHEAT. San Francisco: (Oyez), 1965.
>   Two issues, no priority:
>>   1). Hardcover, no priority:
>>>   a). 21 copies, lettered in Greek, signed by the author, white endpapers.
>>>   b). 3 copies, lettered in Greek, signed by the author, blue endpapers.
>>   2). Wrappers.
>>>   576 copies.

UNTO CAESAR. (San Francisco: Dave Haselwood, 1965).
>   Wrappers.
>   100 copies (reportedly, only 80 copies were actually published).
>   NOTE: Anonymous.

(UNTITLED). (San Francisco: Privately published, ca. 1966).*
>   Broadside.
>   3 copies, signed by the author and illustrator.
>   Illustrated by Bruce Conner.
>   NOTE: Both the poem and illustration are engraved.

DREAM TABLE. San Francisco: Dave Haselwood, 1966.
>   Set of 30 cards, no priority:
>>   1). Trade edition.
>>   2). 20 copies, signed by the author.

(MANDALAS). San Francisco: Dave Haselwood, 1966.
>   Wrappers.
>   NOTE: 1). With Bruce Conner.
>>   2). Untitled, this work is also known as *Black Dot* and *Mantras and Prayers*.

LOVE LION BOOK. San Francisco: Four Seasons Foundation, 1966.
>   Two issues, no priority:
>>   1). Hardcover.
>>>   40 copies, numbered, signed by the author.
>>   2). Wrappers.
>>>   960 copies.
>   Writing 11.

LOBE KEY STILLED LIONMAN LACED WINGED APRIL RAPHAEL DANCE WIRY.
    (San Francisco: Privately published, 1966).
    25 cards, in envelope.
    NOTE: With Bruce Conner.

WAR IS DECOR IN MY CAVERN CAVE. (San Francisco): Communication Company
    (ca. 1967).
    Broadside.

FREEWHEELIN FRANK, SECRETARY OF THE ANGELS. New York: Grove Press (1967).
    Hardcover, dustwrapper.
    "First Printing"
    NOTE: Ostensibly a collaboration, the writing is almost exclusively McClure's.

HAIL THEE WHO PLAY. Los Angeles: Black Sparrow Press, 1968.
    Two issues, no priority:
        1). Hardcover.
          75 copies, with an original drawing by the author.
        2). Wrappers.
          250 copies, numbered, signed by the author (according to the publisher,
          only 233 were actually published).
    ALSO: Berkeley: Sand Dollar, 1974.
        Wrappers, no priority:
          1). Red wrappers.
          600 copies.
          2). Blue wrappers.
          100 copies.
    NOTE: Revised edition.

LITTLE ODES, JAN-MARCH 1961. (New York: Poets Press, 1968).
    Wrappers, no priority:
        1). 150 copies, numbered, signed by the author.
        2). 12 copies, starred, for the use of the author.

THE SERMONS OF JEAN HARLOW & THE CURSES OF BILLY THE KID. San Francisco:
    Four Seasons Foundation/Dave Haselwood Books, 1968.
    Two issues, priority as listed:
        1). Wrappers.
          1200 copies.
        2). Hardcover.
          50 copies, numbered, signed by the author.
    Writing 18.
    NOTE: The wrappers issue preceded the hardcover issue by approximately two years.

MUSCLED APPLE SWIFT. (Topanga, Calif.: Love Press, 1968).
    Wrappers, no priority:
        1). 87 copies.
        2). 63 copies, numbered, signed by the author.

CHILDHOOD MEMORIES ARE LIKE THE SMALLNESS. (London): Cape Goliard Press, 1968.
> Broadside.

THE SURGE. (Buffalo, N.Y.): Frontier Press, 1969.
> Wrappers.

THE SHELL. London: Cape Goliard Press (1969).
> Scroll in tube, no priority:
> > 1). 250 copies, numbered.
> > 2). 50 copies, numbered, signed by the author.

PLANE POMES. New York: Phoenix Bookshop, 1969.
> Wrappers, no priority:
> > 1). 100 copies, numbered, signed by the author.
> > 2). 26 copies, lettered, signed by the author.

LION FIGHT. (New York: Pierrepont Press, 1969).
> Cards in silk bag, boxed; no priority:
> > 1). 300 copies, numbered, signed by the author.
> > 2). 26 copies, lettered, signed by the author.
> > 3). 4 copies, hors commerce, signed by the author.

LITTLE ODES & THE RAPTORS. Los Angeles: Black Sparrow Press, 1969.
> Two issues, no priority:
> > 1). Hardcover, no priority:
> > > a). Acetate dustwrapper.
> > > > 200 copies, numbered, signed by the author.
> > > b). No dustwrapper.
> > > > 26 copies, lettered, signed, with an original drawing by the author.
> > > c). 4 special copies, for the publisher, author, printer and binder.
> > 2). Wrappers.
> > > 1000 copies.

TO JAMES B. RECTOR. (San Francisco: Privately published, 1969).
> Broadside, no priority:
> > 1). Trade edition.
> > 2). 30 copies, numbered, signed by the author.

LIBERATION. (Oakland: Mills College Tape Music Center, 1969).
> Broadside.
> NOTE: Originally laid in bag labeled *Free,* with eight other broadsides.

THE CHERUB. (Berkeley: Privately published) 1969.*
> Broadside.

THE CHERUB. Los Angeles: Black Sparrow Press, 1970.
  Hardcover, acetate dustwrapper; no priority:
      1). 250 copies, numbered, signed by the author.
      2). 26 copies, lettered, signed, with an original drawing by the author.
      3). 4 special copies, for the publisher, author, printer and binder.

THE MAD CUB. New York: Bantam Books (1970).
  Wrappers.
  No statement of first edition.

STAR. New York: Grove Press (1970).
  Two issues, no priority:
      1). Hardcover, dustwrapper.
      2). Wrappers.
  "First Printing"

WE. (San Francisco: Privately published, ca. 1970).
  Mechanically reproduced sheets.

THE ADEPT. New York: Delacorte Press (1971).
  Hardcover, dustwrapper.
  "First Printing"
  NOTE: Uncorrected proofs in spiral-bound wrappers preceded publication.

CROSS SECTION. (Lawrence, Kan.: Cottonwood) 1971.
  Broadside.

ESSAY ON THE MEDIA. (San Francisco: Privately published, ca. 1971).
  Broadside.

GARGOYLE CARTOONS.
  Two issues, no priority:
      1). New York: Delacorte Press (1971).
        Hardcover, dustwrapper.
        "First Printing"
      2). (New York: Dell, 1971).
        Wrappers.
        "First Delta printing—April, 1971"

THE MAMMALS. San Francisco: Cranium Press, 1972.
  Wrappers.

TRIP FOR JOANNA. (San Francisco: Privately published) 1972.
  Broadside.

A SPIRIT OF MT. TAMALPAIS. (San Francisco: Book People, 1972).
  Broadside.

99 THESES. Lawrence, Kan.: Tansy/Wakarusa Press, 1972.
    Broadside.

WOLF NET. (San Francisco: Privately published, ca. 1972).
    Wrappers, spiral-bound.
    20 copies (approximately).
    ALSO: WOLF NET PART ONE. London: Bonefold Imprint (1973).
        Wrappers.
        500 copies.

GORF AND THE BLIND DYKE. (San Francisco: Privately published, ca. 1972).
    Wrappers, ring-bound.
    20 copies, numbered, signed by the author.

KOSMOS. (San Francisco: Privately published, ca. 1972).
    Wrappers.

TRANSFIGURATION. Cambridge, Mass.: Pomegranate Press, 1973.
    Broadside, no priority:
        1). 150 copies, numbered.
        2). 100 copies, numbered, signed by the author and illustrator.
    Illustrated by Karyl Klopp.

GEORGE HERMS: SELECTED WORKS 1960-1973. Davis, Calif.: University of California
    Memorial Union Art Gallery, 1973.
    Wrappers.
    NOTE: With Robert Duncan.

SOLSTICE BLOSSOM. (Berkeley): Arif Press, 1973.
    Two issues, no priority:
        1). 100 copies, signed by the author.
        2). 30 copies, numbered, signed by the author and illustrator, with an original
            watercolor by the illustrator.
    Illustrated by Wesley Tanner.

91 WORDS FOR JOANNA. (Berkeley): Sand Dollar (1973).
    Broadside.

THE BOOK OF JOANNA. Berkeley: Sand Dollar, 1973.
    Wrappers, no priority:
        1). 350 copies.
        2). 50 copies, numbered, signed by the author.
    Sand Dollar 9.

IS THE INSTANT SO COMPLEX? Berkeley: Arif Press, 1973.
>Broadside.
>50 copies, signed by the author.
>NOTE: There were an unknown number of copies unsigned.

RARE ANGEL (WRIT WITH RAVEN'S BLOOD). (San Francisco: Privately published, 1973).
>Wrappers, spiral-bound.
>20 copies (approximately).
>ALSO: Los Angeles: Black Sparrow Press, 1974.
>>Hardcover, acetate dustwrapper; no priority:
>>>1). 200 copies, numbered, signed by the author.
>>>2). 26 copies, lettered, signed, with an original drawing by the author.
>>>3). 4 copies, numbered, signed by the author, for the use of the author.

A FIST-FULL (1956-1957). (Los Angeles): Black Sparrow Press, 1974.
>Wrappers.
>Sparrow 16.

FLEAS 189-195. (New York): Aloe Editions, 1974.
>Wrappers, no priority:
>>1). 124 copies, numbered, signed by the author.
>>2). 26 copies, lettered, signed by the author.

SEPTEMBER BLACKBERRIES. (San Francisco: Privately published, ca. 1974).
>Wrappers, spiral-bound.
>20 copies (approximately).
>ALSO: (New York): New Directions (1974).
>>Two issues, no priority:
>>>1). Hardcover, dustwrapper.
>>>2). Wrappers.
>>No statement of first edition.

THE DERBY. (San Francisco: Privately published, 1974).
>Wrappers, spiral-bound.
>20 copies (approximately), numbered, signed by the author.
>NOTE: There were an unknown number of unsigned copies.

MIND/BODY/SPLIT. (Oakland): Archer Press (1974).
>Broadside.
>20 copies, numbered, signed by the author and illustrator.
>Illustrated by Charles Gill.

ORGANISM. Canton, N.Y.: Institute of Further Studies (1974).
>Wrappers.
>Curriculum of the Soul #24.

FINALLY. (Brockport, N.Y.: Department of English, State University College, 1975).
    Wrappers.
    NOTE: Cover title is *Writer's Forum.*

FLEA 100. (New York: Frank Hallman, 1975).
    Wrappers.
    150 copies.

TWO PLAYS. (San Francisco: Privately published, 1975).
    Wrappers.
    20 copies, numbered, signed by the author.

JAGUAR SKIES. (New York): New Directions (1975).
        Two issues, no priority:
                1). Hardcover, dustwrapper.
                2). Wrappers.
        No statement of first edition.

MAN OF MODERATION. (New York): Frank Hallman, 1975.
        Two issues, priority as listed:
                1). Wrappers, dustwrapper.
                    400 copies.
                2). Hardcover.
                    100 copies, numbered, signed by the author.

Larry McMurtry

HORSEMAN, PASS BY. New York: Harper & Brothers (1961).
    Hardcover, dustwrapper.
    "FIRST EDITION"

TEXAS INSTITUTE OF LETTERS AWARDS DINNER. (Dallas: Texas Institute of Letters, 1962).
    Ditto sheets.
    NOTE: The text of the author's speech upon receiving the award.

LEAVING CHEYENNE. New York: Harper & Row (1963).
    Hardcover, dustwrapper.
    "FIRST EDITION"

DAUGHTER OF THE TEJAS. Greenwich, Conn.: New York Graphic Society Publishers (1965).
    Hardcover, dustwrapper.
    "First edition"
    NOTE: Ghostwritten for Ophelia Ray.

THE LAST PICTURE SHOW. New York: Dial Press, 1966.
    Hardcover, dustwrapper.
    "First Printing"
    NOTE: 1). Reportedly, there were some copies specially bound for presentation.
           2). Review copies, spiral-bound in the trade dustwrapper, preceded publication.
           3). The author assisted in the preparation of the screenplay for the subsequent film of the same title. Hollywood: BPS Productions/Saticoy Productions (1970). Wrappers.

IN A NARROW GRAVE. Austin: Encino Press, 1968.
    Hardcover, dustwrapper.
    "Skycrappers" (instead of "skyscrapers") on page 105.
    NOTE: This printing was almost entirely destroyed due to errors in the text, the above example of which is determinative.
    ALSO: Austin: Encino Press, 1968.
        Hardcover, no priority:
           1). Trade edition, dustwrapper.
           2). 250 copies, numbered, signed by the author, boxed.
    No boldface letter on copyright page (the second printing has a boldface '**B**').

MOVING ON. New York: Simon & Schuster (1970).
    Hardcover, dustwrapper.
    "FIRST PRINTING"

ALL MY FRIENDS ARE GOING TO BE STRANGERS. New York: Simon & Schuster (1972).
    Hardcover, dustwrapper.
    "First printing"
    NOTE: Uncorrected proofs in printed wrappers preceded publication.

TEXAS IS RICH. (Austin): Texas Library Association (1973).
    Broadside.

IT'S ALWAYS WE RAMBLED. New York: Frank Hallman, 1974.
    Hardcover.
    300 copies, numbered, signed by the author.

TERMS OF ENDEARMENT. New York: Simon & Schuster (1975).
    Hardcover, dustwrapper.
    "1 2 3 4 5 6 7 8 9 10" on copyright page.

David Meltzer

AN UNPUBLISHED LETTER TO SOME LOST RELATIVES. (Los Angeles:
   Wallace Berman, ca. 1956).
   Broadside.
   150 copies.
   NOTE: Laid in portfolio entitled *Semina 1*.

POEMS. (San Francisco: Donald and Alice Schenker, 1957).
      Two issues, no priority:
         1). Hardcover, no priority:
            a). 25 copies, numbered, signed by the authors.
            b). 5 copies, numbered, signed and stained by the blood of the authors.
         2). Wrappers.
            470 copies.
   NOTE: 1). With *Poetry* by Donald Schenker.
         2). 25 copies (approximately) of *Poems* were separately bound in wrappers.

RAGAS. (San Francisco): Discovery Books (1959).
   Wrappers.
   1500 copies (approximately).

TWO POEMS FOR MATTHEW JOSEPHSON LOEWINSOHN, AGE: 4 MONTHS, 9 DAYS
   New Haven, Conn.: Penny Poems, 1959.
   Broadside.
   Penny Poems #35.
   NOTE: With *April* by Fred Cogswell.

THE PROPHET. New Haven, Conn.: Penny Poems, 1959.
   Broadside.
   Penny Poems No. 54.

FROM: THE CLOWN, BOOK II AIR & INTERIM. New Haven, Conn.: Penny Poems, 1959.
   Broadside.
   Penny Poems #69.

MORNING POEM. New Haven, Conn.: Penny Poems, 1959.
   Broadside.
   Penny Poems #83.

TODOS SANTOS. VILLA. (Los Angeles: Wallace Berman, 1960).
   Broadside.
   NOTE: Laid in portfolio entitled *Semina 5.*

THE CLOWN. Larkspur, Calif.: (Wallace Berman) 1960.
   Cards in wrappers.
   335 copies.
   Semina VI.

FROM TWO POEMS TO DO MEDITATION ON. New Haven, Conn.: Penny Poems,
   1961.
   Broadside.
   Penny Poems No. 143.
   NOTE: With *Patricia* by Ron Padgett.

WE ALL HAVE SOMETHING TO SAY TO EACH OTHER. San Francisco: Auerhahn Press,
   1962.
   Wrappers.
   750 copies.

BAZASCOPE MOTHER. (Los Angeles): Drekfesser Press (1964).
   Wrappers, priority as listed:
      1). No photograph credits on the cover.
      2). Photograph credits on the cover.
   250 copies, of which 150 copies (approximately) were supposedly destroyed.

STATION. (San Francisco: San Francisco Arts Festival Commission, 1964).
   Broadside.
   300 copies.
   NOTE: Laid in portfolio entitled *A Poetry Folio 1964.*

THE BLACKEST ROSE. (Berkeley): Oyez, 1964.
   Broadside.
   350 copies.
   Oyez 6.
   NOTE: 27 copies, numbered, signed by the author in 1964 but published in 1965 in
      portfolio entitled *Poems in Broadside. Oyez. First Series.*

THE PROCESS. Berkeley: Oyez, 1965.
   Two issues, no priority:
      1). Hardcover, dustwrapper.
         25 copies, numbered, signed by the author.

2). Wrappers.
475 copies.
NOTE: 5 copies, hardcover, signed by the author, publisher and binder, with drawings by the author, were published in 1967.

OYEZ! (Berkeley): Oyez, 1965.
Wrappers.
250 copies (approximately).

THE DARK CONTINENT. (Berkeley): Oyez, 1967.
Two issues, no priority:
1). Hardcover, no priority:
a). 26 copies, lettered, signed by the author.
b). 5 copies, numbered, signed by the author.
2). Wrappers.
969 copies.

NATURE POEM. (Santa Barbara, Calif.): Unicorn Press, 1967.
Broadside, priority as listed:
1). States 226 copies on front, no priority:
a). 200 copies.
b). 26 copies, signed by the author.
2) States 200 copies on front.

JOURNAL OF THE BIRTH. Berkeley: Oyez (1967).
Wrappers.

ORF. North Hollywood, Calif.: Essex House (1968).
Wrappers.

THE AGENT. North Hollywood, Calif.: Essex House (1968).
Wrappers.

THE AGENCY. North Hollywood, Calif.: Essex House (1968).
Wrappers.

HOW MANY BLOCKS IN THE PILE? North Hollywood, Calif.: Essex House (1968).
Wrappers.

THE BEGINNING OF MACHINERY, THE START OF LANGUAGE. (San Francisco: Maya, 1968).
Wrappers.
250 copies.
NOTE: With *A Love Song for Basho and Pound* by Jack Shoemaker.

ROUND THE POEM BOX. Los Angeles: Black Sparrow Press, 1969.
    Two issues, no priority:
        1). Hardcover, acetate dustwrapper; no priority:
            a). 125 copies, numbered, signed by the author.
            b). 26 copies, lettered, signed, with an original drawing by the author.
            c). 4 special copies, for the publisher, author, printer and binder.
        2). Wrappers.
        300 copies, numbered, signed by the author.

YESOD. London: Trigram Press (1969).
    Two issues, no priority:
        1). Hardcover, no priority:
            a). Trade edition, dustwrapper.
            b). 100 copies, numbered, signed by the author, glassine dustwrapper.
        2). Wrappers.

A POEM FOR MY WIFE. (San Francisco): Maya (1969).
    Broadside, no priority:
        1). Trade edition.
        2). 50 copies, numbered, signed by the author.
    Broadside Two.

LOVELY. North Hollywood, Calif.: Essex House (1969).
    Wrappers.

HEALER. North Hollywood, Calif.: Essex House (1969).
    Wrappers.

THE MARTYR. North Hollywood, Calif.: Essex House (1969).
    Wrappers.

GLUE FACTORY. North Hollywood, Calif.: Essex House (1969).
    Wrappers.

OUT. North Hollywood, Calif.: Essex House (1969).
    Wrappers.

FROM EDEN BOOK. (San Francisco): Maya (1969).
    Wrappers, no priority:
        1). 250 copies.
        2). 50 copies, numbered, signed by the author.
    Maya Quarto Four.

ABULAFIA SONG. (Santa Barbara, Calif.: Unicorn Press, 1969).
    Wrappers, no priority:
        1). Maroon wrappers.
           950 copies.
        2). Orange wrappers.
           50 copies, numbered, signed by the author.

DUSK, MY FRIENDS. BACH. (San Francisco: Maya, 1970).
    Wrappers.
    NOTE: With *Stars* by Jack Shoemaker and *Ahead of the Poem* by Clifford Burke.

BRONX LIL. (Portland, Ore.): Yes! Press, 1970.
    Broadside.
    125 copies.

FOR RAYMOND CHANDLER. (Santa Barbara, Calif.: Unicorn Press) 1970.
    Broadside, no priority:
        1). Trade edition.
        2). 15 copies, numbered, signed by the author.
    Unicorn Broadsheet 5.

STAR. North Hollywood, Calif.: Essex House (1970).
    Wrappers.

ISLA VISTA NOTES. (Santa Barbara, Calif.: Christopher Books, 1970).
    Wrappers.
    1000 copies.

LUNA. Los Angeles: Black Sparrow Press, 1970.
    Two issues, no priority:
        1). Hardcover, acetate dustwrapper; no priority:
           a). 200 copies, numbered, signed by the author.
           b). 26 copies, lettered, signed, with an original drawing by the author, boxed.
           c). 4 special copies, for the publisher, author, printer and binder.
        2). Wrappers.
           1000 copies.

GREENSPEECH. (Goleta, Calif.): Christopher Books, 1970.
    Two issues, no priority:
        1). Hardcover, no priority:
           a). 50 copies, numbered, signed by the author.
           b). Unknown number of copies, hors commerce.
        2). Wrappers.
           950 copies.

32 BEAMS OF LIGHT. (Portland, Ore.): Yes! Press, 1970.
    Broadside.
    100 copies.

KNOTS. Bolinas, Calif.: Tree Books, 1971.
    Wrappers.
    500 copies.

IT'S SIMPLE. (Seattle: Michael Wiater) 1971.
    Broadside, no priority:
        1). Trade edition.
        2). 25 copies (approximately), signed by the author.
    NOTE: This is to be differentiated from the broadside of the same title by
        (San Francisco): Mudra Windrose Series (1971).

ON A LEASH. (San Francisco): Panjandrum Press, 1972.
    Broadside.

BARK. Santa Barbara, Calif.: Capra Press, 1973.
    Two issues, no priority:
        1). Hardcover.
            75 copies, numbered, signed by the author.
        2). Wrappers.
    Yes! Capra Chapbook Series Number Six.

HERO/LIL. Los Angeles: Black Sparrow Press, 1973.
    Two issues, no priority:
        1). Hardcover, acetate dustwrapper, boxed; no priority:
            a). 175 copies, numbered, signed by the author.
            b). 26 copies, lettered, signed by the author.
        2). Wrappers.
            1000 copies.
    NOTE: A flyer, printing two poems from the book, preceded publication.

UNTITLED and FROM THE WORDBOOK. (Allendale, Mich.): East Lansing Arts
    Workshop Press, 1973.
    Broadside.

WHAT DO I KNOW OF JOURNEY. London: Trigram Press, 1973.
    Broadside.
    75 copies, signed by the author and illustrator.
    Illustrated by Pip Benveniste.

TENS. New York: McGraw-Hill (1973).
    Hardcover, dustwrapper.
    "First edition"
    NOTE: Uncorrected proofs in printed wrappers, indicating Herder & Herder as the
        publisher, preceded publication.

FRENCH BROOM. (Berkeley): Oyez, 1973.
    Wrappers.
    250 copies.

THE EYES, THE BLOOD. San Francisco: Mudra, 1973.
    Wrappers.
    500 copies.

IN CELEBRATION OF THE WEDDING OF ALLEN SAY & DEIRDRE MYLES. San Francisco: (Privately published) 1974.
    Wrappers.
    26 copies.

AMULET. Cambridge, Mass.: Pomegranate Press, 1974.
    Broadside, no priority:
        1). 80 copies, numbered.
        2). 100 copies, numbered, signed by the author and illustrator.
    Illustrated by Karyl Klopp.

BLUE RAGS. Berkeley: Oyez, 1974.
    Two issues, no priority:
        1). Hardcover, dustwrapper; no priority:
            a). 250 copies.
            b). 100 copies, numbered, signed by the author.
        2). Wrappers.
            1000 copies.

HARPS. (Berkeley): Oyez, 1975.
    Two issues, no priority:
        1). Hardcover, dustwrapper.
            500 copies.
        2). Wrappers.
            1000 copies.

Translation.

Shiga Naoya.
MORNING GLORIES. (Berkeley): Oyez (1975).
    Wrappers.
    note: Translated with Allen Say.

Josephine Miles

LINES AT INTERSECTION. New York: Macmillan, 1939.
>Hardcover, dustwrapper.
>"FIRST PRINTING"

POEMS ON SEVERAL OCCASIONS. Norfolk, Conn.: New Directions (1941).
>Wrappers.
>No statement of first edition.

WORDSWORTH AND THE VOCABULARY OF EMOTION. Berkeley: University of
California Press, 1942.
>Wrappers.
>No statement of first edition.
>ALSO: New York: Octagon Books, 1965.
>>Hardcover, dustwrapper.
>>No statement of first edition.
>>NOTE: New preface by the author.

PATHETIC FALLACY IN THE NINETEENTH CENTURY. Berkeley: University of
California Press, 1942.
>Wrappers.
>No statement of first edition.
>ALSO: New York: Octagon Books, 1965.
>>Hardcover, dustwrapper.
>>No statement of first edition.
>>NOTE: New preface by the author.

LOCAL MEASURES. New York: Reynal & Hitchcock (1946).
>Hardcover, dustwrapper.
>No statement of first edition.

MAJOR ADJECTIVES IN ENGLISH POETRY. Berkeley: University of California Press,
1946.
>Wrappers.
>No statement of first edition.

THE VOCABULARY OF POETRY. Berkeley: University of California Press, 1946.
Hardcover.
NOTE: Comprises the 1942 publications of *Wordsworth and the Vocabulary of Emotion* and *Pathetic Fallacy in the Nineteenth Century* in addition to *Major Adjectives in English Poetry*, all three bound together.

AFTER THIS, SEA. (San Francisco): Book Club of California, 1947.
Single sheet, folded.
750 copies.

THE PRIMARY LANGUAGE OF POETRY IN THE 1640's. Berkeley: University of California Press, 1948.
Wrappers.
No statement of first edition.
University of California Publications in English, Vol. 19, No. 1.

THE PRIMARY LANGUAGE OF POETRY IN THE 1740's and 1840's. Berkeley: University of California Press, 1950.
Wrappers.
No statement of first edition.
University of California Publications in English, Vol. 19, No. 2.

THE PRIMARY LANGUAGE OF POETRY IN THE 1940's. Berkeley: University of California Press, 1951.
Wrappers.
No statement of first edition.
University of California Publications in English, Vol. 19, No. 3.

THE CONTINUITY OF POETIC LANGUAGE. Berkeley: University of California Press, 1951.
Hardcover, dustwrapper.
No statement of first edition.
ALSO: New York: Octagon Books, 1965.
Hardcover, dustwrapper.
No statement of first edition.
NOTE: New preface by the author.

PREFABRICATIONS. Bloomington, Ind.: Indiana University Press, 1955.
Hardcover, dustwrapper.
No statement of first edition.

ERAS AND MODES IN ENGLISH POETRY. Berkeley: University of California Press, 1957.
Hardcover, dustwrapper.
No statement of first edition.
ALSO: Berkeley: University of California Press, 1964.
Wrappers.
No statement of first edition.
NOTE: Revised edition.

POEMS 1930-1960. Bloomington, Ind. : Indiana University Press, 1960.
    Hardcover, dustwrapper.
    No statement of first edition.

RENAISSANCE, EIGHTEENTH-CENTURY, AND MODERN LANGUAGE IN ENGLISH.
    Berkeley : University of California Press, 1960.
    Wrappers.
    No statement of first edition.

IN IDENTITY. (Berkeley) : Oyez, 1964.
    Broadside.
    350 copies.
    Oyez 3.
    NOTE : 27 copies, numbered, signed by the author in 1964 but published in 1965 in
        portfolio entitled *Poems in Broadside. Oyez. First Series.*

RALPH WALDO EMERSON. Minneapolis, Minn. : University of Minnesota Press (1964).
    Wrappers.
    No statement of first edition.
    University of Minnesota Pamphlets on American Writers #41.

CIVIL POEMS. (Berkeley) : Oyez (1966).
    Wrappers, no priority :
        1). 500 copies.
        2). 40 copies, uncut, for the use of the author.

BENT. (Santa Barbara, Calif. : Unicorn Press, 1967).
    Wrappers, no priority :
        1). 450 copies, brown wrappers.
        2). 26 copies, lettered, signed by the author, orange wrappers.

SAVING THE BAY. San Francisco : White Rabbit / Open Space, 1967.
    Wrappers.

KINDS OF AFFECTION. Middletown, Conn. : Wesleyan University Press (1967).
    Hardcover, dustwrapper.
    "First edition"

STYLE AND PROPORTION. Boston : Little, Brown (1967).
    Hardcover, dustwrapper.
    "FIRST EDITION"

FIELDS OF LEARNING. Berkeley : Oyez, 1968.
    Wrappers.

POETRY AND CHANGE. Berkeley : University of California Press, 1974.
    Hardcover, dustwrapper.
    No statement of first edition.

TO ALL APPEARANCES. (Urbana, Ill.: University of Illinois Press, 1974).
Two issues, no priority:
1). Hardcover, dustwrapper.
2). Wrappers.
No statement of first edition.

Warren Miller

THE SLEEP OF REASON. London: Secker & Warburg, 1956.
    Hardcover, dustwrapper.
    No statement of first edition.

LOVE ME LITTLE. New York: McGraw-Hill (1957).
    Hardcover, dustwrapper.
    No statement of first edition.
    NOTE: Written as "Amanda Vail."

THE BRIGHT YOUNG THINGS. Boston: Little, Brown (1958).
    Hardcover, dustwrapper.
    "FIRST EDITION"
    NOTE: Written as "Amanda Vail."

THE WAY WE LIVE NOW. Boston: Little, Brown (1958).
    Hardcover, dustwrapper.
    "FIRST EDITION"

KING CARLO OF CAPRI. New York: Harcourt, Brace and Company (1958).
    Hardcover, dustwrapper.
    "First Edition"

THE COOL WORLD. Boston: Little, Brown (1959).
    Hardcover, dustwrapper.
    "FIRST EDITION"

PABLO PAINTS A PICTURE. Boston: Little, Brown (1959).
    Hardcover, dustwrapper.
    "FIRST EDITION"

THE GOINGS ON AT THE LITTLE WISHFUL. Boston: Little, Brown (1959).
    Hardcover, dustwrapper.
    "FIRST EDITION"

90 MILES FROM HOME. Boston: Little, Brown (1961).
    Hardcover, dustwrapper.
    "FIRST EDITION"
    NOTE: The British edition is retitled *The Lost Plantation*.

FLUSH TIMES. Boston: Little, Brown (1962).
    Hardcover, dustwrapper.
    "FIRST EDITION"

LOOKING FOR THE GENERAL. New York: McGraw-Hill (1964).
    Hardcover, dustwrapper.
    "FIRST EDITION"

THE SIEGE OF HARLEM. New York: McGraw-Hill (1964).
    Hardcover, dustwrapper.
    "FIRST EDITION"

Wright Morris

MY UNCLE DUDLEY. New York: Harcourt, Brace (1942).
   Hardcover, dustwrapper.
   "first edition"

THE MAN WHO WAS THERE. New York: Scribner's, 1945.
   Hardcover, dustwrapper.
   "A" on copyright page.

THE INHABITANTS. New York: Scribner's, 1946.
   Hardcover, dustwrapper.
   "A" on copyright page.
   ALSO: New York: DaCapo Press, 1972.
      Hardcover, dustwrapper.
      "Second Edition"
      NOTE: New preface by the author.

THE HOME PLACE. New York: Scribner's, 1948.
   Hardcover, dustwrapper.
   "A" on copyright page.

THE WORLD IN THE ATTIC. New York: Scribner's, 1949.
   Hardcover, dustwrapper.
   "A" on copyright page.

MAN AND BOY. New York: Knopf, 1951.
   Hardcover, dustwrapper; priority as listed:
      1). Yellow dustwrapper, stating "Advance Copy."
      2). Blue dustwrapper.
   "FIRST EDITION"

THE WORKS OF LOVE. New York: Knopf, 1952.
   Hardcover, dustwrapper.
   "FIRST EDITION"

THE DEEP SLEEP. New York: Scribner's, 1953.
>   Hardcover, dustwrapper.
>   "A" on copyright page.

THE HUGE SEASON. New York: Viking Press (1954).
>   Hardcover, dustwrapper.
>   No statement of first edition.
>   NOTE: Uncorrected proofs, tied in printed wrappers, preceded publication and contained some text not in the published book.

THE FIELD OF VISION. New York: Harcourt, Brace and Company (1956).
>   Hardcover, dustwrapper; priority as listed:
>>   1). Plain black dustwrapper with blue letters.
>>   2). Pictorial dustwrapper, with yellow background.
>>   3). Pictorial dustwrapper, with orange background.
>>   4). Pictorial dustwrapper, with excerpts from reviews on rear of dustwrapper, instead of quote by J. Aldridge.
>>   5). As 4) with National Book Award seal.
>   "first edition"

LOVE AMONG THE CANNIBALS. New York: Harcourt, Brace and Company (1957).
>   Hardcover, dustwrapper.
>   "first edition"

THE TERRITORY AHEAD. (New York): Harcourt, Brace and Company (1958).
>   Hardcover, dustwrapper.
>   "first edition"

CEREMONY IN LONE TREE. New York: Atheneum, 1960.
>   Hardcover, dustwrapper; priority as listed:
>>   1). Unevenly stamped gold on cloth spine.
>>   2). Unblemished gold on cloth spine.
>   "FIRST EDITION"

WHAT A WAY TO GO. New York: Atheneum, 1962.
>   Hardcover, dustwrapper.
>   "First Edition"

CAUSE FOR WONDER. New York: Atheneum, 1963.
>   Hardcover, dustwrapper; priority as listed:
>>   1). Text of pages 50 and 119 transposed but integral.
>>   2). Errata slip variously tipped or laid in at page 50.
>>   3). Text of pages 49 and 119 cancelled incorrectly.
>>   NOTE: Though unknown to the publisher, some copies are reported to have had pages 49/50 cancelled in backwards, so pagination reads 50/49.
>   "First Edition"

ONE DAY. New York: Atheneum, 1965.
  Hardcover, dustwrapper.
  "First Edition"

IN ORBIT. (New York): New American Library (1967).
  Hardcover, dustwrapper.
  "First Printing"

GOD'S COUNTRY AND MY PEOPLE. New York: Harper & Row (1968).
  Hardcover, dustwrapper; priority as listed:
      1). "$7.95" on front flap of dustwrapper.
      2). "$10.95" on front flap of dustwrapper.
  "FIRST EDITION"

A BILL OF RITES, A BILL OF WRONGS, A BILL OF GOODS. (New York): New American
  Library (1968).
  Hardcover, dustwrapper.
  "First Printing"

GREEN GRASS, BLUE SKY, WHITE HOUSE. Los Angeles: Black Sparrow Press, 1970.
  Two issues, no priority:
      1). Hardcover, acetate dustwrapper.
      200 copies, numbered, signed by the author.
      2). Wrappers.
      1000 copies (according to the publisher, only 972 copies were actually
      published).

WRIGHT MORRIS: A READER. New York: Harper & Row (1970).
  Hardcover, dustwrapper.
  "FIRST EDITION"

FIRE SERMON. New York: Harper & Row (1971).
  Hardcover, dustwrapper.
  "FIRST EDITION"

WAR GAMES. Los Angeles: Black Sparrow Press, 1972.
  Two issues, no priority:
      1). Hardcover, acetate dustwrapper; no priority:
          a). 300 copies, numbered, signed by the author.
          b). 26 copies, lettered, signed by the author.
      2). Wrappers.
      1500 copies.

LOVE AFFAIR—A VENETIAN JOURNAL. New York: Harper & Row (1972).
  Hardcover, dustwrapper.
  "FIRST EDITION 1972"
      NOTE: Uncorrected proofs, without photographs, in printed wrappers, preceded
      publication.

HERE IS EINBAUM. Los Angeles: Black Sparrow Press, 1973.
    Two issues, no priority;
        1). Hardcover, no priority:
            a). Dustwrapper.
                500 copies.
            b). Acetate dustwrapper.
                200 copies, numbered, signed by the author.
            c). Acetate dustwrapper.
                26 copies, lettered, signed by the author.
        2). Wrappers.
            1499 copies.

A LIFE. New York: Harper & Row (1973).
    Hardcover, dustwrapper.
    "FIRST EDITION"

ABOUT FICTION. New York: Harper & Row (1975).
    Hardcover, dustwrapper.
    "FIRST EDITION"
    NOTE: Uncorrected proofs in printed wrappers preceded publication.

THE CAT'S MEOW. Los Angeles: Black Sparrow Press, 1975.
    Two issues, no priority:
        1). Hardcover, acetate dustwrapper; no priority:
            a). 100 copies, numbered, signed by the author.
            b). 25 copies, numbered, for the use of the author.
        2). Wrappers.
            200 copies.

Joyce Carol Oates

BY THE NORTH GATE. New York: Vanguard Press (1963).
  Hardcover, dustwrapper.
  No statement of first edition.

WITH SHUDDERING FALL. New York: Vanguard Press (1964).
  Hardcover, dustwrapper.
  No statement of first edition.
  NOTE: Sewn signatures, laid in finished dustwrapper, preceded publication.

THE SWEET ENEMY. (New York: Actors Studio, 1965).
  Photocopied sheets.
  NOTE: A playscript for the use of the cast.

UPON THE SWEEPING FLOOD. New York: Vanguard Press (1966).
  Hardcover, dustwrapper.
  No statement of first edition.

A GARDEN OF EARTHLY DELIGHTS. New York: Vanguard Press (1967).
  Hardcover, dustwrapper.
  No statement of first edition.
  NOTE: Uncorrected proofs in printed wrappers, ringbound, preceded publication.

EXPENSIVE PEOPLE. New York: Vanguard Press (1968).
  Hardcover, dustwrapper.
  No statement of first edition.
  NOTE: Uncorrected proofs in printed wrappers preceded publication.

WOMEN IN LOVE. New York: Albondocani Press, 1968.
  Wrappers, no priority:
      1). 150 copies, numbered, signed by the author.
      2). 26 copies, lettered, signed by the author.

THEM. New York: Vanguard Press (1969).
  Hardcover, dustwrapper.
  No statement of first edition.
  NOTE: Uncorrected proofs in printed wrappers preceded publication.

ANONYMOUS SINS. Baton Rouge: Louisiana State University Press (1969).
    Hardcover, dustwrapper.
    No statement of first edition.

SUNDAY DINNER. New York: American Place Theatre (1970).
    Ditto sheets.
    NOTE: A playscript for the use of the cast.

ACCEPTANCE REMARKS. (New York: National Book Award Committee) 1970.
    Mechanically reproduced sheets.
    NOTE: Precedes *Remarks by Joyce Carol Oates Accepting the National Book Award*
        in Fiction for 'Them', New York: Vanguard Press (1970), mimeographed sheets;
        however, the text is identical.

CUPID AND PSYCHE. New York: Albondocani Press, 1970.
    Wrappers, no priority:
        1). 200 copies, numbered, signed by the author.
        2). 26 copies, lettered, signed by the author.

THE WHEEL OF LOVE. New York: Vanguard Press (1970).
    Hardcover, dustwrapper.
    No statement of first edition.
    NOTE: Uncorrected proofs in printed wrappers preceded publication.

LOVE AND ITS DERANGEMENTS. Baton Rouge: Louisiana State University Press (1970).
    Hardcover, dustwrapper.
    No statement of first edition.

WOMAN IS THE DEATH OF THE SOUL. (Toronto: Coach House Press, 1970).
    Broadside.
    500 copies.
    NOTE: Laid in folder entitled *Orange Bear Reader Number Two*.

WONDERLAND. New York: Vanguard Press (1971).
    Hardcover, dustwrapper.
    No statement of first edition.
    NOTE: Uncorrected proofs in printed wrappers preceded publication.
    ALSO: London: Gollancz, 1972.
        Hardcover, dustwrapper.
        No statement of first edition.
        NOTE: Revised edition.

THE EDGE OF IMPOSSIBILITY. New York: Vanguard Press (1972).
    Hardcover, dustwrapper.
    No statement of first edition.

MARRIAGES AND INFIDELITIES. New York: Vanguard Press (1972).
    Hardcover, dustwrapper.
    No statement of first edition.
    NOTE: Uncorrected proofs in printed wrappers preceded publication.

IN CASE OF ACCIDENTAL DEATH. Cambridge, Mass.: Pomegranate Press, 1972.
    Broadside, no priority:
        1). 150 copies, numbered.
        2). 100 copies, numbered, signed by the author and illustrator.
    Illustrated by Karyl Klopp.

ANGEL FIRE. Baton Rouge: Louisiana State University Press, 1973.
    Hardcover, dustwrapper.
    No statement of first edition.

WOODED FORMS. (New York: Albondocani Press, 1972).
    Wrappers, no priority:
        1). "Albondocani Books/Ampersand Books" on greeting page.
        2). No names on greeting page.

A POSTHUMOUS SKETCH. (Los Angeles): Black Sparrow Press, 1973.
    Wrappers.
    Sparrow 10.

THE HOSTILE SUN. Los Angeles: Black Sparrow Press, 1973.
    Two issues, no priority:
        1). Hardcover, acetate dustwrapper; no priority:
            a). 300 copies, numbered, signed by the author.
            b). 26 copies, lettered, signed by the author.
        2). Wrappers.
        1453 copies.

DO WITH ME WHAT YOU WILL. New York: Vanguard Press (1973).
    Hardcover, dustwrapper.
    No statement of first edition.
    NOTE: Uncorrected proofs, with a new ending tipped in, in printed wrappers preceded
        publication.

DREAMING AMERICA. (New York): Aloe Editions, 1973.
    Wrappers, no priority:
        1). 150 copies, numbered, signed by the author.
        2). 26 copies, lettered, signed by the author.
    NOTE: Uncorrected proofs, stapled, preceded publication; priority as listed:
        1). Includes "Fireflies" instead of "Flight".
        2). Includes "Flight", as issued.

MIRACLE PLAY. New York: Phoenix Theatre (1973).
    Xeroxed sheets, clasped.
    NOTE: Playscript for the use of the cast.
    ALSO: Los Angeles: Black Sparrow Press, 1974.
        Two issues, no priority:
            1). Hardcover, acetate dustwrapper; no priority:
                a). 1000 copies (according to the publisher, 1251 copies were
                    actually published).
                b). 350 copies, numbered, signed by the author.
                c). 50 copies, numbered, signed by the author, boxed.
            2). Wrappers.
                3760 copies.

THE HUNGRY GHOSTS. Los Angeles: Black Sparrow Press, 1974.
    Two issues, no priority:
        1). Hardcover, acetate dustwrapper; no priority:
            a). 1000 copies (according to the publisher, 1131 copies were actually
                published.
            b). 350 copies, numbered, signed by the author.
            c). 50 copies, numbered, signed by the author, boxed.
        2). Wrappers.
            4116 copies.

THE TRIUMPH OF THE SPIDER MONKEY (Yellow Springs, Ohio: Antioch Review, 1974).
    Wrappers.
    NOTE: Suppressed before being publicly released, this is in newspaper tabloid format
        (*The Sunday Sentinel Magazine*) and poses as *The Exclusive First-Person Con-
        fession of the Maniac Bobbie Gotteson by Bobbie Gotteson as told to Joyce
        Carol Oates.* In fact, it is solely Ms. Oates' creation.

PLAGIARIZED MATERIAL. (Los Angeles): Black Sparrow Press, 1974.
    Wrappers.
    Sparrow 19.
    NOTE: Although the cover states "by Fernandes 'translated' by Joyce Carol Oates,"
        the work is wholly by Oates.

THE GODDESS. New York: Vanguard Press (1974).
    Hardcover, dustwrapper.
    No statement of first edition.
    NOTE: Uncorrected proofs in printed wrappers preceded publication.

NEW HEAVEN, NEW EARTH. New York: Vanguard Press (1974).
    Hardcover, dustwrapper.
    No statement of first edition.
    NOTE: Uncorrected proofs in printed wrappers preceded publication.

WHERE ARE YOU GOING, WHERE HAVE YOU BEEN? Greenwich, Conn.: Fawcett
    (1974).
    Wrappers.
    No statement of first edition.

THE GIRL. Cambridge, Mass.: Pomegranate Press, 1974.
    Two issues, no priority:
        1). Hardcover.
           50 copies, numbered, signed by the author and illustrator.
        2). Wrappers.
           250 copies, numbered, signed by the author and illustrator.
    Illustrated by Karyl Klopp.

THE SEDUCTION. Los Angeles: Black Sparrow Press, 1975.
    Two issues, no priority:
        1). Hardcover, acetate dustwrapper; no priority:
           a). 1500 copies.
           b). 350 copies, numbered, signed by the author.
           c). 50 copies, numbered, signed by the author, boxed.
        2). Wrappers.
           4180 copies.

THE POISONED KISS. New York: Vanguard Press (1975).
    Hardcover, dustwrapper.
    No statement of first edition.
    NOTE: 1). "Fernandes" is credited as co-author but the work is wholly by Oates.
           2). Uncorrected proofs in printed wrappers preceded publication.

THE ASSASSINS. New York: Vanguard Press (1975).
    Hardcover, dustwrapper.
    No statement of first edition.

THE FABULOUS BEASTS. Baton Rouge: Louisiana State University Press, 1975.
    Hardcover, dustwrapper.
    No statement of first edition.

Frank O'Hara

A CITY WINTER. New York: Tibor de Nagy Gallery, 1951.
>   Two issues, no priority:
>>   1). Hardcover.
>>   20 copies, numbered, with an original drawing signed by the illustrator.
>>   2). Wrappers.
>>   130 copies, numbered.
>   Illustrated by Larry Rivers.
>   NOTE: There were an unknown number of unnumbered copies, both bound and unbound.

ORANGES. New York: Tibor de Nagy, 1953.
>   Wrappers.
>   20 copies.

THE HUNTER HUNTED. N.p., n.d.
>   Wrappers.

MEDITATIONS IN AN EMERGENCY. New York: Grove Press (1957).
>   Two issues, no priority:
>>   1). Hardcover, no priority:
>>>   a). 75 copies, numbered, boxed.
>>>   b). 15 copies, numbered, signed by the author, with an original drawing by Grace Hartigan.
>>>   NOTE: Copy #18 was examined, although the colophon calls for only 15.
>>   2). Wrappers.
>   No statement of first edition.
>   NOTE: There were an unknown number of unnumbered copies.

JACKSON POLLOCK. New York: George Braziller, 1959.
>   Two issues, no priority:
>>   1). Hardcover, dustwrapper.
>>   2). Wrappers.
>   No statement of first edition.

STONES. (East Islip, N.Y.: Universal Limited Art Editions, ca. 1959).*
Portfolio, boxed.
NOTE: 12 lithographed sheets with text by O'Hara, illustrated by Larry Rivers and
O'Hara.

HARTIGAN AND RIVERS WITH O'HARA. (New York: Tibor de Nagy Gallery, 1959).
Wrappers.

ODES. New York: Tiber Press (1960).
Hardcover, acetate dustwrapper; no priority:
1). 200 copies, numbered in Arabic, signed by the author and illustrator.
2). 25 copies, numbered in Roman, signed by the author and illustrator.
Illustrated by Michael Goldberg.
NOTE: Issued in box with *The Poems* by John Ashbery, *Permanently* by Kenneth Koch
and *Salute* by James Schuyler.

SECOND AVENUE. New York: Totem Press/Corinth Books (1960).
Wrappers, priority as listed:
1). Cover printed in red and black; publisher's imprint at the base of the
copyright page.
2). Cover printed in black and grey; publisher's imprint removed.

AWAKE IN SPAIN. New York: American Theatre For Poets, 1960.
Mimeographed sheets, stapled.

NEW SPANISH PAINTING AND SCULPTURE. New York: Museum of Modern Art
(1960).
Wrappers.
No statement of first edition.

ARTISTS' THEATRE: FOUR PLAYS. New York/London: Grove Press/Evergreen Books
(1960).
Wrappers.
"First Evergreen Edition 1960"
NOTE: Plays by four authors; O'Hara contributed *Try! Try!*

LOVES LABOR. New York: American Theatre For Poets (ca. 1961).
Stapled sheets.

A CORDIAL INVITATION TO CELEBRATE THE SIXTIETH BIRTHDAY OF EDWIN
DENBY AT A DINNER TO BE GIVEN BY HIS FRIENDS. New York: (Privately
published) 1963.
Wrappers.
NOTE: Contains the author's *Edwin's Hand* as the only text.

LUNCH POEMS. (San Francisco): City Lights Books (1964).
  Wrappers.
  No statement of first edition.
  Pocket Poets Series: Number 19.

THE GENERAL RETURNS FROM ONE PLACE TO ANOTHER. (New York:
  Present Stages, 1964).
  Mechanically reproduced sheets.
  NOTE: Contrary to the notice on the cover sheet, *The Baptism* by LeRoi Jones is not
    included.

ARSHILE GORKY: DRAWINGS. (London): Arts Council (ca. 1964).
  Wrappers.
  NOTE: All text by the author.

FRANZ KLINE: A RETROSPECTIVE EXHIBITION. London: Whitechapel Gallery, 1964.
  Wrappers.
  NOTE: All text by the author.

LARRY RIVERS. New York: October House (for Brandeis University) (1965).
  Hardcover, dustwrapper.
  No statement of first edition.

LOVE POEMS (TENTATIVE TITLE). New York: Tibor de Nagy Editions, 1965.
  Wrappers, no priority:
    1). Trade edition.
    2). 20 copies, numbered, signed by the author.

ROBERT MOTHERWELL: WITH SELECTIONS FROM THE ARTIST'S WRITINGS.
  New York: Museum of Modern Art (1965).
  Two issues, no priority:
    1). Hardcover, dustwrapper.
    2). Wrappers.
  No statement of first edition.

NAKIAN. New York: Museum of Modern Art (1966).
  Two issues, no priority:
    1). Hardcover, dustwrapper.
    2). Wrappers.
  No statement of first edition.

WHY I AM NOT A PAINTER. New York: Martha Jackson Gallery, 1966.
  Wrappers.
  NOTE: Exhibition catalogue of Michael Goldberg's painting; all text by the author.

HOMAGE TO ANTONIO MACHADO. (New York: Spanish Refugee Aid, 1966).
  Wrappers.

NATURE AND NEW PAINTING. (New York: Tiber Press, ca. 1967).
  Wrappers.

HOTEL PARTICULIER. Pleasant Valley, N.Y.: Kriya Press, 1967.
  Broadside.
  100 copies, numbered.

IN MEMORY OF MY FEELINGS. New York: Museum of Modern Art, 1967.*
  Portfolio, boxed.
  2500 copies, numbered.

TWO PIECES. (London: Long Hair Books, 1969).
  Wrappers.

THE COLLECTED POEMS OF FRANK O'HARA. New York: Knopf, 1971.
  Hardcover, dustwrapper; priority as listed:
        1). Dustwrapper with drawing by Larry Rivers.
        2). Dustwrapper with lettering only.
  "First Edition"

BELGRADE, NOVEMBER 19, 1963. (New York): Adventures In Poetry (ca. 1973).
  Wrappers.
  500 copies.

THE SELECTED POEMS OF FRANK O'HARA. New York: Random House (1974).
  Two issues, no priority:
        1). Hardcover, dustwrapper.
          "First Edition"
        2). Wrappers.
          "First Vintage Books Edition January 1974"

HYMNS OF ST. BRIDGET. (New York): Adventures In Poetry (1974).
  Wrappers.
  NOTE: With Bill Berkson.

THE END OF THE FAR WEST. (London: Privately published, 1974).
  Wrappers.

MACARONI. Calais, Vt.: Z Press, 1974.
  Broadside.
  NOTE: With *In Memoriam* by Patsy Southgate.

ART CHRONICLES 1954-1966. New York: George Braziller (1975).
  Hardcover, dustwrapper.
  No statement of first edition.

STANDING STILL AND WALKING IN NEW YORK. Bolinas, Calif. : Grey Fox Press
    (1975).
    Two issues, no priority :
        1). Hardcover, dustwrapper.
        2). Wrappers.

Reynolds Price

ONE SUNDAY IN LATE JULY. (N.p.: Privately published) 1960.
   Wrappers.
   50 copies.
   NOTE: An offprint from *Encounter* magazine.

A LONG AND HAPPY LIFE. New York: Atheneum, 1962.
   Hardcover, dustwrapper; priority as listed:
      1). Names of Spender, Cecil and Patton printed in pale green on rear cover of
         dustwrapper.
      2). Names in dark green on rear cover of dustwrapper.
   "First Edition"
   NOTE: 1). Review copies in printed wrappers preceded publication, priority as listed:
      a). Bound in yellow wrappers.
      b). Bound in the trade dustwrapper.
      2). A Formosan piracy of the first edition, in reduced format, has been examined.

THE NAMES AND FACES OF HEROES. New York: Atheneum, 1963.
   Hardcover, dustwrapper.
   "First Edition"

THE THING ITSELF. (Durham, N.C.: Privately published, 1966).
   Wrappers.
   500 copies.

A GENEROUS MAN. New York: Atheneum, 1966.
   Hardcover, dustwrapper.
   "First Edition"
   NOTE: Review copies in printed wrappers preceded publication.

LOVE AND WORK. New York: Atheneum, 1968.
   Hardcover, dustwrapper.
   "First Edition"

LATE WARNING. New York: Albondocani Press, 1968.
    Wrappers, no priority:
        1). 150 copies, numbered, signed by the author.
        2). 26 copies, lettered, signed by the author.
    Albondocani Press Publication No. 4.

PERMANENT ERRORS. New York: Atheneum, 1970.
    Hardcover, dustwrapper.
    "First Edition"

THINGS THEMSELVES. New York: Atheneum, 1972.
    Hardcover, dustwrapper.
    "First Edition"

THE SURFACE OF EARTH. New York: Atheneum, 1975.
    Hardcover, dustwrapper.
    "First Edition"

ANNUNCIATION. (Durham, N.C.: Privately published) 1975.
    Wrappers.

Translations.

TORSO OF AN ARCHAIC APOLLO. (New York) : Albondocani Press (1969).
    Wrappers, no priority :
        1). "Ampersand Books" omitted on first leaf.
        2). "Ampersand Books" credited on first leaf.
    300 copies.

TWO THEOPHANIES. (Durham, N.C. : Privately published, 1971).
    Wrappers, no priority :
        1). Grey wrappers.
        2). Purple wrappers.
    200 copies.

THE FOURTH ECLOGUE OF VERGIL. (Durham, N.C. : Privately published) 1972.
    Wrappers.
    200 copies.

PRESENCE AND ABSENCE. (Bloomfield Hills, Mich. : Bruccoli Clark, 1973).
    Signatures in box, no priority :
        1). 300 copies, numbered, signed by the author.
        2). 20 copies, unnumbered, signed by the author.
    NOTE : Not released until mid-1974.

AN APOCRYPHAL HYMN OF JESUS. (Durham, N.C. : Privately published) 1973.
    Wrappers.
    200 copies.

A NATIVITY FROM THE APOCRYPHAL BOOK OF JAMES. (Durham, N.C. : Privately
    published) 1974.
    Wrappers.
    200 copies.

James Purdy

DON'T CALL ME BY MY RIGHT NAME. New York: William-Frederick Press, 1956.
   Wrappers.

63: DREAM PALACE. New York: William-Frederick Press, 1956.
   Wrappers.

COLOR OF DARKNESS. (New York): New Directions (1957).
   Hardcover, dustwrapper.
   No statement of first edition.

MALCOLM. New York: Farrar, Straus & Cudahy (1959).
   Hardcover, dustwrapper.
   No statement of first edition.

THE NEPHEW. New York: Farrar, Straus & Cudahy (1960).
   Hardcover, dustwrapper.
   "First Printing, 1960"

CHILDREN IS ALL. (New York): New Directions (1961).
   Hardcover, dustwrapper.
   No statement of first edition.

CABOT WRIGHT BEGINS. New York: Farrar, Straus & Giroux (1964).
   Hardcover, dustwrapper.
   "First printing, 1964"

EUSTACE CHISHOLM AND THE WORKS. New York: Farrar, Straus & Giroux (1967).
   Hardcover, dustwrapper.
   "First printing, 1967"

AN OYSTER IS A WEALTHY BEAST. (Los Angeles) : Black Sparrow Press (1967).
 Two issues, priority as listed:
  1). Wrappers.
   200 copies, numbered, signed by the author; priority as listed:
    a). 50 copies (approximately) with an original drawing by the author.
    b). 150 copies (approximately) with no drawing.
  2). Hardcover, no priority:
    a). 50 copies, numbered, signed, with an original drawing by the author.
    b). 4 special copies, for the publisher, author, printer and binder.

MR. EVENING. Los Angeles: Black Sparrow Press, 1968.
 Two issues, no priority:
  1). Hardcover, no priority:
    a). 75 copies, numbered, signed, with an original drawing by the author.
    b). 4 special copies, for the publisher, author, printer and binder.
  2). Wrappers.
   300 copies, numbered, signed by the author.

JEREMY'S VERSION. Garden City, N.Y.: Doubleday, 1970.
 Hardcover, dustwrapper.
 "FIRST EDITION"

ON THE REBOUND. Los Angeles: Black Sparrow Press, 1970.
 Hardcover, acetate dustwrapper; no priority:
  1). 300 copies, numbered, signed by the author.
  2). 26 copies, lettered, signed by the author.
  3). 4 special copies, for the publisher, author, printer and binder.

THE RUNNING SUN. (New York: Privately published, 1971).
 Wrappers.
 300 copies, numbered, signed by the author.
 NOTE: 150 copies (approximately) were reportedly never issued.

I AM ELIJAH THRUSH. Garden City, N.Y.: Doubleday, 1972.
 Hardcover, dustwrapper.
 "First Edition"

SUNSHINE IS AN ONLY CHILD. New York: Aloe Editions, 1973.
 Wrappers, no priority:
  1). 124 copies, numbered, signed by the author.
  2). 26 copies, lettered, signed by the author.

THE HOUSE OF THE SOLITARY MAGGOT. Garden City, N.Y.: Doubleday, 1974.
 Hardcover, dustwrapper.
 "First Edition"

Philip Roth

GOODBYE COLUMBUS. Boston: Houghton Mifflin, 1959.
    Hardcover, dustwrapper.
    "First printing"

LETTING GO. New York: Random House (1962).
    Hardcover, dustwrapper.
    "FIRST PRINTING"

WHEN SHE WAS GOOD. New York: Random House (1967).
    Hardcover, dustwrapper.
    "First Printing"

PORTNOY'S COMPLAINT. New York: Random House (1969).
    Hardcover, no priority:
        1). Trade edition, yellow dustwrapper.
        2). 600 copies, numbered, signed by the author, white dustwrapper, boxed.
    "First Printing"

ON THE AIR. (New York): New American Review (1970).
    Wrappers.
    1500 copies.

OUR GANG. New York: Random House (1971).
    Hardcover, dustwrapper.
    "FIRST EDITION"
    ALSO: New York: Bantam Books (1973).
        Wrappers.
        NOTE: 1). Contains a new preface by the author.
            2). The fifth Bantam printing, entitled *Watergate Edition*, noted on the
               copyright page as "New Bantam Edition."
    ALSO: New York: Bantam Books (1974).
        Wrappers.
        NOTE: 1). Contains another new preface by the author.
            2). The eighth Bantam printing, entitled *Special Pre-Impeachment
               Edition*, noted on the copyright page as "New Bantam Edition."

THE BREAST. New York: Holt, Rinehart & Winston (1973).
>   Hardcover, dustwrapper.
>   "First Edition"

THE GREAT AMERICAN NOVEL. New York: Holt, Rinehart & Winston (1973).
>   Hardcover, dustwrapper.
>   "FIRST EDITION"
>   NOTE: Uncorrected proofs in printed wrappers preceded publication.

ELI, THE FANATIC. Tel Aviv: The Colour System For Teaching Languages, 1973.
>   Wrappers.
>   NOTE: English text and Hebrew text, color coded for language instruction.

MY LIFE AS A MAN. New York: Holt, Rinehart & Winston (1974).
>   Hardcover, dustwrapper.
>   "First Edition"
>   NOTE: Uncorrected proofs in printed wrappers preceded publication.

READING MYSELF AND OTHERS. New York: Farrar, Straus and Giroux (1975).
>   Hardcover, dustwrapper.
>   "First printing, 1975"
>   NOTE: Uncorrected proofs in printed wrappers preceded publication.

Jerome Rothenberg

WHITE SUN BLACK SUN. (New York): Hawk's Well Press (1960).
    Wrappers.

THE SEVEN HELLS OF THE JIGOKU ZOSHI. New York: Trobar (1962).
    Wrappers.

SIGHTINGS. (New York: Hawk's Well Press, 1964).
    Wrappers.
    NOTE: With *Lunes* by Robert Kelly.

THE GORKY POEMS. (Mexico City): El Corno Emplumado (1966).
    Wrappers.
    1000 copies.

RITUAL. New York: (Something Else Press) 1966.
    Wrappers.
    A Great Bear Pamphlet.

BETWEEN. London: Fulcrum Press (1967).
    Two issues, no priority:
        1). Hardcover, dustwrapper; no priority:
            a). 100 copies.
            b). 50 copies, numbered, signed by the author.
        2). Wrappers.

POLAND/1931: THE WEDDING. (New York: Ikon, 1967).
    Broadside.

CONVERSATIONS. Los Angeles: Black Sparrow Press, 1968.
    Two issues, no priority:
        1). Hardcover, dustwrapper; no priority:
            a). 50 copies, numbered, signed by the author.
            b). 4 special copies, for the publisher, author, printer and binder.
        2). Wrappers.
            250 copies, numbered, signed by the author.

POEMS 1964-1967. Los Angeles: Black Sparrow Press, 1968.
    Two issues, no priority:
        1). Hardcover, no priority:
            a). 125 copies, numbered, signed by the author.
            b). 4 special copies, for the publisher, author, printer and binder.
        2). Wrappers.
            750 copies.

SIGHTINGS I-IX & RED EASY A COLOR. (London: Circle Press, 1968).
    Wrappers in portfolio in case.
    125 copies, numbered, signed by the author and illustrator.
    Illustrated by Ian Tyson.

OFFERING FLOWERS. No known priority:
        1). (Santa Barbara, Calif.: Unicorn Press, 1968).
           Broadside.
           NOTE: 1). "Arranged by" Rothenberg.
                2). Laid in portfolio entitled *Unicorn Folio: Series Two, Number One,* numbered.
        2). (London: Circle Press, 1968).
           Broadside.
           100 copies, signed by the author.
           Circle 3.

THE CONNOISSEUR OF JEWS. (Stony Brook, N.Y.: Stony Brook Poetics Foundation, 1968).
    Broadside.
    10 copies, signed by the author.
    NOTE: Laid in portfolio entitled *Stony Brook Holographs 1968.*

THE YELLOW BIRD OF SLEEP WHOSE. (London: Circle Press, 1968).
    Broadside.
    150 copies.
    Circle 8.

THE DIRECTIONS. (London: Tetrad Press, 1969).
    Broadside, no priority:
        1). 450 copies.
        2). 50 copies, signed by the author and illustrator.
    Illustrated by Tom Phillips.

POLAND/1931. (Santa Barbara, Calif.): Unicorn Press (1969).
    Sheets in portfolio, no priority:
        1). 500 copies.
        2). 50 copies, numbered, signed by the author.
        3). 10 copies, lettered.

NOTE: Flyer, containing one poem, preceded publication.
ALSO: (New York): New Directions (1974).
   Two issues, no priority:
      1). Hardcover, dustwrapper.
      2). Wrappers.
   NOTE: Expanded edition.

A BOOK OF NARRATIVES & REALTHEATER PIECES. (Brooklyn: Pierrepont Press, 1969).*
   Wrappers, boxed.
   NOTE: Cancelled after printing, but some copies reportedly escaped.

POLISH ANECDOTES. (Santa Barbara, Calif.): Unicorn Press (1970).
   Wrappers.
   250 copies, numbered, signed by the author.

POLISH ANECDOTE: THE BANQUET. (Santa Barbara, Calif.: Unicorn Press, 1970).
   Broadside.
   Unicorn Broadsheet Series One Number Nine.

A BOOK OF TESTIMONY. (Bolinas, Calif.): Tree Books, 1971.
   Wrappers.
   300 copies.

POEMS FOR THE GAME OF SILENCE. New York: Dial Press, 1971.
   Two issues, no priority:
      1). Hardcover, dustwrapper.
      2). Wrappers.
   "First Printing"
   NOTE: Uncorrected proofs in printed wrappers preceded publication.

NET OF SUN NET OF MOON. (Santa Barbara, Calif.: Unicorn Press) 1971.
   Broadside.
   Unicorn Broadsheet Series II Number 9.

CRAZY DOG EVENTS. (Detroit): Alternative Press (ca. 1971).
   Broadside.
   NOTE: "Arranged by" Rothenberg.

OTO INDIAN: BUFFALO INDIAN NARRATIVE. (Santa Barbara, Calif.: Unicorn Press, 1972).*
   Postcard.

A VALENTINE NO A VALEDICTORY FOR GERTRUDE STEIN. (London: Judith Walker, ca. 1972).*
   Broadside.

THE NIGHT THE MOON WAS A SPIDER. (Brockport, N.Y.: Department of
    English, State University College, 1973).
    Wrappers.
    NOTE: Cover title is *Writer's Forum.*

ESTHER K. COMES TO AMERICA. (Greensboro, N.C.): Unicorn Press (1973).
    Wrappers.
    2000 copies.

A POEM OF BEAVERS: SENECA JOURNAL 1. Blue Mounds Township, Wisc.: Perishable
    Press, 1973.
    Wrappers.
    97 copies, numbered, signed by the author.

OLD MAN BEAVER'S BLESSING SONG. (New York): Alcheringa, 1973.
    Broadside.
    NOTE: Laid in *Alcheringa*, No. 4, but copies were also distributed separately.

MME SHEKINAH. New York: (Privately published, 1973).
    Broadside.
    20 copies.

COKBOY (PART TWO). (Amsterdam: Uitgeverij Athanaeum-Polak & Van Gennep, 1973).
    Wrappers.
    NOTE: 1). With *Kennis Van Die Aand* by Andre P. Brink.
          2). An offprint from *Raster*, vol. VI, no. 4.

FROM SENECA JOURNAL: "ALPHA & OMEGA". (Norwich, Conn.: Stone Press,
    1974).
    Postcard.

THE CARDS. (Los Angeles): Black Sparrow Press, 1974.
    Wrappers.
    Sparrow 24.

THE PIRKE & THE PEARL. Berkeley: Tree, 1975.
    Wrappers, dustwrapper.

FOR THE LOVE OF THE SERPENT. (Milwaukee: Membrane Press, 1975).
    Postcard.

SENECA JOURNAL MID-WINTER. Saint Louis, Mo.: Singing Bone Press, 1975.
    Hardcover, box; no priority:
          1). 60 copies, numbered, signed by the author.
          2). 41 copies, hors commerce.
    NOTE: Also in the 4 1/8″ x 3 1/8″ box is an assortment of items, to include beaver fur,
          corn husk, a map, 6 old photos, a small sheet of music and 4 corn kernels.

Translations.

Martin Buber.
TALES OF ANGELS, SPIRITS AND DEMONS. New York: Hawk's Well Press, 1958.*
    Wrappers.
    NOTE: Translated with David Antin.

NEW YOUNG GERMAN POETS. San Francisco: City Lights Books (1959).
    Wrappers.
    No statement of first edition.
    Pocket Poets Series No. 11.

Rolf Hochhuth.
THE DEPUTY. New York: Samuel French (1964).
    Wrappers.
    Price is $1.25.

THE FLIGHT OF QUETZALCOATL. Brighton: Unicorn Press, 1967.
    Wrappers, no priority:
        1). 324 copies.
        2). 50 copies, numbered, signed by the translator.
        3). 26 copies, lettered, hors commerce.

Hans Magnus Enzensberger.
POEMS FOR PEOPLE WHO DON'T READ POEMS. New York: Atheneum, 1968.
    Two issues, no priority:
        1). Hardcover, dustwrapper.
        2). Wrappers.
   "First Edition"
    NOTE: Translated with Michael Hamburger and the author.

Eugen Gomringer.
THE BOOK OF HOURS AND CONSTELLATIONS.. New York: Something Else Press,
    1968.
    Two issues, no priority:
        1). Hardcover, dustwrapper.
        2). Wrappers.
    No statement of first edition.

THE 17 HORSE SONGS OF FRANK MITCHELL NOS. X-XII. (London: Tetrad Press, 1969).
    Sheets in box, no priority:
        1). 200 copies.
        2). 50 copies, numbered, signed by the translator and illustrator.
    Illustrated by Ian Tyson.

THE OWL. (Detroit: Alternative Press, 1971).*
    Postcard.

I WAS SURPRISED TO FIND MYSELF OUT HERE AND ACTING LIKE A CROW.
(London: Tetrad Press, 1972).
Wrappers.
NOTE: Translated with Richard Johnny John.

I WAS GOING THROUGH THE BIG SMOKE. (London: Tetrad Press, 1973).
Broadside.
50 copies, numbered, signed by the translator and publisher (Ian Tyson).

I WAS GOING THROUGH THE BIG EARTH. (London: Tetrad Press, 1973).*
Broadside.
50 copies, numbered, signed by the translator and publisher (Ian Tyson).

THREE FRIENDLY WARNINGS. (London: Tetrad Press, 1973).*
Cards in envelope in folio, no priority:
  1). 100 copies.
  2). 25 copies, signed by the translators and publisher (Ian Tyson).
NOTE: Translated with Richard Johnny John.

Gary Snyder

RIPRAP. (Ashland, Mass.): Origin Press, 1959.
    Wrappers.
    500 copies.
    ALSO: (Santa Barbara, Calif.: Allen Schiller, ca. 1970).
        Broadside.
        NOTE: Laid in the magazine *Stooge,* no. 5.

MYTHS AND TEXTS. New York: Totem Press/Corinth Books (1960).
    Wrappers.
    Publisher's name on copyright page.

RYOSEN-AN: ZENDO PRACTICES. Kyoto: First Zen Institute of America in Japan, 1960.*
    Wrappers.
    NOTE: Anonymous.

AMERICA FIVE HUNDRED YEARS AGO. Cambridge, Mass.: Paterson Society, 1961.
    Mimeographed sheet.

THE FIRING. New York: R. L. Ross, 1964.*
    Broadside.
    7 copies, numbered, signed by the publisher.

NANAO KNOWS. (San Francisco: Four Seasons Foundation, 1964).
    Broadside.
    300 copies, signed by the author.

ACROSS LAMARCK COL. (San Francisco: San Francisco Arts Festival Commission, 1964).
    Broadside, no priority:
        1). 30 copies (approximately).
        2). 270 copies (approximately), signed by the author and illustrator.
    Illustrated by Francesca Green.
    NOTE: Laid in portfolio entitled *San Francisco Arts Festival: A Poetry Folio: 1964.*

HOP, SKIP AND JUMP. (Berkeley): Oyez, 1964.
>Broadside.
>350 copies.
>Oyez 9.
>NOTE: 27 copies, numbered, signed by the author in 1964 but published in 1965 in
>>portfolio entitled *Poems in Broadside. Oyez. First Series.*

DEAR MR. PRESIDENT. (San Francisco: C. Plymell & Ari Publications, 1965).
>Broadside.
>500 copies.

RIPRAP AND COLD MOUNTAIN POEMS. (San Francisco: Four Seasons Foundation,
>1965).
>Wrappers.
>No price on rear cover.
>Writing 7.
>NOTE: 1). (San Francisco: Allen Schiller, ca. 1972). Title page and six pages of poems,
>>printed in clay. 7 sets (approximately).
>>2). See translations.

SIX SECTIONS FROM MOUNTAINS AND RIVERS WITHOUT END. San Francisco:
>Four Seasons Foundation, 1965.
>Wrappers.
>"1965" on title page.
>Writing 9.
>ALSO: London: Fulcrum Press (1967).
>>Hardcover, dustwrapper; no priority:
>>>1). Trade edition.
>>>2). 100 copies, numbered, signed by the author.
>NOTE: The 1970 Four Seasons Foundation is arguably "expanded," but the ad-
>>ditional poem (*The Blue Sky*) had appeared earlier as a separate title (see below).

A RANGE OF POEMS. London: Fulcrum Press (1966).
>Hardcover, dustwrapper; no priority:
>>1). Trade edition.
>>2). Numbered issue, no priority:
>>>a). 50 copies.
>>>b). 50 copies, signed by the author.
>"First Edition March 1966"
>NOTE: 1). Uncorrected proofs in plain wrappers preceded publication.
>>2). A Formosan piracy of the first printing, in reduced format, has been examined.

THREE WORLDS, THREE REALMS, SIX ROADS. Marlboro, Vt.: Griffin Press (1966).
>Wrappers.
>200 copies.

GO ROUND. (Santa Barbara, Calif.: Unicorn Press, 1967).
    Broadside.
    325 copies.
    NOTE: 1). Laid in portfolio entitled *Unicorn Folio: Series One, Number One,*
        numbered.
        2). A postcard printing of this poem was produced later in 1967; the first print-
        ing measures 5 x 7¼."

REGARDING WAVE. (San Francisco): Donald Allen, 1967.
    Broadside.
    125 copies.

THE BACK COUNTRY. London: Fulcrum Press (1967).
    Two issues, no priority:
        1). Hardcover, dustwrapper; no priority:
          a). Trade edition.
          b). 100 copies, numbered, signed by the author.
        2). Wrappers.
    No statement of first edition.
    ALSO: (New York): New Directions (1968).
        Two issues, no priority:
        1). Hardcover, dustwrapper.
        2). Wrappers.
    No statement of first edition.
    NOTE: Expanded edition.

THE BED IN THE SKY. (Isla Vista, Calif.: Privately published, 1968).
    Broadside.
    12 copies (25 copies is more likely).

A CURSE ON THE MEN IN WASHINGTON, PENTAGON. New York: Communications
    Company (ca. 1968).
    Broadside.
    NOTE: This is to be differentiated from the 1970 publication: (Santa Barbara, Calif.:
    Unicorn Press) 1968 (but is 1970).
        Broadside, no priority:
        1). Trade edition, priority as listed:
          a). "Buddah" on line 16.
          b). "Buddha" on line 16.
        2). 30 copies, signed by the author.
        All of the "Buddah" state.
    Unicorn Broadsheet One.

THE BLUE SKY. New York: Phoenix Book Shop, 1969.
    Wrappers, no priority:
        1). 100 copies, numbered, signed by the author.
        2). 26 copies, lettered, signed by the author.
    NOTE: An unknown number of copies were labeled "out of series," unnumbered,
    unsigned.

EARTH HOUSE HOLD. (New York): New Directions (1969).
> Two issues, no priority:
>> 1). Hardcover, dustwrapper.
>> 2). Wrappers.
> No statement of first edition.
> NOTE: Uncorrected proofs in printed wrappers preceded publication.

REGARDING WAVE. Iowa City, Iowa: Windhover Press (1969).
> Hardcover.
> 280 copies, numbered, signed by the author.
> ALSO: (New York): New Directions (1970).
>> Two issues, no priority:
>>> 1). Hardcover, dustwrapper.
>>> 2). Wrappers.
>> No statement of first edition.
>> NOTE: Expanded edition.

SMOKEY THE BEAR SUTRA. (Privately published, 1969).
> Mimeographed sheets.
> NOTE: This is to be differentiated from subsequent broadside printings (e.g. Adler Off-set Printing, ca. 1969, in double column; Cottonwood, 1972, in single column) and from the printing in wrappers (Yellow Springs, Ohio: Moon of the Snowblind, 1974).

SOURS OF THE HILLS. (Brooklyn, N.Y.): Sam Charters (1969).
> Wrappers.
> 300 copies.
> Portents #15.

FOUR CHANGES. (Berkeley: Privately published, 1969).
> Photocopied sheets.
> 30 copies (approximately).
> NOTE: This was Snyder's first draft for what became a group effort.
> ALSO: (Berkeley): Earth-Read Out, 1969.
>> Mimeographed sheets; black letters on gold stock.
>> NOTE: This was the first printing of the collaborative work, with Snyder the major contributor. There have since been several independent printings (e.g. the edition printed in green ink on buff stock, by an unknown publisher; and the edition published by the Ecology Center).

CHANGES CHANGES 4 CHANGES CHANGES. (Santa Barbara, Calif.): Unicorn Book Shop, 1969.
> Broadside.
> The sun is colored in the first edition.
> NOTE: Written as "Chofu," the author's Zen name.

EVERYBODY LYING ON THEIR STOMACHS HEAD TOWARD THE CANDLE, READING, SLEEPING, DRAWING. (San Francisco): Maya (1969).
  Broadside, no priority:
      1). Trade edition.
      2). 50 copies, numbered, signed by the author.
  Maya Broadside One.

SPEL AGAINST DEMONS. (Berkeley: Moe's Books) 1970.
  Broadside (letterpress).
  NOTE: There are several piracies of this title; none are letterpress.

ENERGY IS ETERNAL DELIGHT. (Berkeley: Privately published, 1971).
  Broadside.
  NOTE: This is a photo-offset (not Xerox) edition of the author's article in the *New York Times*, 12 January 1971.

PRAYER FOR THE GREAT FAMILY. (San Francisco: Committee of Concern For the Traditional Indian, ca. 1971).
  Broadside, no priority:
      1). Trade edition.
      2). 200 copies, numbered, signed by the author.
      3). 26 copies, lettered, signed by the author.
  NOTE: There is reportedly a first state, which consists of border illustrations which were rejected and changed before publication of the above.

MANZANITA. (Kent, Ohio: Kent State University Library, 1971).
  Wrappers.

ANASAZI. Portland, Ore.: Yes! Press, 1971.
  Broadside.

FOR HEMP, HANAEP, HANAF. (San Francisco: C.M.I., ca. 1972).
  Broadside.

MANZANITA. Bolinas, Calif.: Four Seasons Foundation, 1972.
  Wrappers.
  NOTE: This is a group of poems, unlike the single poem of 1971.

PIUTE CREEK. (Brockport, N.Y.: Department of English, State University College, 1972).
  Wrappers.
  NOTE: Cover title is *Writer's Forum*.

THE FUDO TRILOGY. Berkeley: Shaman Drum, 1973.
> Two issues, no priority:
>> 1). Hardcover, glassine dustwrapper.
>>> 108 copies, numbered, signed by the author and illustrator, with original woodcuts by the illustrator tipped in.
>> 2). Wrappers.
> Illustrated by Michael Corr.

TWO LOGGING SONGS. (Berkeley): Serendipity Books, 1973.
> Broadside.

WHY LOG TRUCK DRIVERS RISE EARLIER THAN STUDENTS OF ZEN. (San Francisco: Privately published) 1973.
> Broadside.

THE CALL OF THE WILD. (Privately published, ca. 1973).
> Broadsides in portfolio.
> NOTE: This title is the title on the portfolio; the five broadsides inside each contain a single untitled poem.

THE USES OF LIGHT. (San Francisco: Privately published, ca. 1974).
> Broadside.

NORTH SEA ROAD. (San Francisco: Planet/Drum Foundation, 1974).
> Wrappers.
> NOTE: Originally laid with other contributions in folder which in turn is enclosed in envelope entitled *North Pacific Rim Alive,* which is Planet/Drum 3.

TURTLE ISLAND. (New York): New Directions (1974).
> Two issues, no priority:
>> 1). Hardcover, dustwrapper.
>> 2). Wrappers.
> No statement of first edition.

SWIMMING NAKED IN THE YUBA RIVER. (Nevada City, Calif.: Maidu, 1974).
> Broadside.
> NOTE: Anonymous.

CLEAR CUT. (Detroit: Alternative Press, ca. 1974).
> Postcard.

ONE WHO WOULD NOT TALK TO A SKILLED HUNTER ABOUT WHAT IS FORBIDDEN BY THE BUDDHA. (Port Townsend, Wash.): Copper Canyon Press, 1974.
> Broadside.
> 100 copies.
> Copperhead Broadside 4.
> NOTE: Laid in box entitled *Copperhead: A Giftbox for Kenneth Rexroth.*

NORTH BEACH. (San Francisco: Canessa Gallery, 1975).
    Broadside.
    NOTE: Anonymous.

ALL IN THE FAMILY. (Davis, Calif.: University of California Library, 1975).
    Wrappers.
    200 copies, numbered, signed by the author and illustrator.
    Illustrated by Mimi Osborne.
    Fine Arts Series Number Two.

Translations.

Rinzai Zen.
THE WOODEN FISH. (Kyoto): Zen Institute of America in Japan, 1961.
    Wrappers, no known priority:
        1). Title on cover printed in black.
        2). Title on cover printed in red.
    NOTE: Translated with Kanetsuki Gutesu.

Han-Shan.
COLD MOUNTAIN POEMS. (Portland, Ore.: Press-22, 1970).
    Wrappers.
    1000 copies, numbered.
    "first separate printing."

Jack Spicer

AFTER LORCA. (San Francisco: White Rabbit Press, 1957).
    Wrappers, no priority:
        1). 474 copies.
        2). 26 copies, lettered, signed by the author.
    NOTE: Some copies were circulated without covers, unstapled.

HOMAGE TO CREELEY. (Annapolis, Calif.: Privately published, 1959).
    Mimeographed sheets, stapled.

BILLY THE KID. (Privately published, ca. 1959).
    Mimeographed sheets, stapled.
    ALSO: (Stinson Beach, Calif.: Enkidu Surrogate, 1959).
        Wrappers, priority as listed:
            1). One word, "Face," omitted on page 8, last line.
            2). One word, "Face," added in fountain pen (by author) or ballpoint pen
               (by illustrator).
        750 copies.
        Illustrated by Jess (Collins).

THE HEADS OF THE TOWN UP TO THE AETHER. San Francisco: Auerhahn Society,
    1962.
    Two issues, no priority:
        1). Hardcover.
        "No more than 50" copies signed by the author and illustrator.
        2). Wrappers.
            750 copies.
    Illustrated by Fran Herndon.

DEAR FERLINGHETTI. (San Francisco): White Rabbit Press (1962).
    Wrappers.
    NOTE: With Lawrence Ferlinghetti.

LAMENT FOR THE MAKERS. (Oakland: White Rabbit Press, 1962).*
    Wrappers.
    100 copies.

THE HOLY GRAIL. San Francisco: White Rabbit Press, 1964.
>   Two issues, no priority:
>>   1). Hardcover.
>>>   13 copies, numbered, signed by the author (according to the printer, 4 copies were destroyed).
>>   2). Wrappers.

LANGUAGE. San Francisco: White Rabbit Press (1965).
>   Wrappers.
>   950 copies.

A REDWOOD FOREST. (San Francisco): White Rabbit Press, 1965.
>   Broadside.

BOOK OF MAGAZINE VERSE. (San Francisco): White Rabbit Press (1966).
>   Wrappers.
>   1500 copies.

THE DAY FIVE THOUSAND FISH DIED IN THE CHARLES RIVER. Pleasant Valley, N.Y.: Kriya Press, 1967.
>   Broadside.
>   100 copies, numbered.

THE RED WHEELBARROW. (St. Aubyn's, Hove, Sussex: Peter Riley, 1968).*
>   Wrappers.
>   12 copies (approximately).
>   NOTE: An offprint from the periodical *Collection One*.
>   ALSO: (Berkeley): Arif Press, 1971.
>>   Wrappers, no priority:
>>>   1). 475 copies, numbered.
>>>   2). 25 copies, numbered, with hand-colored frontispiece, signed by the publisher/illustrator.
>>   Illustrated by Wesley Tanner.

A BOOK OF MUSIC.
>   Wrappers, priority as listed:
>>   1). San Francisco: White Rabbit Press, 1969.
>>>   Title page has a poorly printed silver monogram and author's name is blind-stamped.
>>   2). (San Francisco): White Rabbit Press, 1969.
>>>   Title page printed in red and black only; sewn in wrappers.
>>   3). As 2); stapled in wrappers.
>   1800 copies.
>   NOTE: There were 150 copies, not restricted to any state of issue, with an additional leaf indicating "For Friends of White Rabbit, Oyez, and the Author."

INDIAN SUMMER: MINNEAPOLIS 1950. (Brooklyn, N.Y.): Samuel Charters (1970).
  Broadside.
  1000 copies.
  Portents 16.

BOOK OF MUSIC WITH WORDS. (Vancouver, B.C.: Vancouver Free Press/Georgia
  Straight, 1970).
  Newspaper.
  NOTE: The January 28—February 4, 1970 issue of the *Free Press*, all by Spicer.

THE BALLAD OF THE DEAD WOODCUTTER. (Berkeley: Arif Press, 1972).
  Wrappers.

SOME THINGS FROM JACK. (Verona, Italy): Plain Wrapper Press (1972).
  Wrappers.
  91 copies, numbered.
  Plain Wrapper Keepsakes: Three.

POSTSCRIPT. Albuquerque: Billy Goat Press (ca. 1973).
  Broadside.
  100 copies, numbered.

15 FALSE PROPOSITIONS ABOUT GOD. (South San Francisco: ManRoot Books, 1974).
  Wrappers.

ADMONITIONS. (New York): Adventures In Poetry (1974).
  Wrappers.

BERKELEY IN A TIME OF PLAGUE. (Berkeley: No Signe of the Pide Bull/Arif Press, 1974).
  Broadside, priority as listed:
        1). Grey stock.
            100 copies.
        2). White stock.
            50 copies.

AN ODE AND ARCADIA. Berkeley: Ark Press, 1974.
  Wrappers.
  1000 copies.
  NOTE: With Robert Duncan.

A LOST POEM. (Verona, Italy): Plain Wrapper Press (1975).
  Hardcover.
  114 copies, numbered, signed by the illustrator.
  Illustrated by Ariel (Parkinson).
  Quartus 1.

THE COLLECTED BOOKS OF JACK SPICER. Los Angeles: Black Sparrow Press, 1975.
    Two issues, no priority:
        1). Hardcover, acetate dustwrapper; no priority:
            a). 1000 copies.
            b). 100 copies, numbered, signed by the editor (Robin Blaser).
        2). Wrappers.

THERE IS AN INNER NERVOUSNESS IN VIRGINS. (Eureka, Ca.): Spotted Pig Press
    (ca. 1975).
    Wrappers.
    50 copies.

William Styron

LIE DOWN IN DARKNESS. Indianapolis: Bobbs-Merrill (1951).
> Hardcover, dustwrapper.
> "First Edition"
> NOTE: 1). An entirely unlettered binding has been examined.
>   2). Uncorrected proofs in printed wrappers preceded publication.

THE LONG MARCH. New York: Modern Library (1952).
> Wrappers.
> "95¢" on front cover.
> ALSO: The first Norwegian edition has an introduction, written by the author, which has never appeared in English.

SET THIS HOUSE ON FIRE. New York: Random House (1960).
> Hardcover, priority as listed:
>   1). Light green dustwrapper lettered in red; flaps without text (author, title, publisher and price only).
>   2). Dark green dustwrapper lettered in white, with additional wording; text on flaps.
> "First Printing"

THE FOUR SEASONS. (University Park, Penn.: Pennsylvania State University Press, 1965).*
> Sheets in box.
> 75 copies, numbered, signed by the artist.
> Illustrated by Harold Altman.
> NOTE: All text is by Styron.

THIS QUIET DUST. (New York: Random House, 1967).
> Wrappers.

THE CONFESSIONS OF NAT TURNER. New York: Random House (1967).
> Hardcover, no priority:
>> 1). Trade edition, dustwrapper.
>> 2). 500 copies, numbered, signed by the author, no dustwrapper, boxed.
> "First Printing"
> NOTE: 1). Uncorrected proofs in printed wrappers preceded publication.
>> 2). A Formosan piracy of the first edition, in reduced format, has been examined.

THE CLAP SHACK. New York: Random House (1973).
> Hardcover, dustwrapper.
> No statement of first edition.
> NOTE: Uncorrected proofs in printed wrappers preceded publication.

Harvey Swados

OUT WENT THE CANDLE. New York: Viking Press, 1955.
> Hardcover, dustwrapper.
> No statement of first edition.

ON THE LINE. Boston: Little, Brown (1957).
> Hardcover, dustwrapper.
> "FIRST EDITION"

FALSE COIN. Boston: Little, Brown (1959).
> Hardcover, dustwrapper.
> "FIRST EDITION"

NIGHTS IN THE GARDENS OF BROOKLYN. Boston: Little, Brown (1960).
> Hardcover, dustwrapper.
> "FIRST EDITION"

A RADICAL'S AMERICA. Boston: Little, Brown (1962).
> Hardcover, dustwrapper.
> "FIRST EDITION"

THE WILL. Cleveland: World (1963).
> Hardcover, dustwrapper.
> "FIRST EDITION"

A STORY FOR TEDDY. New York: Simon & Schuster (1965).
> Hardcover, dustwrapper.
> "FIRST PRINTING"

THE EMERGENCE OF AN ARTIST: BERNARD MALAMUD. Iowa City, Iowa: N.d.*
> Wrappers.
> NOTE: An offprint from *The Western Review*.

ON THE LINE: AN ADDRESS. Washington, D.C.: U.S. Dept. of Labor, Management Administration, Office of Manpower Policy, Evaluation and Research, 1966.
> Wrappers.

A RADICAL AT LARGE. London: Rupert Hart-Davis, 1968.
    Hardcover, dustwrapper.
    No statement of first edition.

STANDING FAST. Garden City, N.Y.: Doubleday, 1970.
    Hardcover, dustwrapper.
    "First Edition"
    NOTE: A Formosan piracy of the first edition, in reduced format, has been examined.

STANDING UP FOR THE PEOPLE: THE LIFE AND WORK OF ESTES KEFAUVER.
    New York: Dutton, 1972.
    Hardcover, dustwrapper.
    "First Edition"

CELEBRATION. New York: Simon & Schuster (1974).
    Hardcover, dustwrapper.
    "1 2 3 4 5 6 7 8 9 10" on copyright page.
    NOTE: 1). Uncorrected proofs in printed wrappers preceded publication.
        2). Review copies in printed wrappers preceded publication.

Translation.

Jacques Prevert.
BIM, THE LITTLE DONKEY. Garden City, N.Y. : Doubleday, 1973.*
    Hardcover, dustwrapper.

Paul Theroux

WALDO. Boston: Houghton Mifflin (1967).
    Hardcover, dustwrapper.
    "First Printing"

FONG AND THE INDIANS. Boston: Houghton Mifflin, 1968.
    Hardcover, dustwrapper.
    "First Printing"

GIRLS AT PLAY. Boston: Houghton Mifflin, 1969.
    Hardcover, dustwrapper.
    "First Printing"

MURDER IN MOUNT HOLLY. London: Alan Ross, 1969.
    Hardcover, dustwrapper.
    No statement of first edition.

JUNGLE LOVERS. Boston: Houghton Mifflin, 1971.
    Hardcover, dustwrapper.
    "First Printing"

SINNING WITH ANNIE. Boston: Houghton Mifflin, 1972.
    Hardcover, dustwrapper.
    "FIRST PRINTING"
    NOTE: Uncorrected proofs in printed wrappers preceded publication.

V.S. NAIPAUL. (London): Andre Deutsch (1972).
    Hardcover, dustwrapper.
    No statement of first edition.

SAINT JACK. Boston: Houghton Mifflin, 1973.
    Hardcover, dustwrapper.
    "FIRST PRINTING"
    NOTE: Uncorrected proofs in printed wrappers preceded publication.

THE BLACK HOUSE. Boston: Houghton Mifflin, 1974.
    Hardcover, dustwrapper.
    "FIRST PRINTING"
    NOTE: Uncorrected proofs in printed wrappers preceded publication.

THE GREAT RAILWAY BAZAAR. Boston: Houghton Mifflin, 1975.
    Hardcover, dustwrapper.
    "10 9 8 7 6 5 4 3 2 1" on copyright page.
    NOTE: Uncorrected proofs, in two volumes, in printed wrappers preceded publication.

John Updike

THE CARPENTERED HEN AND OTHER TAME CREATURES. New York: Harper &
Brothers (1958).
   Hardcover, dustwrapper.
   "FIRST EDITION"
   ALSO: London: Gollancz, 1959.
      Hardcover, dustwrapper.
      No statement of first edition.
      NOTE: 1). Retitled *Hoping for a Hoopoe.*
            2). The contents of *The Carpentered Hen,* with the addition of
                an "Author's Note"

THE POORHOUSE FAIR. New York: Knopf, 1959.
   Hardcover, dustwrapper.
   "First Edition"

THE SAME DOOR. New York: Knopf, 1959.
   Hardcover, dustwrapper.
   "First Edition"

RABBIT, RUN. New York: Knopf, 1960.
   Hardcover, dustwrapper.
   "First Edition"
   ALSO: (Harmondsworth, Middlesex, England): Penguin Books (1964).
      Wrappers.
      No statement of first edition.
      NOTE: Revised edition.
   ALSO: New York: Modern Library (1965).
      Hardcover, dustwrapper.
      "First MODERN LIBRARY Edition, 1965"
      NOTE: 1). Entitled *The Poorhouse Fair/Rabbit, Run.*
            2). The Penguin revision, with a new introduction by the author.

PIGEON FEATHERS. New York: Knopf, 1962.
   Hardcover, dustwrapper.
   "First Edition"

THE MAGIC FLUTE. New York: Knopf (1962).
>   Hardcover, no priority:
>   >   1). Trade edition, dustwrapper.
>   >   2). Reinforced library binding, no dustwrapper.
>   No statement of first edition.

THE CENTAUR. New York: Knopf, 1963.
>   Hardcover, dustwrapper.
>   "First Edition"

TELEPHONE POLES. New York: Knopf, 1963.
>   Hardcover, dustwrapper.
>   "First Edition"

OLINGER STORIES. New York: Vintage Books (1964).
>   Wrappers.
>   "First Vintage Edition, September, 1964"

THE RING. New York: Knopf (1964).
>   Hardcover, no priority:
>   >   1). Trade edition, dustwrapper.
>   >   2). Reinforced library binding, no dustwrapper.
>   No statement of first edition.

ASSORTED PROSE. New York: Knopf, 1965.
>   Hardcover, dustwrapper; no priority:
>   >   1). Trade edition.
>   >   2). Unknown number of copies, signed by the author on sheet tipped in before
>   >   title page.
>   "FIRST EDITION"

OF THE FARM. New York: Knopf, 1965.
>   Hardcover, dustwrapper.
>   "FIRST EDITION"

A CHILD'S CALENDAR. New York: Knopf (1965).
>   Hardcover, dustwrapper.
>   No statement of first edition.

DOG'S DEATH. (Cambridge, Mass.: Lawrence Scott) 1965.
>   Broadside.
>   100 copies, numbered, signed by the author.

VERSE. Greenwich, Conn.: Crest Book/Fawcett Publications (1965).
>   Wrappers.
>   "First Crest Printing, February 1965"

THE MUSIC SCHOOL. New York: Knopf, 1966.
>Hardcover, dustwrapper; priority as listed:
>>1). Page 46, lines 15 and 16 inverted to read:
>>>The state of both his universities
>>>"The King, observing with judicious eyes,
>>2). Corrected page tipped in.
>>3). Corrected page integral.
>"FIRST EDITION"

COUPLES. New York: Knopf, 1968.
>Hardcover, dustwrapper.
>"FIRST EDITION"

BATH AFTER SAILING. (Stevenson, Conn.: Country Squires Books, 1968).
>Two issues, priority as listed:
>>1). Broadside, no known priority:
>>>a). Printed in Roman.
>>>>3 copies (approximately).
>>>b). Printed in italic.
>>>>15 copies (approximately).
>>2). Wrappers.
>>>125 copies, numbered, signed by the author.

THE ANGELS. Pensacola, Fla.: King & Queen Press, 1968.
>Wrappers.
>150 copies.

THREE TEXTS FROM EARLY IPSWICH. Ipswich, Mass.: The 17th Century Day
Committee of the Town of Ipswich, 1968.
>Wrappers, no priority:
>>1). 950 copies.
>>2). 50 copies, numbered, signed by the author.

ON MEETING AUTHORS. Newburyport, Mass.: Wickford Press, 1968.*
>Wrappers.
>250 copies, numbered.

MIDPOINT. New York: Knopf, 1969.
>Hardcover, dustwrapper; no priority:
>>1). Trade edition, dustwrapper with white lettering.
>>2). 350 copies, numbered, signed by the author, dustwrapper with black letter-
>>ing, boxed.
>"FIRST EDITION"

BOTTOM'S DREAM. New York: Knopf (1969).
> Hardcover, no priority:
>> 1). Trade edition, dustwrapper.
>> 2). Reinforced library binding, no dustwrapper.
> No statement of first edition.

BECH. New York: Knopf, 1970.
> Hardcover, dustwrapper; no priority:
>> 1). Trade edition, yellow dustwrapper.
>> 2). 500 copies, numbered, signed by the author, orange dustwrapper, boxed.
> "FIRST EDITION"

THE DANCE OF THE SOLIDS. (New York: Scientific American, ca. 1970).
> Wrappers.

THE INDIAN. (Marvin, S.D.: Blue Cloud Abbey, 1971).
> Wrappers.
> NOTE: Comprises the whole of *The Blue Cloud Quarterly*, XVII, 1.

RABBIT REDUX. New York: Knopf, 1971.
> Hardcover, dustwrapper; no priority:
>> 1). Trade edition, printed dustwrapper.
>> 2). 350 copies, numbered, signed by the author, acetate dustwrapper, boxed.
> "FIRST EDITION"

A CONVERSATION WITH JOHN UPDIKE. (Schenectady, N.Y.: Union College, 1971).
> Wrappers.
> NOTE: A special issue of *The Idol*, Spring 1971.

MUSEUMS AND WOMEN. New York: Knopf, 1972.
> Hardcover, dustwrapper; no priority:
>> 1). Trade edition, dustwrapper with photograph.
>> 2). 350 copies, numbered, signed by the author, dustwrapper with drawings.
> "FIRST EDITION"
> NOTE: Uncorrected proofs in printed wrappers preceded publication.

PHI BETA KAPPA POEM, HARVARD, 1973. Cambridge, Mass.: Harvard University
> News Office, 1973.
> Mimeographed sheets.

WARM WINE. New York: Albondocani Press, 1973.
> Wrappers, no priority:
>> 1). 250 copies, numbered, signed by the author.
>> 2). 26 copies, lettered, signed by the author.

A GOOD PLACE. (New York): Aloe Editions, 1973.
> Wrappers, no priority:
>> 1). 100 copies, numbered, signed by the author.
>> 2). 26 copies, lettered, signed by the author.

SIX POEMS. (New York): Aloe Editions, 1973.
> Wrappers, no priority:
>> 1). 100 copies, numbered, signed by the author.
>> 2). 26 copies, lettered, signed by the author.

BUCHANAN DYING. New York: Knopf, 1974.
> Hardcover, dustwrapper.
> "FIRST EDITION"
> NOTE: Uncorrected proofs in printed wrappers preceded publication.

CUNTS. New York: Frank Hallman (1974).
> Hardcover, no priority:
>> 1). 250 copies, numbered, signed by the author.
>> 2). 26 copies, lettered, signed by the author.

QUERY. (New York: Albondocani Press/Ampersand Books, 1974).
> Wrappers, no priority:
>> 1). Albondocani Press/Ampersand Books on greeting page.
>> 2). No names on greeting page.
> 400 copies.

A MONTH OF SUNDAYS. New York: Knopf, 1975.
> Hardcover, dustwrapper; no priority:
>> 1). Trade edition, black dustwrapper.
>> 2). 450 copies, numbered, signed by the author, maroon dustwrapper, boxed.
> "FIRST EDITION"
> NOTE: Uncorrected proofs in printed wrappers preceded publication.

SUNDAY IN BOSTON. (Derry, Penn.: Rook Press, 1975).
> Broadside, no priority:
>> 1). 100 copies, numbered, signed by the author and illustrator.
>> 2). 100 copies, numbered, signed by the author.
>> 3). 100 copies, unnumbered, unsigned and unillustrated.
> Illustrated by William Lint.

PICKED-UP PIECES. New York: Knopf, 1975.
> Hardcover, no priority:
>> 1). Trade edition, dustwrapper with photographs.
>> 2). 250 copies, numbered, signed by the author, cream dustwrapper, boxed.
> "First Edition"
> NOTE: Uncorrected proofs in printed wrappers preceded publication.

Diane Wakoski

JUSTICE IS REASON ENOUGH. (Berkeley: Privately published) 1959.
    Mimeographed sheets.
    50 copies (approximately).

FOUR YOUNG LADY POETS. New York: Totem Press/Corinth Books (1962).
    Wrappers.
    No statement of first edition.
    NOTE: Carol Berge, Barbara Moraff and Rochelle Owens also contributed.

COINS AND COFFINS. (New York): Hawk's Well Press (1962).
    Wrappers.

DISCREPANCIES AND APPARITIONS. Garden City, N.Y.: Doubleday, 1966.
    Hardcover, dustwrapper.
    "First Edition"

GEORGE WASHINGTON POEMS. New York: Riverrun Press (1967).
    Wrappers, priority as listed:
        1). Picture of a dollar bill on page 1.
        2). "2" stamped to the left of the dollar bill.

THE MAGELLANIC CLOUDS. (New York: Letter Edged in Black Press, ca. 1968).
    Wrappers.
    NOTE: This is one sheet, folded, the cover of which is a plastic record.

GREED: PARTS ONE AND TWO. Los Angeles: Black Sparrow Press, 1968.
    Two issues, no priority:
        1). Hardcover, dustwrapper; no priority:
            a). 50 copies, numbered, signed by the author.
            b). 4 special copies, for the publisher, author, printer and binder.
        2). Wrappers.
            250 copies, numbered, signed by the author.

INSIDE THE BLOOD FACTORY. Garden City, N.Y.:Doubleday, 1968.
  Hardcover, dustwrapper; priority as listed:
    1). Red endpapers.
    2). White endpapers.
  "FIRST EDITION"

THE DIAMOND MERCHANT. Cambridge, Mass.: Sans Souci Press (1968).
  Hardcover, dustwrapper.
  99 copies, numbered, signed by the author.

A PLAY AND TWO POEMS. Los Angeles: Black Sparrow Press, 1968.
  Wrappers, no priority:
    1). 300 copies (according to the publisher, only 224 were actually published).
    2). 100 copies, numbered, signed by the authors.
  NOTE: Robert Kelly and Ron Loewinsohn also contributed.

INSIDE OUT. (Brockport, N.Y.: Department of English, State University College, 1968).
  Wrappers.
  NOTE: Cover title is *Department of English, State University College, Brockport.*

THANKING MY MOTHER FOR PIANO LESSONS. Mt. Horeb, Wisc.: Perishable Press,
  1969.
  Wrappers.
  250 copies.

GREED: PARTS 3 AND 4. Los Angeles: Black Sparrow Press, 1969.
  Two issues, no priority:
    1). Hardcover, acetate dustwrapper; no priority:
      a). 150 copies, numbered, signed by the author.
      b). 4 special copies, for the publisher, author, printer and binder.
    2). Wrappers, no priority:
      a). 250 copies.
      b). 300 copies, numbered, signed by the author.

THE LAMENT OF THE LADY BANK DICK. Cambridge, Mass.: Sans Souci Press (1969).
  Hardcover, glassine dustwrapper; no priority:
    1). 99 copies, numbered, signed by the author.
    2). 10 copies, "For Presentation," signed by the author and publisher.

THE MOON HAS A COMPLICATED GEOGRAPHY. (Palo Alto, Calif.: D. Alexander,
  1969).
  Wrappers.
  Odda Tala, Number Three.

REVIEWS. (New York: Privately published, ca. 1969).
  Mimeographed sheets.
  NOTE: Book reviews of *Songs* by Robert Kelly, *The Floor Keeps Turning* by Shirley
    Kaufman & *Somewhere Among Us A Stone Is Taking Notes* by Charles Simic.

THE MAGELLANIC CLOUDS. Los Angeles: Black Sparrow Press, 1970.
Two issues, priority as listed:
  1). Wrappers, priority as listed:
    a). No correction slip laid in.
    b). Correction slip, noting "Georgraphy" on page 1, laid in.
    1000 copies (according to the publisher, 1017 were actually published).
  2). Hardcover, acetate dustwrapper; no priority:
    a). 250 copies, numbered, signed by the author.
    b). 4 special copies, for the publisher, author, printer and binder.

BLACK DREAM DITTY FOR BILLY "THE KID" M SEEN IN DR. GENEROSITY'S BAR
RECRUITING FOR HELL'S ANGELS AND BLACK MAFIA. (Los Angeles: Black
Sparrow Press, 1970).
Two issues, no priority:
  1). Hardcover, acetate dustwrapper; no priority:
    a). 26 copies, lettered, signed by the author.
    b). 4 special copies, for the publisher, author, printer and binder.
  2). Wrappers.
    a). 300 copies.
    b). 100 copies, numbered, signed by the author.

REVIEWS. (New York: Privately published, ca. 1970).
Mimeographed sheets.
NOTE: Book reviews of *Altars* by Clayton Eshleman and *Threads* by David Bromige.

A FEW SUGGESTIONS BY DIANE WAKOSKI FOR CONCERNED ACTIONS BY
PEOPLE WHO LOVE POETRY. New York: (Privately published) 1970.
Multilithed sheet.

SOME BOOKS RECOMMENDED BY DIANE WAKOSKI — PERTAINING TO POETRY.
(New York: Privately published) 1970.
Mimeographed sheet.

LOVE, YOU BIG FAT SNAIL. San Francisco: Tenth Muse, 1970.
Broadside, no priority:
  1). 200 copies.
  2). 18 copies, numbered, signed by the author.

EXORCISM. (Cambridge, Mass.): My Dukes, 1970.
Broadside, no priority:
  1). Trade edition.
  2). 10 copies (approximately) with the last line changed and then signed by the author.

A TERRIBLE WAR. (Brockport, N.Y.: Far Point, 1970).
Wrappers.
NOTE: An offprint from *The Far Point No. 4*, Spring-Summer 1970, and so noted on the cover.

ON BARBARA'S SHORE. Los Angeles: Black Sparrow Press, 1971.
    Two issues, no priority:
        1). Hardcover, acetate dustwrapper; no priority:
            a). 100 copies, numbered, signed by the author.
            b). 4 special copies, for the publisher, author, printer and binder.
        2). Wrappers.
           404 copies.

GREED: PARTS 5-7. Los Angeles: Black Sparrow Press, 1971.
    Two issues, no priority:
        1). Hardcover, acetate dustwrapper; no priority:
            a). 200 copies, numbered, signed by the author.
            b). 26 copies, lettered, signed by the author with holograph poem.
            c). 4 special copies, for the publisher, author, printer and binder.
        2). Wrappers.
           1000 copies (according to the publisher, 1011 were actually published).

THIS WATER BABY. (Santa Barbara, Calif.: Unicorn Press, 1971).
    Postcard, no priority:
        1). Trade edition, on lavender stock.
        2). 50 copies, signed by the author, in plastic cover entitled *Signed Edition of Fifty Copies.*

THE MOTORCYCLE BETRAYAL POEMS. New York: Simon & Schuster (1971)
    Hardcover, dustwrapper.
    "First printing"
    NOTE: Uncorrected proofs in printed wrappers preceded publication.

THE WISE MEN DRAWN TO KNEEL IN WONDER AT THE FACT SO OF ITSELF.
    Los Angeles: Black Sparrow Press, 1971.
    Two issues, no priority:
        1). Hardcover, acetate dustwrapper; no priority:
            a). 100 copies, numbered, signed by the authors.
            b). 6 special copies, for the publisher, authors, printer and binder.
        2). Wrappers.
           525 copies.
    NOTE: David Bromige and Robert Kelly also contributed.

SMUDGING. Los Angeles: Black Sparrow Press, 1972.
    Two issues, no priority:
        1). Hardcover, acetate dustwrapper; no priority:
            a). 250 copies, numbered, signed by the author.
            b). 30 copies, signed, with holograph poem by the author.
            c). 4 special copies, for the publisher, author, printer and binder.
        2). Wrappers.
           2510 copies.
    NOTE: Advertising flyer (*Broadside/Flyer No.1*), printing one poem from the book, preceded publication; of those, 100 copies were numbered, signed by the author.

REVIEW. (New York: Privately published, 1972).
    Photo-offset sheets.
    NOTE: Book review of *The Tablets, I-XV* by Armand Schwerner.

SOMETIMES A POET WILL HIJACK THE MOON. Providence, R.I.: Burning Deck, 1972.
    Broadside, no priority:
        1). Trade edition.
        2). 20 copies (approximately), signed by the author.

FORM IS AN EXTENSION OF CONTENT. (Charlottesville, Va.: Privately published, 1972).
    Mimeographed sheets.
    50 copies (approximately).
    ALSO: Los Angeles: Black Sparrow Press, 1972.
        Wrappers.
        Sparrow 3.

THE PURPLE FINCH SONG. (Mt. Horeb, Wisc.): Perishable Press, 1972.
    Broadside.
    97 copies.

THE PUMPKIN PIE. (Los Angeles: Black Sparrow Press, 1972).
    Two issues, no priority:
        1). Hardcover, acetate dustwrapper; no priority:
            a). 100 copies, numbered, signed by the author.
            b). 26 copies, lettered, signed by the author.
            c). 4 special copies, for the publisher, author, printer and binder.
        2). Wrappers.
            431 copies.

A LOVER DISREGARDS NAMES. (Providence, R.I.): Burning Deck (ca. 1972).
    Postcard.
    NOTE: There were an unknown number of copies signed by the author.

CLAWS. (Providence, R.I.): Burning Deck (ca. 1972).
    Postcard.
    NOTE: There were an unknown number of copies signed by the author.

THE OWL AND THE SNAKE. Mt. Horeb, Wisc.: Perishable Press, 1973.
    Broadside.
    73 copies.

COMPARISONS. (Providence, R.I.): Burning Deck (1973).
    Postcard.
    NOTE: There were an unknown number of copies signed by the author.

GREED/PARTS 8, 9, 11. Los Angeles: Black Sparrow Press, 1973.
Two issues, no priority:
1). Hardcover, acetate dustwrapper; no priority:
a). 250 copies, numbered, signed by the author.
b). 50 copies, signed, with holograph poem by the author.
c). 4 special copies, for the publisher, author, printer and binder.
2). Wrappers.
2497 copies.
NOTE: An advertising flyer (*Broadside/Flyer No.6*), printing one poem from the book, preceded publication; of those, 100 copies were numbered, signed by the author.

DANCING ON THE GRAVE OF A SON OF A BITCH. Los Angeles: Black Sparrow Press, 1973.
Two issues, no priority:
1). Hardcover, acetate dustwrapper; no priority:
a). 300 copies, numbered, signed by the author.
b). 50 copies, numbered, signed, with holograph poem by the author.
c). 4 special copies, for the publisher, author, printer and binder.
2). Wrappers.
2530 copies.

STILLIFE: MICHAEL, SILVER FLUTE AND VIOLETS. (Storrs, Conn.: University of Connecticut, 1973).
Wrappers.
250 copies.

WINTER SEQUENCES. (Los Angeles): Black Sparrow Press (1973).
Wrappers, no priority:
1). 500 copies.
2). 100 copies, numbered, signed by the author.
3). 26 copies, lettered, signed by the author.

MARRIAGE POEM. (Ann Arbor, Mich.: Old Marble Press, 1974).
Broadside, no known priority:
1). Italic title, 8½ x 11", printed on stock of varying colors, hors commerce.
2). Roman title, 11 x 17", printed on imitation vellum.

BIRTHING THE MYTH OF MYSELF. (Laguna Beach, Calif.: Privately published, 1974).
Mimeographed sheets.
NOTE: A book review of *Coils* by Eshleman.

DIANE WAKOSKI. (La Grande, Ore.: Eastern Oregon State College, ca. 1974).
Broadside.
NOTE: An autobiographical sketch.

TRILOGY. Garden City, N.Y.: Doubleday, 1974.
    Two issues, no priority:
        1). Hardcover, dustwrapper.
        2). Wrappers.
    No statement of first edition.

LOOKING FOR THE KING OF SPAIN. (Los Angeles): Black Sparrow Press, 1974.
    Wrappers.
    Sparrow 21.

THE WISTERIA PROMISES. (Austin: Cold Mountain Press, 1974).
    Postcard.
    Cold Mountain Press Poetry Post Card Series II, Number 6.

ABALONE. Los Angeles: Black Sparrow Press, 1974.
    Two issues, no priority:
        1). Hardcover, dustwrapper; no priority:
            a). 100 copies, numbered, signed by the author.
            b). 26 copies, lettered, signed by the author.
        2). Wrappers.
            500 copies.
    NOTE: Cover title is *A New Year's End Poem From the Black Sparrow Press 1974* and
        . . . . *1975.*

THE WANDERING TATTLER. Driftless, Wisc.: Perishable Press, 1974.
    Hardcover, no priority:
        1). 115 copies, numbered, signed by the author; blue leather spine.
        2). 5 copies, numbered, signed by the author; green leather spine.
        3). 10 copies, numbered, signed by the author; "on pure white & slightly
            narrower."

THE LIAR. (New York): L. Lutes, 1974.
    Broadside.
    200 copies, numbered, signed by the author.

VIRTUOSO LITERATURE FOR TWO AND FOUR HANDS. Garden City, N.Y.:
    Doubleday, 1974.
    Two issues, no priority:
        1). Hardcover, dustwrapper.
        2). Wrappers.
    "First Edition"
    NOTE: 1). A flyer in advance of publication printed biographical information and one
        poem, *The Liar*, the text of which is identical with the broadside of the same
        title.
        2). Uncorrected proofs in printed wrappers preceded publication.

THE FABLE OF THE LION & THE SCORPION. (Milwaukee: Pentagram Press, 1975).
  Wrappers, no priority:
      1). 900 copies.
      2). 100 copies, numbered, signed by the author.

LOVE THE LIZARD. Providence (R.I.): Burning Deck, 1975.
  Broadside.
    NOTE: 1). An unknown number of copies were signed by the author.
          2). Some copies were gathered with *Sometimes a Poet Will Hijack the Moon,*
              A Lover Disregards Names, Claws, and *Comparisons* in a folder entitled
              DIANE WAKOSKI/2 broadsides, 3 postcards, distributed by Burning Deck.

Edward Lewis Wallant

THE HUMAN SEASON. New York: Harcourt, Brace and Company (1960).
  Hardcover, dustwrapper.
  "first edition"

THE PAWNBROKER. New York: Harcourt, Brace and World (1961).
  Hardcover, dustwrapper.
  "FIRST EDITION"

THE TENANTS OF MOONBLOOM. New York: Harcourt, Brace and World (1963).
  Hardcover, dustwrapper.
  "first edition"

THE ARTIST'S EYESIGHT. (New York): Harcourt, Brace & World School Department,
  1963.
  Wrappers.
  NOTE: Teacher's Notebook in English.

THE CHILDREN AT THE GATE. New York: Harcourt, Brace and World (1964).
  Hardcover, dustwrapper.
  "First edition"

Lew Welch

WOBBLY ROCK. (San Francisco): Auerhahn Press, 1960.
   Wrappers.
   500 copies.

EARLY SUMMER HERMIT SONG. (San Francisco: San Francisco Arts Festival Commission, 1963).
   Broadside.
   300 copies, signed by the author and illustrator.
   Illustrated by W. Weber.
   NOTE: Laid in portfolio entitled *San Francisco Arts Festival: A Poetry Folio: 1963.*

STEP OUT ONTO THE PLANET. (San Francisco: Four Seasons Foundation, 1964).
   Broadside.
   300 copies, signed by the author.

RICHER THAN THE RICHEST FALCONER. (San Francisco): Auerhahn (1965).
   Broadside, no priority:
      1). 50 copies.
      2). 25 copies, initialed in red by Philip Whalen.

ON OUT. Berkeley: Oyez, 1965.
   Wrappers.
   500 copies.

HERMIT POEMS. San Francisco: Four Seasons Foundation, 1965.
   Wrappers, no priority:
      1). 974 copies.
      2). 26 copies, numbered, signed by the author.
   Writing 8.

AT TIMES WE'RE ALMOST ABLE TO SEE. (San Francisco): Don Carpenter, 1965.
   Wrappers.
   125 copies.

A MOVING TARGET IS HARD TO HIT. San Francisco: Communication Company, 1967.
    Broadside.

THE BASIC CON. (Santa Barbara, Calif.: Unicorn Press, 1967).
    Wrappers, no priority:
        1). Cover printed in brown and black; no priority:
            a). Trade edition.
            b). 26 copies, lettered, signed by the author.
        2). Cover printed in red and black.
    450 copies.

COURSES. San Francisco: Dave Haselwood, 1968.
    Leather wrappers.
    50 copies (approximately).
    NOTE: The Cranium Press "facsimile edition" (1968) states that there were 100 copies;
        50 copies is more accurate.

SAUSALITO TRASH PRAYER. (Sausalito, Calif.: Lew Welch) 1969.
    Photocopied sheet.
    40 copies.
    NOTE: Xeroxed by the author at the Public Library in Sausalito and given away.
    ALSO: (San Francisco: Cranium Press) 1969.
        Postcard.

THE SONG MT. TAMALPAIS SINGS. (San Francisco): Maya (1969).
    Wrappers, no priority:
        1). 250 copies.
        2). 50 copies, numbered, signed by the author.
    Maya Quarto Five.
    ALSO: Berkeley: Sand Dollar (1970).
        Wrappers.
        1000 copies.
        Sand Dollar 3.
        NOTE: Expanded edition.

FROM WOBBLY ROCK. (San Francisco: Cranium Press, ca. 1969).
    Broadside.

INFLATION FOR NEIL DAVIS, INNKEEPER. (Portland, Ore.): Yes! Press, 1970.
    Broadside.

NO BARS. (San Francisco): Cranium Press, 1970.
    Broadside.
    NOTE: Not written as a poem; assembled extracts from a letter by the author to
        Clifford Burke (Cranium); never formally published.

GETTING BALD. (San Francisco: Cranium Press, ca. 1970).
    Postcard.

I SOMETIMES TALK TO KEROUAC WHEN I DRIVE. Portland, Ore.: Yes! Press, 1971.
  Broadside.

SPRINGTIME IN THE ROCKIES, LICHEN. San Francisco: Cranium (1971).
  Broadside, no priority:
    1). Light pink stock.
    2). Light grey stock.
    3). Light green stock.

REDWOOD HAIKU. (San Francisco: Cranium Press, ca. 1972).
  Broadside.
  NOTE: Printed on stock of varying colors and sizes.

REDWOOD HAIKU & OTHER POEMS. San Francisco:.Cranium Press, 1972.
  Wrappers.
  250 copies.

RING OF BONE. Bolinas, Calif.: Grey Fox Press, 1973.
  Two issues, no priority:
    1). Hardcover, dustwrapper.
    2). Wrappers.
  "First Edition"

TRIP TRAP. Bolinas, Calif.: Grey Fox Press, 1973.
  Wrappers.
  No statement of first edition.
  NOTE: With Jack Kerouac and Albert Saijo.

HOW I WORK AS A POET. Bolinas, Calif.: Grey Fox Press, 1973.
  Two issues, no priority:
    1). Hardcover, dustwrapper.
    2). Wrappers.
  No statement of first edition.

Philip Whalen

THREE SATIRES. Portland, Ore.: (Privately published) 1951.*
  Wrappers.
  13 copies.

SONG. (Portland, Ore.: Privately published, 1951).*
  Broadside.
  2 copies.

SELF-PORTRAIT FROM ANOTHER DIRECTION. (San Francisco): Auerhahn Press,
  1959.
  Wrappers.

THE END, OF A MONTH OF SUNDAYS. (San Francisco): Auerhahn Press (1959).
  Wrappers.
  NOTE: 1). Cover title of only "Auerhahn Press" for this folded broadside, which is also
            encountered without wrappers.
        2). With John Wieners, Philip Lamantia and Michael McClure.
        3). Commonly referred to by Wieners' title, *Bag Dad By the Bay.*

MEMOIRS OF AN INTERGLACIAL AGE. (San Francisco): Auerhahn Press, 1960.
  Two issues, no priority:
      1). Hardcover, no priority:
          a). 60 copies.
          b). 25 copies, with an original drawing and holograph poem by the author.
          c). 15 copies, signed by the author.
      2). Wrappers.

FROM MEMOIRS OF AN INTERGLACIAL AGE. Cambridge, Mass.: Paterson Society
  (ca. 1960).
  Mimeographed sheet.

LIKE I SAY. New York: Totem Press/Corinth Books (1960).
  Grey wrappers.
  Publishers' names on copyright page.

HYMNUS AD PATREM SINENSIS. San Francisco: (San Francisco Arts Festival Commission) 1963.
  Broadside.
  300 copies, most of which were signed by the author.
  NOTE: Laid in portfolio entitled *San Francisco Arts Festival: A Poetry Folio: 1963.*

THREE MORNINGS. (San Francisco: Four Seasons Foundation, 1964).
  Broadside.

MONDAY IN THE EVENING, 21: VII: 61. Milan: (Privately published, 1964).
  Wrappers, no priority:
      1). 291 copies, numbered.
      2). 18 copies, hors commerce.

GODDESS. (San Francisco): Don Carpenter, 1964.
  Broadside, no priority:
      1). 100 copies.
      2). 25 copies, without colophon, for the use of the author.

DEAR MR. PRESIDENT. (San Francisco: Impressions Productions) 1965.
  Broadside.
  500 copies.

EVERY DAY. (Eugene, Ore.): Coyote's Journal, 1965.
  Wrappers.
  Coyote Book #1.

NOBODY LISTENING TO YOU? San Francisco: Philip Whalen, 1965.
  Broadside.
  NOTE: Issued to celebrate "Gentle Thursday" and often listed by that title.

HIGHGRADE. (San Francisco): Coyote's Journal, 1966.
  Wrappers.

YOU DIDN'T EVEN TRY. (San Francisco): Coyote, 1967.
  Wrappers.

THE INVENTION OF THE LETTER. (New York: Irving Rosenthal, 1967).
  Hardcover, ring-bound.

T/O. San Francisco: David Haselwood, 1967.
  Wrappers.
  80 copies.

ON BEAR'S HEAD. New York: Harcourt, Brace & World/Coyote (1969).
    Two issues, no priority:
        1). Hardcover, dustwrapper.
        2). Wrappers.
   "First edition"

SEVERANCE PAY. San Francisco: Four Seasons Foundation, 1970.
    Two issues, no priority:
        1). Hardcover, no priority:
           a). Trade edition.
           b). 50 copies, signed by the author.
        2). Wrappers.
   Writing 24.

SCENES OF LIFE AT THE CAPITAL. (San Francisco: Maya) 1970.
    Wrappers, no priority:
        1). 250 copies.
        2). 50 copies, numbered, signed by the author.
    Maya Quarto Ten.
    ALSO: Bolinas, Calif.: Grey Fox Press, 1971.
       Wrappers.
       "First edition"
       NOTE: Expanded edition.

IMAGINARY SPEECHES FOR A BRAZEN HEAD. Los Angeles: Black Sparrow Press,
   1972.
    Two issues, no priority:
        1). Hardcover, acetate dustwrapper; no priority:
           a). 200 copies, numbered, signed by the author.
           b). 26 copies, lettered, signed by the author.
        2). Wrappers.
          1500 copies.

LOOKING FOR HELP. (San Francisco): Panjandrum Press, 1972.
   Broadside.

IN THE NIGHT. (N.p.: Privately published, ca. 1972).
   Broadside.

John Wieners

THE HOTEL WENTLEY POEMS. (San Francisco: Auerhahn Press) 1958.
>   Wrappers, priority as listed:
>   1). Blank spaces in place of "censorable" words.
>   2). Unexpurgated text.
>   ALSO: San Francisco: Dave Haselwood, 1965.
>   Wrappers.
>   "Second edition, revised."

AND WHAT IS NOTHINGNESS. (San Francisco: Wallace Berman, 1959).
>   Broadside.
>   NOTE: Laid in portfolio entitled *Semina 4.*

BAG DAD BY THE BAY. (San Francisco): Auerhahn Press (1959).
>   Wrappers.
>   NOTE: 1). Cover title of only "Auerhahn Press" for this folded broadside, which is also
>   encountered without wrappers.
>   2). With Michael McClure, Philip Lamantia and Philip Whalen.

PEYOTE POEM. (Los Angeles: Wallace Berman, ca. 1960).
>   Broadside.
>   NOTE: Laid in portfolio entitled *Semina 5.*

OF ASPHODEL, IN HELL'S DESPITE. New York: Judson Poets Theatre, n.d.
>   Mechanically reproduced sheets.

ACE OF PENTACLES. New York: James F. Carr and Robert A. Wilson, 1964.
>   Three issues, no priority:
>   1). Hardcover, glassine dustwrapper; no priority:
>   a). Trade edition.
>   b). 75 copies, numbered, signed by the author, with a page of manuscript
>   added.
>   2). Leather.
>   12 copies, signed by the author and publishers, with a poem tipped in.
>   3). Wrappers.

YOU TALK OF GOING, BUT DON'T EVEN HAVE A SUITCASE. Spoleto, Italy: Spoleto
    Festival, ca. 1965.*
    Mimeographed sheets, stapled.

CHINOISERIE. San Francisco: Dave Haselwood, 1965.
    Wrappers.
    100 copies.

HART CRANE, HARRY CROSBY, I SEE YOU GOING OVER THE EDGE. (Detroit:
    Artists Workshop Press, ca. 1966).
    Broadside.
    Free Poem Among Friends #10.
    NOTE: This is to be differentiated from this title's 1966 publication as *Artist's Work-
        shop Press Broadside #2*.

PRESSED WAFER. (Buffalo, N.Y.: Gallery Upstairs Press, 1967).
    Two issues, no priority:
        1). Hardcover.
            100 copies, numbered, signed by the author.
        2). Wrappers.
            900 copies.

KING SOLOMON'S MAGNETIC QUIZ. Pleasant Valley, N.Y.: Kriya Press, 1967.
    Broadside.
    100 copies, numbered.

LONG DISTANCE. (Mt. Horeb, Wisc.): Perishable Press, 1968.
    Broadside.
    250 copies.

UNHIRED. (Mt. Horeb, Wisc.): Perishable Press (1968).
    Wrappers.
    250 copies.

L'ABYSSE. (New York: George Robert Minkoff, 1968).
    Broadside.
    250 copies, numbered, signed by the author.

ACCEPTANCE. (Detroit): Mail Press, 1968.
    Broadside.
    Free Poems Among Friends #4.

ON LOOKING IN THE MIRROR. (New York: Brownstone Press, 1968).
    Broadside, no priority:
        1). 200 copies.
        2). 50 copies, signed by the author.
    NOTE: Also referred to as *Pisces*; it is one of a set of broadsides laid in portfolio
        entitled *The Zodiac*. 250 numbered copies of *The Zodiac* were published.

A LETTER TO CHARLES OLSON. (Brooklyn): Samuel Charters, 1968.
  Broadside.
  Portents #11.

IDYLL. (Santa Barbara, Calif.: Unicorn Press, 1968).
  Broadside.
  350 copies.
  NOTE: Laid in portfolio entitled *Unicorn Folio: Series Two, Number One*, numbered.

TO DO. (Stony Brook, N.Y.: Stony Brook Poetics Foundation, 1968).
  Broadside.
  10 copies, signed by the author.
  NOTE: Laid in portfolio entitled *Stony Brook Holographs 1968*.

ASYLUM POEMS. (New York): Angel Hair Books, 1969.
  Wrappers, no priority:
    1). 190 copies.
    2). 10 copies, numbered, signed by the author.
  NOTE: Precedes the pirated edition by the Press of the Black Flag Raised, also 1969.

INVITATION. (Santa Barbara, Calif.: Unicorn Press, 1970).
  Two issues, no priority:
    1). Hardcover, no priority:
        a). 200 copies, numbered, signed by the author.
        b). 26 copies, lettered, signed by the author.
    2). Wrappers.
        300 copies.

YOUTH. New York: Phoenix Book Shop, 1970.
  Wrappers, no priority:
    1). 100 copies, numbered, signed by the author.
    2). 26 copies, lettered, signed by the author.
  NOTE: 1). An unknown number of copies were labeled "hors commerce," signed by the
            author.
        2). Six copies of stapled page proofs were used for review.

NERVES. (London): Cape Goliard Press (1970).
  Two issues, no priority:
    1). Hardcover, dustwrapper; no priority:
        a). Trade edition.
        b). 100 copies, numbered, signed by the author.
    2). Wrappers.
  NOTE: Copies for American distribution say "Cape Goliard Press in association with
        Grossman Publishers New York" on the title page and "Cape
        Goliard/Grossman" on the spine.

LARDERS. Cambridge, Mass.: Restau Press, 1970.
>Broadside, priority as listed:
>>1). Author's name spelled "Weiners."
>>2). Author's name spelled "Wieners,"no priority:
>>>a). Trade edition.
>>>b). 74 copies, numbered, signed by the author.
>>>c). 26 copies, lettered, signed by the author.

READING IN BED. (San Francisco): White Rabbit Press, 1970.
>Broadside.
>40 copies, numbered, signed by the author.

SELECTED POEMS.
>No priority:
>>1). New York: Grossman Publishers, 1972.
>>Two issues, no priority:
>>>a). Hardcover, dustwrapper.
>>>b). Wrappers.
>>2). London: Cape Goliard Press, 1972.
>>Hardcover, dustwrapper.
>>NOTE: Uncorrected proofs of earlier typesetting by Cape Goliard Press preceded publication.

PLAYBOY. (Boston: Good Gay Poets, 1972).
>Wrappers, no known priority:
>>1). Cover of red stock.
>>2). Cover of pink stock.
>>3). Cover of green stock.
>NOTE: Also known by the cover title *We Were There*.

WOMAN. (Canton, N.Y.): Institute of Further Studies (1972).
>Wrappers.
>A Curriculum of the Soul 3.

THE LANTERNS ALONG THE WALL. (Buffalo, N.Y.): Other Publications, 1972.
>Wrappers.
>100 copies.

YONNIE. (New York): Athanor Books, 1973.
>Wrappers.
>NOTE: Laid in *Athanor 4*, Spring, 1973.

GOD IS THE ORGAN OF NOVELTY. Cambridge, Mass.: Pomegranate Press (1973).
>Broadside, no priority:
>>1). 150 copies, numbered.
>>2). 100 copies, numbered, signed by the author and illustrator.
>Illustrated by Karyl Klopp.

YES, YOUTH ARE MARCHING ON AGAINST THE WORLD. Philadelphia : Middle Earth
 Bookstore, 1973.
 Broadside.
 300 copies.

HOTELS. (New York) : Angel Hair Books (1974).
 Wrappers, no priority :
  1). 500 copies.
  2). 10 copies, signed by the author and illustrator.
 Illustrated by Gordon Baldwin.

BEHIND THE STATE CAPITOL. (Boston) : Good Gay Poets (1975).
 Two issues, priority as listed :
  1). Wrappers.
   1500 copies.
  2). Hardcover.
   100 copies.

John
Tom
Robert
Cid Cor
Robert
James
Diane
Robert
Clayton
William
Lawrence
Bruce Jay
John Gard
William
Herbert